TRIATHLON
TRAINING JOURNAL

Training Log and Planner
for Multisport Athletes

Name: _Kristen Sorensen_

Year: _2014_

If found, please contact me at:
SORENSKT@GMAIL.COM

©DESIGNED & WRITTEN BY DARIUSZ JANCZEWSKI
RUNALOGS

WWW.RUNALOGS.COM

FIRST EDITION, MAY 2009.

CONTENTS

* CUT THESE PAGES OUT AND MAKE COPIES FOR REPEAT USE

PERSONAL PROFILE

NAME: _____

ADDRESS: _____

EMAIL: _____

EMERGENCY CONTACT INFO: _____

MONTH					YEAR

MONTH					YEAR

MONTH					YEAR

MONTH					YEAR

MONTH					YEAR

MONTH					YEAR

JANUARY _____

FEBRUARY _____

MARCH _____

APRIL _____

MAY _____

JUNE _____

JULY _____

AUGUST _____

SEPTEMBER _____

OCTOBER _____

NOVEMBER _____

DECEMBER _____

#	race name	date	distance	time	place	notes
1	GOOCHLAND SPRINT www:	8/10 2013				
	www:					
	www:					
	www:					
	www:					
	www:					
	www:					
	www:					
	www:					
	www:					
	www:					
	www:					
	www:					
	www:					
	www:					
	www:					
	www:					
	www:					
	www:					
	www:					
	www:					
	www:					

my racing calendar

#	race name	date	distance	time	place	notes
	www:					
	www:					
	www:					
	www:					
	www:					
	www:					
	www:					
	www:					
	www:					
	www:					
	www:					
	www:					
	www:					
	www:					
	www:					
	www:					
	www:					
	www:					
	www:					
	www:					
	www:					
	www:					
	www:					

TRIATHLON
TRAINING JOURNAL

NAME: Kristen Sorensen

ADDRESS:

EMAIL: sorenskt@gmail.com

EMERGENCY CONTACT:

RUNALOG® FOR TRIATHLETES

TODAY'S DATE _____

MY LONG-TERM GOAL(S) _____
_____

TODAY'S MEAL PLAN	BREAKFAST	SNACK	LUNCH	SNACK	DINNER
	_____	_____	_____	_____	_____
	_____	_____	_____	_____	_____

weekly planner

	SUNDAY	MONDAY	TUESDAY	WEDNESDAY	THURSDAY	FRIDAY	SATURDAY	TOTAL
a.m.								
p.m.								

daily planner

5 a.m. _____	2 p.m. _____
6 a.m. _____	3 p.m. _____
7 a.m. _____	4 p.m. _____
8 a.m _____	5 p.m. _____
9 a.m. _____	6 p.m. _____
10 a.m. _____	7 p.m. _____
11 a.m. _____	8 p.m. _____
12 p.m. _____	9 p.m. _____
1 p.m. _____	10 p.m. _____

my training journal

my training log

SWIMMING WORKOUT:	distance
a.m.	
p.m.	
	total

BIKING WORKOUT:	distance
a.m.	
p.m.	
	total

RUNNING WORKOUT:	distance
a.m.	
p.m.	
	total

CROSS-TRAINING:	time
a.m.	
p.m.	
	total

TOMORROW'S TO DO

√RUNALOG® FOR TRIATHLETES

TODAY'S DATE _____

MY LONG-TERM GOAL(S) _____
_____

TODAY'S MEAL PLAN	BREAKFAST	SNACK	LUNCH	SNACK	DINNER
	_____	_____	_____	_____	_____
	_____	_____	_____	_____	_____

weekly planner

	SUNDAY	MONDAY	TUESDAY	WEDNESDAY	THURSDAY	FRIDAY	SATURDAY	TOTAL
a.m.								
p.m.								

daily planner

5 a.m. _____	2 p.m. _____
6 a.m. _____	3 p.m. _____
7 a.m. _____	4 p.m. _____
8 a.m _____	5 p.m. _____
9 a.m. _____	6 p.m. _____
10 a.m. _____	7 p.m. _____
11 a.m. _____	8 p.m. _____
12 p.m. _____	9 p.m. _____
1 p.m. _____	10 p.m. _____

my training journal

my training log

SWIMMING WORKOUT:		*distance*
a.m.		
p.m.		
		total

BIKING WORKOUT:		*distance*
a.m.		
p.m.		
		total

RUNNING WORKOUT:		*distance*
a.m.		
p.m.		
		total

CROSS-TRAINING:		*time*
a.m.		
p.m.		
		total

TOMORROW'S TO DO

MY LONG-TERM GOAL(S) _____

_____

TODAY'S MEAL PLAN	BREAKFAST	SNACK	LUNCH	SNACK	DINNER
	_____	_____	_____	_____	_____
	_____	_____	_____	_____	_____

weekly planner

	SUNDAY	MONDAY	TUESDAY	WEDNESDAY	THURSDAY	FRIDAY	SATURDAY	TOTAL
a.m.								
p.m.								

daily planner

5 a.m. _____	2 p.m. _____
6 a.m. _____	3 p.m. _____
7 a.m. _____	4 p.m. _____
8 a.m _____	5 p.m. _____
9 a.m. _____	6 p.m. _____
10 a.m. _____	7 p.m. _____
11 a.m. _____	8 p.m. _____
12 p.m. _____	9 p.m. _____
1 p.m. _____	10 p.m. _____

my training journal

my training log

SWIMMING WORKOUT:	*distance*
a.m.	
p.m.	
	total

BIKING WORKOUT:	*distance*
a.m.	
p.m.	
	total

RUNNING WORKOUT:	*distance*
a.m.	
p.m.	
	total

CROSS-TRAINING:	*time*
a.m.	
p.m.	
	total

TOMORROW'S To Do

MY LONG-TERM GOAL(S) _____

Today's Meal Plan	Breakfast	Snack	Lunch	Snack	Dinner
	_____	_____	_____	_____	_____
	_____	_____	_____	_____	_____

weekly planner

	SUNDAY	MONDAY	TUESDAY	WEDNESDAY	THURSDAY	FRIDAY	SATURDAY	TOTAL
a.m.								
p.m.								

daily planner

5 a.m. _____	2 p.m. _____
6 a.m. _____	3 p.m. _____
7 a.m. _____	4 p.m. _____
8 a.m _____	5 p.m. _____
9 a.m. _____	6 p.m. _____
10 a.m. _____	7 p.m. _____
11 a.m. _____	8 p.m. _____
12 p.m. _____	9 p.m. _____
1 p.m. _____	10 p.m. _____

my training journal

my training log

SWIMMING WORKOUT:	distance
a.m.	
p.m.	
	total

BIKING WORKOUT:	distance
a.m.	
p.m.	
	total

RUNNING WORKOUT:	distance
a.m.	
p.m.	
	total

CROSS-TRAINING:	time
a.m.	
p.m.	
	total

Tomorrow's To Do

√RUNALOG® FOR TRIATHLETES

MY LONG-TERM GOAL(S) _____
_____

TODAY'S MEAL PLAN	BREAKFAST	SNACK	LUNCH	SNACK	DINNER
	_____	_____	_____	_____	_____
	_____	_____	_____	_____	_____

weekly planner

	SUNDAY	MONDAY	TUESDAY	WEDNESDAY	THURSDAY	FRIDAY	SATURDAY	TOTAL
a.m.								
p.m.								

daily planner

5 a.m. _____	2 p.m. _____
6 a.m. _____	3 p.m. _____
7 a.m. _____	4 p.m. _____
8 a.m _____	5 p.m. _____
9 a.m. _____	6 p.m. _____
10 a.m. _____	7 p.m. _____
11 a.m. _____	8 p.m. _____
12 p.m. _____	9 p.m. _____
1 p.m. _____	10 p.m. _____

my training journal

my training log

SWIMMING WORKOUT:	*distance*
a.m.	
p.m.	
	total

BIKING WORKOUT:	*distance*
a.m.	
p.m.	
	total

RUNNING WORKOUT:	*distance*
a.m.	
p.m.	
	total

CROSS-TRAINING:	*time*
a.m.	
p.m.	
	total

TOMORROW'S TO DO

√RUNALOG® FOR TRIATHLETES

TODAY'S DATE _____

MY LONG-TERM GOAL(S) _____
_____

TODAY'S MEAL PLAN	BREAKFAST	SNACK	LUNCH	SNACK	DINNER
	_____	_____	_____	_____	_____
	_____	_____	_____	_____	_____

weekly planner

	SUNDAY	MONDAY	TUESDAY	WEDNESDAY	THURSDAY	FRIDAY	SATURDAY	TOTAL
a.m.								
p.m.								

daily planner

5 a.m. _____	2 p.m. _____
6 a.m. _____	3 p.m. _____
7 a.m. _____	4 p.m. _____
8 a.m _____	5 p.m. _____
9 a.m. _____	6 p.m. _____
10 a.m. _____	7 p.m. _____
11 a.m. _____	8 p.m. _____
12 p.m. _____	9 p.m. _____
1 p.m. _____	10 p.m. _____

my training journal

my training log

SWIMMING WORKOUT:	*distance*
a.m.	
p.m.	
	total

BIKING WORKOUT:	*distance*
a.m.	
p.m.	
	total

RUNNING WORKOUT:	*distance*
a.m.	
p.m.	
	total

CROSS-TRAINING:	*time*
a.m.	
p.m.	
	total

TOMORROW'S TO DO

⚡RUNALOG® FOR TRIATHLETES

TODAY'S DATE _____

MY LONG-TERM GOAL(S) _____

TODAY'S MEAL PLAN	BREAKFAST	SNACK	LUNCH	SNACK	DINNER
	_____	_____	_____	_____	_____
	_____	_____	_____	_____	_____

weekly planner

	SUNDAY	MONDAY	TUESDAY	WEDNESDAY	THURSDAY	FRIDAY	SATURDAY	TOTAL
a.m.								
p.m.								

🕐 daily planner

5 a.m. _____	2 p.m. _____
6 a.m. _____	3 p.m. _____
7 a.m. _____	4 p.m. _____
8 a.m _____	5 p.m. _____
9 a.m. _____	6 p.m. _____
10 a.m. _____	7 p.m. _____
11 a.m. _____	8 p.m. _____
12 p.m. _____	9 p.m. _____
1 p.m. _____	10 p.m. _____

✍ my training journal

my training log

SWIMMING WORKOUT:	*distance*
a.m.	
p.m.	
	total

BIKING WORKOUT:	*distance*
a.m.	
p.m.	
	total

RUNNING WORKOUT:	*distance*
a.m.	
p.m.	
	total

CROSS-TRAINING:	*time*
a.m.	
p.m.	
	total

TOMORROW's To Do

⚡RUNALOG® FOR TRIATHLETES

TODAY'S DATE _____

MY LONG-TERM GOAL(S) _____

_____

TODAY'S MEAL PLAN	BREAKFAST	SNACK	LUNCH	SNACK	DINNER
	_____	_____	_____	_____	_____
	_____	_____	_____	_____	_____

weekly planner

	SUNDAY	MONDAY	TUESDAY	WEDNESDAY	THURSDAY	FRIDAY	SATURDAY	TOTAL
a.m.								
p.m.								

🕐 daily planner

5 a.m. _____	2 p.m. _____
6 a.m. _____	3 p.m. _____
7 a.m. _____	4 p.m. _____
8 a.m _____	5 p.m. _____
9 a.m. _____	6 p.m. _____
10 a.m. _____	7 p.m. _____
11 a.m. _____	8 p.m. _____
12 p.m. _____	9 p.m. _____
1 p.m. _____	10 p.m. _____

✍ my training journal

my training log

SWIMMING WORKOUT:	*distance*
a.m.	
p.m.	
	total

🚴 BIKING WORKOUT:	*distance*
a.m.	
p.m.	
	total

🏃 RUNNING WORKOUT:	*distance*
a.m.	
p.m.	
	total

CROSS-TRAINING:	*time*
a.m.	
p.m.	
	total

TOMORROW'S TO DO

RUNALOG® FOR TRIATHLETES

TODAY'S DATE _____

MY LONG-TERM GOAL(S) _____

_____

TODAY'S MEAL PLAN	BREAKFAST	SNACK	LUNCH	SNACK	DINNER
	_____	_____	_____	_____	_____
	_____	_____	_____	_____	_____

weekly planner

	SUNDAY	MONDAY	TUESDAY	WEDNESDAY	THURSDAY	FRIDAY	SATURDAY	TOTAL
a.m.								
p.m.								

daily planner

5 a.m. _____	2 p.m. _____
6 a.m. _____	3 p.m. _____
7 a.m. _____	4 p.m. _____
8 a.m _____	5 p.m. _____
9 a.m. _____	6 p.m. _____
10 a.m. _____	7 p.m. _____
11 a.m. _____	8 p.m. _____
12 p.m. _____	9 p.m. _____
1 p.m. _____	10 p.m. _____

my training journal

my training log

SWIMMING WORKOUT: *distance*

a.m.	
p.m.	
	total

BIKING WORKOUT: *distance*

a.m.	
p.m.	
	total

RUNNING WORKOUT: *distance*

a.m.	
p.m.	
	total

CROSS-TRAINING: *time*

a.m.	
p.m.	
	total

TOMORROW'S TO DO

MY LONG-TERM GOAL(S)_____

TODAY'S DATE _____

TODAY'S MEAL PLAN	BREAKFAST	SNACK	LUNCH	SNACK	DINNER
	_____	_____	_____	_____	_____
	_____	_____	_____	_____	_____

weekly planner

	SUNDAY	MONDAY	TUESDAY	WEDNESDAY	THURSDAY	FRIDAY	SATURDAY	TOTAL
a.m.								
p.m.								

daily planner

5 a.m. _____	2 p.m. _____
6 a.m. _____	3 p.m. _____
7 a.m. _____	4 p.m. _____
8 a.m _____	5 p.m. _____
9 a.m. _____	6 p.m. _____
10 a.m. _____	7 p.m. _____
11 a.m. _____	8 p.m. _____
12 p.m. _____	9 p.m. _____
1 p.m. _____	10 p.m. _____

my training journal

my training log

SWIMMING WORKOUT:	*distance*
a.m.	
p.m.	
	total

BIKING WORKOUT:	*distance*
a.m.	
p.m.	
	total

RUNNING WORKOUT:	*distance*
a.m.	
p.m.	
	total

CROSS-TRAINING:	*time*
a.m.	
p.m.	
	total

TOMORROW'S TO DO

21

RUNALOG® FOR TRIATHLETES

TODAY'S DATE _____

MY LONG-TERM GOAL(S) _____

TODAY'S MEAL PLAN	BREAKFAST	SNACK	LUNCH	SNACK	DINNER

weekly planner

	SUNDAY	MONDAY	TUESDAY	WEDNESDAY	THURSDAY	FRIDAY	SATURDAY	TOTAL
a.m.								
p.m.								

daily planner

5 a.m. _____	2 p.m. _____
6 a.m. _____	3 p.m. _____
7 a.m. _____	4 p.m. _____
8 a.m _____	5 p.m. _____
9 a.m. _____	6 p.m. _____
10 a.m. _____	7 p.m. _____
11 a.m. _____	8 p.m. _____
12 p.m. _____	9 p.m. _____
1 p.m. _____	10 p.m. _____

my training journal

my training log

SWIMMING WORKOUT:	distance
a.m.	
p.m.	
	total

BIKING WORKOUT:	distance
a.m.	
p.m.	
	total

RUNNING WORKOUT:	distance
a.m.	
p.m.	
	total

CROSS-TRAINING:	time
a.m.	
p.m.	
	total

TOMORROW'S TO DO

√RUNALOG® FOR TRIATHLETES

TODAY'S DATE _____

MY LONG-TERM GOAL(S) _____
_____

TODAY'S MEAL PLAN	BREAKFAST	SNACK	LUNCH	SNACK	DINNER
	_____	_____	_____	_____	_____
	_____	_____	_____	_____	_____

weekly planner

	SUNDAY	MONDAY	TUESDAY	WEDNESDAY	THURSDAY	FRIDAY	SATURDAY	TOTAL
a.m.								
p.m.								

daily planner

5 a.m. _____	2 p.m. _____
6 a.m. _____	3 p.m. _____
7 a.m. _____	4 p.m. _____
8 a.m _____	5 p.m. _____
9 a.m. _____	6 p.m. _____
10 a.m. _____	7 p.m. _____
11 a.m. _____	8 p.m. _____
12 p.m. _____	9 p.m. _____
1 p.m. _____	10 p.m. _____

my training journal

my training log

SWIMMING WORKOUT:	*distance*
a.m.	
p.m.	
	total

BIKING WORKOUT:	*distance*
a.m.	
p.m.	
	total

RUNNING WORKOUT:	*distance*
a.m.	
p.m.	
	total

CROSS-TRAINING:	*time*
a.m.	
p.m.	
	total

TOMORROW'S TO DO

MY LONG-TERM GOAL(S) _____

TODAY'S MEAL PLAN	BREAKFAST	SNACK	LUNCH	SNACK	DINNER
	_____	_____	_____	_____	_____
	_____	_____	_____	_____	_____

weekly planner

	SUNDAY	MONDAY	TUESDAY	WEDNESDAY	THURSDAY	FRIDAY	SATURDAY	TOTAL
a.m.								
p.m.								

daily planner

5 a.m. _____	2 p.m. _____
6 a.m. _____	3 p.m. _____
7 a.m. _____	4 p.m. _____
8 a.m _____	5 p.m. _____
9 a.m. _____	6 p.m. _____
10 a.m. _____	7 p.m. _____
11 a.m. _____	8 p.m. _____
12 p.m. _____	9 p.m. _____
1 p.m. _____	10 p.m. _____

my training journal

my training log

SWIMMING WORKOUT:	*distance*
a.m.	
p.m.	
	total

BIKING WORKOUT:	*distance*
a.m.	
p.m.	
	total

RUNNING WORKOUT:	*distance*
a.m.	
p.m.	
	total

CROSS-TRAINING:	*time*
a.m.	
p.m.	
	total

TOMORROW'S To Do

√RUNALOG® FOR TRIATHLETES

TODAY'S DATE _____

MY LONG-TERM GOAL(S) _____
_____

TODAY'S MEAL PLAN	BREAKFAST	SNACK	LUNCH	SNACK	DINNER
	_____	_____	_____	_____	_____
	_____	_____	_____	_____	_____
	_____	_____	_____	_____	_____

weekly planner

	SUNDAY	MONDAY	TUESDAY	WEDNESDAY	THURSDAY	FRIDAY	SATURDAY	TOTAL
a.m.								
p.m.								

daily planner

5 a.m. _____	2 p.m. _____
6 a.m. _____	3 p.m. _____
7 a.m. _____	4 p.m. _____
8 a.m _____	5 p.m. _____
9 a.m. _____	6 p.m. _____
10 a.m. _____	7 p.m. _____
11 a.m. _____	8 p.m. _____
12 p.m. _____	9 p.m. _____
1 p.m. _____	10 p.m. _____

my training journal

my training log

SWIMMING WORKOUT:	distance
a.m.	
p.m.	
	total

BIKING WORKOUT:	distance
a.m.	
p.m.	
	total

RUNNING WORKOUT:	distance
a.m.	
p.m.	
	total

CROSS-TRAINING:	time
a.m.	
p.m.	
	total

TOMORROW'S TO DO

RUNALOG® FOR TRIATHLETES

TODAY'S DATE _____

MY LONG-TERM GOAL(S) _____
_____

TODAY'S MEAL PLAN	BREAKFAST	SNACK	LUNCH	SNACK	DINNER
	_____	_____	_____	_____	_____
	_____	_____	_____	_____	_____

weekly planner

	SUNDAY	MONDAY	TUESDAY	WEDNESDAY	THURSDAY	FRIDAY	SATURDAY	TOTAL
a.m.								
p.m.								

daily planner

5 a.m. _____	2 p.m. _____
6 a.m. _____	3 p.m. _____
7 a.m. _____	4 p.m. _____
8 a.m _____	5 p.m. _____
9 a.m. _____	6 p.m. _____
10 a.m. _____	7 p.m. _____
11 a.m. _____	8 p.m. _____
12 p.m. _____	9 p.m. _____
1 p.m. _____	10 p.m. _____

my training journal

my training log

SWIMMING WORKOUT: distance

a.m.	
p.m.	
	total

BIKING WORKOUT: distance

a.m.	
p.m.	
	total

RUNNING WORKOUT: distance

a.m.	
p.m.	
	total

CROSS-TRAINING: time

a.m.	
p.m.	
	total

TOMORROW'S To Do

√RUNALOG® *FOR TRIATHLETES*   **TODAY'S DATE** _____

MY LONG-TERM GOAL(S) _____
_____

TODAY'S MEAL PLAN	BREAKFAST	SNACK	LUNCH	SNACK	DINNER
	_____	_____	_____	_____	_____
	_____	_____	_____	_____	_____

weekly planner

	SUNDAY	MONDAY	TUESDAY	WEDNESDAY	THURSDAY	FRIDAY	SATURDAY	TOTAL
a.m.								
p.m.								

daily planner

5 a.m. _____	2 p.m. _____
6 a.m. _____	3 p.m. _____
7 a.m. _____	4 p.m. _____
8 a.m _____	5 p.m. _____
9 a.m. _____	6 p.m. _____
10 a.m. _____	7 p.m. _____
11 a.m. _____	8 p.m. _____
12 p.m. _____	9 p.m. _____
1 p.m. _____	10 p.m. _____

my training journal

my training log

SWIMMING WORKOUT:	*distance*
a.m.	
p.m.	
	total

BIKING WORKOUT:	*distance*
a.m.	
p.m.	
	total

RUNNING WORKOUT:	*distance*
a.m.	
p.m.	
	total

CROSS-TRAINING:	*time*
a.m.	
p.m.	
	total

TOMORROW'S TO DO

✓RUNALOG® FOR TRIATHLETES

TODAY'S DATE _____

MY LONG-TERM GOAL(S) _____
_____

TODAY'S MEAL PLAN	BREAKFAST	SNACK	LUNCH	SNACK	DINNER
	_____	_____	_____	_____	_____
	_____	_____	_____	_____	_____

weekly planner

	SUNDAY	MONDAY	TUESDAY	WEDNESDAY	THURSDAY	FRIDAY	SATURDAY	TOTAL
a.m.								
p.m.								

daily planner

5 a.m. _____	2 p.m. _____
6 a.m. _____	3 p.m. _____
7 a.m. _____	4 p.m. _____
8 a.m _____	5 p.m. _____
9 a.m. _____	6 p.m. _____
10 a.m. _____	7 p.m. _____
11 a.m. _____	8 p.m. _____
12 p.m. _____	9 p.m. _____
1 p.m. _____	10 p.m. _____

my training log

SWIMMING WORKOUT:	distance
a.m.	
p.m.	
	total

BIKING WORKOUT:	distance
a.m.	
p.m.	
	total

RUNNING WORKOUT:	distance
a.m.	
p.m.	
	total

CROSS-TRAINING:	time
a.m.	
p.m.	
	total

my training journal

TOMORROW'S TO DO

⩔RUNALOG® FOR TRIATHLETES

TODAY'S DATE _____

MY LONG-TERM GOAL(S) _____
_____

TODAY'S MEAL PLAN	BREAKFAST	SNACK	LUNCH	SNACK	DINNER
	_____	_____	_____	_____	_____
	_____	_____	_____	_____	_____

weekly planner

	SUNDAY	MONDAY	TUESDAY	WEDNESDAY	THURSDAY	FRIDAY	SATURDAY	TOTAL
a.m.								
p.m.								

🕐 daily planner

5 a.m. _____	2 p.m. _____
6 a.m. _____	3 p.m. _____
7 a.m. _____	4 p.m. _____
8 a.m _____	5 p.m. _____
9 a.m. _____	6 p.m. _____
10 a.m. _____	7 p.m. _____
11 a.m. _____	8 p.m. _____
12 p.m. _____	9 p.m. _____
1 p.m. _____	10 p.m. _____

✍ my training journal

my training log

SWIMMING WORKOUT:	*distance*
a.m.	
p.m.	
	total

🚴 BIKING WORKOUT:	*distance*
a.m.	
p.m.	
	total

🏃 RUNNING WORKOUT:	*distance*
a.m.	
p.m.	
	total

CROSS-TRAINING:	*time*
a.m.	
p.m.	
	total

TOMORROW'S TO DO

29

RUNALOG° *FOR TRIATHLETES*

TODAY'S DATE _____

MY LONG-TERM GOAL(S) _____

_____

TODAY'S MEAL PLAN	BREAKFAST	SNACK	LUNCH	SNACK	DINNER
	_____	_____	_____	_____	_____
	_____	_____	_____	_____	_____

weekly planner

	SUNDAY	MONDAY	TUESDAY	WEDNESDAY	THURSDAY	FRIDAY	SATURDAY	TOTAL
a.m.								
p.m.								

daily planner

5 a.m. _____	2 p.m. _____
6 a.m. _____	3 p.m. _____
7 a.m. _____	4 p.m. _____
8 a.m _____	5 p.m. _____
9 a.m. _____	6 p.m. _____
10 a.m. _____	7 p.m. _____
11 a.m. _____	8 p.m. _____
12 p.m. _____	9 p.m. _____
1 p.m. _____	10 p.m. _____

my training journal

my training log

SWIMMING WORKOUT:	*distance*
a.m.	
p.m.	
	total

BIKING WORKOUT:	*distance*
a.m.	
p.m.	
	total

RUNNING WORKOUT:	*distance*
a.m.	
p.m.	
	total

CROSS-TRAINING:	*time*
a.m.	
p.m.	
	total

TOMORROW'S TO DO

√RUNALOG® FOR TRIATHLETES

TODAY'S DATE _____

MY LONG-TERM GOAL(S) _____

TODAY'S MEAL PLAN	BREAKFAST	SNACK	LUNCH	SNACK	DINNER
	_____	_____	_____	_____	_____
	_____	_____	_____	_____	_____
	_____	_____	_____	_____	_____

weekly planner

SUNDAY	MONDAY	TUESDAY	WEDNESDAY	THURSDAY	FRIDAY	SATURDAY	TOTAL
a.m.							
p.m.							

daily planner

5 a.m. _____	2 p.m. _____
6 a.m. _____	3 p.m. _____
7 a.m. _____	4 p.m. _____
8 a.m _____	5 p.m. _____
9 a.m. _____	6 p.m. _____
10 a.m. _____	7 p.m. _____
11 a.m. _____	8 p.m. _____
12 p.m. _____	9 p.m. _____
1 p.m. _____	10 p.m. _____

my training journal

my training log

SWIMMING WORKOUT:	*distance*
a.m.	
p.m.	
	total

BIKING WORKOUT:	*distance*
a.m.	
p.m.	
	total

RUNNING WORKOUT:	*distance*
a.m.	
p.m.	
	total

CROSS-TRAINING:	*time*
a.m.	
p.m.	
	total

TOMORROW'S TO DO

√RUNALOG® FOR TRIATHLETES

TODAY'S DATE _____

MY LONG-TERM GOAL(S) _____

TODAY'S MEAL PLAN	BREAKFAST	SNACK	LUNCH	SNACK	DINNER
	_____	_____	_____	_____	_____
	_____	_____	_____	_____	_____

weekly planner

	SUNDAY	MONDAY	TUESDAY	WEDNESDAY	THURSDAY	FRIDAY	SATURDAY	TOTAL
a.m.								
p.m.								

daily planner

5 a.m. _____	2 p.m. _____
6 a.m. _____	3 p.m. _____
7 a.m. _____	4 p.m. _____
8 a.m _____	5 p.m. _____
9 a.m. _____	6 p.m. _____
10 a.m. _____	7 p.m. _____
11 a.m. _____	8 p.m. _____
12 p.m. _____	9 p.m. _____
1 p.m. _____	10 p.m. _____

my training journal

my training log

SWIMMING WORKOUT:	*distance*
a.m.	
p.m.	
	total

BIKING WORKOUT:	*distance*
a.m.	
p.m.	
	total

RUNNING WORKOUT:	*distance*
a.m.	
p.m.	
	total

CROSS-TRAINING:	*time*
a.m.	
p.m.	
	total

TOMORROW'S To Do

32

TODAY'S DATE _____

MY LONG-TERM GOAL(S)_____
_____

TODAY'S MEAL PLAN	BREAKFAST	SNACK	LUNCH	SNACK	DINNER
	_____	_____	_____	_____	_____

weekly planner

	SUNDAY	MONDAY	TUESDAY	WEDNESDAY	THURSDAY	FRIDAY	SATURDAY	TOTAL
a.m.								
p.m.								

daily planner

5 a.m.	_____	2 p.m.	_____
6 a.m.	_____	3 p.m.	_____
7 a.m.	_____	4 p.m.	_____
8 a.m	_____	5 p.m.	_____
9 a.m.	_____	6 p.m.	_____
10 a.m.	_____	7 p.m.	_____
11 a.m.	_____	8 p.m.	_____
12 p.m.	_____	9 p.m.	_____
1 p.m.	_____	10 p.m.	_____

my training journal

my training log

SWIMMING WORKOUT:	*distance*
a.m.	
p.m.	
	total

BIKING WORKOUT:	*distance*
a.m.	
p.m.	
	total

RUNNING WORKOUT:	*distance*
a.m.	
p.m.	
	total

CROSS-TRAINING:	*time*
a.m.	
p.m.	
	total

TOMORROW'S TO DO

33

⅋RUNALOG® FOR TRIATHLETES

TODAY'S DATE _____

MY LONG-TERM GOAL(S) _____

_____

TODAY'S MEAL PLAN	BREAKFAST	SNACK	LUNCH	SNACK	DINNER
	_____	_____	_____	_____	_____
	_____	_____	_____	_____	_____

weekly planner

	SUNDAY	MONDAY	TUESDAY	WEDNESDAY	THURSDAY	FRIDAY	SATURDAY	TOTAL
a.m.								
p.m.								

daily planner

5 a.m. _____	2 p.m. _____
6 a.m. _____	3 p.m. _____
7 a.m. _____	4 p.m. _____
8 a.m _____	5 p.m. _____
9 a.m. _____	6 p.m. _____
10 a.m. _____	7 p.m. _____
11 a.m. _____	8 p.m. _____
12 p.m. _____	9 p.m. _____
1 p.m. _____	10 p.m. _____

my training journal

my training log

SWIMMING WORKOUT: *distance*

a.m.

p.m.

total

BIKING WORKOUT: *distance*

a.m.

p.m.

total

RUNNING WORKOUT: *distance*

a.m.

p.m.

total

CROSS-TRAINING: *time*

a.m.

p.m.

total

TOMORROW'S To Do

√RUNALOG® FOR TRIATHLETES

TODAY'S DATE _____

MY LONG-TERM GOAL(S) _____

_____

TODAY'S MEAL PLAN	BREAKFAST	SNACK	LUNCH	SNACK	DINNER
	___	___	___	___	___
	___	___	___	___	___

weekly planner

	SUNDAY	MONDAY	TUESDAY	WEDNESDAY	THURSDAY	FRIDAY	SATURDAY	TOTAL
a.m.								
p.m.								

daily planner

5 a.m. _____	2 p.m. _____
6 a.m. _____	3 p.m. _____
7 a.m. _____	4 p.m. _____
8 a.m _____	5 p.m. _____
9 a.m. _____	6 p.m. _____
10 a.m. _____	7 p.m. _____
11 a.m. _____	8 p.m. _____
12 p.m. _____	9 p.m. _____
1 p.m. _____	10 p.m. _____

my training journal

my training log

SWIMMING WORKOUT:	*distance*
a.m.	
p.m.	
	total

BIKING WORKOUT:	*distance*
a.m.	
p.m.	
	total

RUNNING WORKOUT:	*distance*
a.m.	
p.m.	
	total

CROSS-TRAINING:	*time*
a.m.	
p.m.	
	total

TOMORROW'S TO DO

ᔦRUNALOG® FOR TRIATHLETES

TODAY'S DATE _____

MY LONG-TERM GOAL(S) _____

TODAY'S MEAL PLAN	BREAKFAST	SNACK	LUNCH	SNACK	DINNER
	_____	_____	_____	_____	_____

weekly planner

	SUNDAY	MONDAY	TUESDAY	WEDNESDAY	THURSDAY	FRIDAY	SATURDAY	TOTAL
a.m.								
p.m.								

daily planner

5 a.m. _____	2 p.m. _____
6 a.m. _____	3 p.m. _____
7 a.m. _____	4 p.m. _____
8 a.m _____	5 p.m. _____
9 a.m. _____	6 p.m. _____
10 a.m. _____	7 p.m. _____
11 a.m. _____	8 p.m. _____
12 p.m. _____	9 p.m. _____
1 p.m. _____	10 p.m. _____

my training journal

my training log

SWIMMING WORKOUT:	*distance*
a.m.	
p.m.	
	total

BIKING WORKOUT:	*distance*
a.m.	
p.m.	
	total

RUNNING WORKOUT:	*distance*
a.m.	
p.m.	
	total

CROSS-TRAINING:	*time*
a.m.	
p.m.	
	total

TOMORROW'S TO DO

√RUNALOG® FOR TRIATHLETES   TODAY'S DATE _____

MY LONG-TERM GOAL(S) _____

TODAY'S MEAL PLAN	BREAKFAST	SNACK	LUNCH	SNACK	DINNER
	_____	_____	_____	_____	_____

weekly planner

	SUNDAY	MONDAY	TUESDAY	WEDNESDAY	THURSDAY	FRIDAY	SATURDAY	TOTAL
a.m.								
p.m.								

daily planner

5 a.m. _____	2 p.m. _____
6 a.m. _____	3 p.m. _____
7 a.m. _____	4 p.m. _____
8 a.m _____	5 p.m. _____
9 a.m. _____	6 p.m. _____
10 a.m. _____	7 p.m. _____
11 a.m. _____	8 p.m. _____
12 p.m. _____	9 p.m. _____
1 p.m. _____	10 p.m. _____

my training journal

my training log

SWIMMING WORKOUT:	*distance*
a.m.	
p.m.	
	total

BIKING WORKOUT:	*distance*
a.m.	
p.m.	
	total

RUNNING WORKOUT:	*distance*
a.m.	
p.m.	
	total

CROSS-TRAINING:	*time*
a.m.	
p.m.	
	total

TOMORROW'S To Do

37

RUNALOG® FOR TRIATHLETES

TODAY'S DATE _____

MY LONG-TERM GOAL(S) _____

TODAY'S MEAL PLAN	BREAKFAST	SNACK	LUNCH	SNACK	DINNER
	_____	_____	_____	_____	_____
	_____	_____	_____	_____	_____

weekly planner

	SUNDAY	MONDAY	TUESDAY	WEDNESDAY	THURSDAY	FRIDAY	SATURDAY	TOTAL
a.m.								
p.m.								

daily planner

5 a.m. _____	2 p.m. _____
6 a.m. _____	3 p.m. _____
7 a.m. _____	4 p.m. _____
8 a.m _____	5 p.m. _____
9 a.m. _____	6 p.m. _____
10 a.m. _____	7 p.m. _____
11 a.m. _____	8 p.m. _____
12 p.m. _____	9 p.m. _____
1 p.m. _____	10 p.m. _____

my training journal

my training log

SWIMMING WORKOUT:	*distance*
a.m.	
p.m.	
	total

BIKING WORKOUT:	*distance*
a.m.	
p.m.	
	total

RUNNING WORKOUT:	*distance*
a.m.	
p.m.	
	total

CROSS-TRAINING:	*time*
a.m.	
p.m.	
	total

TOMORROW'S TO DO

⩔RUNALOG® FOR TRIATHLETES

TODAY'S DATE _____

MY LONG-TERM GOAL(S) _____

_____

TODAY'S MEAL PLAN	BREAKFAST	SNACK	LUNCH	SNACK	DINNER
	_____	_____	_____	_____	_____

weekly planner

	SUNDAY	MONDAY	TUESDAY	WEDNESDAY	THURSDAY	FRIDAY	SATURDAY	TOTAL
a.m.								
p.m.								

🕐 daily planner

5 a.m. _____	2 p.m. _____
6 a.m. _____	3 p.m. _____
7 a.m. _____	4 p.m. _____
8 a.m _____	5 p.m. _____
9 a.m. _____	6 p.m. _____
10 a.m. _____	7 p.m. _____
11 a.m. _____	8 p.m. _____
12 p.m. _____	9 p.m. _____
1 p.m. _____	10 p.m. _____

✎ my training journal

my training log

SWIMMING WORKOUT:	*distance*
a.m.	
p.m.	
	total

🚴 BIKING WORKOUT:	*distance*
a.m.	
p.m.	
	total

🏃 RUNNING WORKOUT:	*distance*
a.m.	
p.m.	
	total

CROSS-TRAINING:	*time*
a.m.	
p.m.	
	total

TOMORROW'S TO DO

✔RUNALOG° *FOR TRIATHLETES*   *TODAY'S DATE* _____

MY LONG-TERM GOAL(S) _____
_____

TODAY'S MEAL PLAN	BREAKFAST	SNACK	LUNCH	SNACK	DINNER
	_____	_____	_____	_____	_____
	_____	_____	_____	_____	_____

weekly planner

	SUNDAY	MONDAY	TUESDAY	WEDNESDAY	THURSDAY	FRIDAY	SATURDAY	TOTAL
a.m.								
p.m.								

daily planner

5 a.m. _____	2 p.m. _____
6 a.m. _____	3 p.m. _____
7 a.m. _____	4 p.m. _____
8 a.m _____	5 p.m. _____
9 a.m. _____	6 p.m. _____
10 a.m. _____	7 p.m. _____
11 a.m. _____	8 p.m. _____
12 p.m. _____	9 p.m. _____
1 p.m. _____	10 p.m. _____

my training journal

my training log

SWIMMING WORKOUT:	*distance*
a.m.	
p.m.	
	total

BIKING WORKOUT:	*distance*
a.m.	
p.m.	
	total

RUNNING WORKOUT:	*distance*
a.m.	
p.m.	
	total

CROSS-TRAINING:	*time*
a.m.	
p.m.	
	total

TOMORROW'S TO DO

MY LONG-TERM GOAL(S) _____
_____

TODAY'S MEAL PLAN	BREAKFAST	SNACK	LUNCH	SNACK	DINNER

weekly planner

	SUNDAY	MONDAY	TUESDAY	WEDNESDAY	THURSDAY	FRIDAY	SATURDAY	TOTAL
a.m.								
p.m.								

🕐 *daily planner*

5 a.m. _____	2 p.m. _____
6 a.m. _____	3 p.m. _____
7 a.m. _____	4 p.m. _____
8 a.m _____	5 p.m. _____
9 a.m. _____	6 p.m. _____
10 a.m. _____	7 p.m. _____
11 a.m. _____	8 p.m. _____
12 p.m. _____	9 p.m. _____
1 p.m. _____	10 p.m. _____

✍ *my training journal*

my training log

SWIMMING WORKOUT:	*distance*
a.m.	
p.m.	
	total

🚴 BIKING WORKOUT:	*distance*
a.m.	
p.m.	
	total

🏃 RUNNING WORKOUT:	*distance*
a.m.	
p.m.	
	total

CROSS-TRAINING:	*time*
a.m.	
p.m.	
	total

TOMORROW'S To Do

RUNALOG° *FOR TRIATHLETES*   ***TODAY'S DATE*** _____

MY LONG-TERM GOAL(S) _____

TODAY'S MEAL PLAN	BREAKFAST	SNACK	LUNCH	SNACK	DINNER
	_____	_____	_____	_____	_____
	_____	_____	_____	_____	_____

weekly planner

	SUNDAY	MONDAY	TUESDAY	WEDNESDAY	THURSDAY	FRIDAY	SATURDAY	TOTAL
a.m.								
p.m.								

daily planner

5 a.m. _____	2 p.m. _____
6 a.m. _____	3 p.m. _____
7 a.m. _____	4 p.m. _____
8 a.m _____	5 p.m. _____
9 a.m. _____	6 p.m. _____
10 a.m. _____	7 p.m. _____
11 a.m. _____	8 p.m. _____
12 p.m. _____	9 p.m. _____
1 p.m. _____	10 p.m. _____

my training journal

my training log

SWIMMING WORKOUT: *distance*
a.m.
p.m.
total

BIKING WORKOUT: *distance*
a.m.
p.m.
total

RUNNING WORKOUT: *distance*
a.m.
p.m.
total

CROSS-TRAINING: *time*
a.m.
p.m.
total

TOMORROW'S To Do

42

√RUNALOG® FOR TRIATHLETES

TODAY'S DATE _____

MY LONG-TERM GOAL(S) _____

_____

TODAY'S MEAL PLAN	BREAKFAST	SNACK	LUNCH	SNACK	DINNER
	_____	_____	_____	_____	_____

weekly planner

	SUNDAY	MONDAY	TUESDAY	WEDNESDAY	THURSDAY	FRIDAY	SATURDAY	TOTAL
a.m.								
p.m.								

daily planner

5 a.m. _____	2 p.m. _____
6 a.m. _____	3 p.m. _____
7 a.m. _____	4 p.m. _____
8 a.m _____	5 p.m. _____
9 a.m. _____	6 p.m. _____
10 a.m. _____	7 p.m. _____
11 a.m. _____	8 p.m. _____
12 p.m. _____	9 p.m. _____
1 p.m. _____	10 p.m. _____

my training journal

my training log

SWIMMING WORKOUT:	distance
a.m.	
p.m.	
	total

BIKING WORKOUT:	distance
a.m.	
p.m.	
	total

RUNNING WORKOUT:	distance
a.m.	
p.m.	
	total

CROSS-TRAINING:	time
a.m.	
p.m.	
	total

TOMORROW'S To Do

43

⚓RUNALOG® FOR TRIATHLETES   TODAY'S DATE _____

MY LONG-TERM GOAL(S) _____

_____

TODAY'S MEAL PLAN	BREAKFAST	SNACK	LUNCH	SNACK	DINNER
	_____	_____	_____	_____	_____
	_____	_____	_____	_____	_____

weekly planner

	SUNDAY	MONDAY	TUESDAY	WEDNESDAY	THURSDAY	FRIDAY	SATURDAY	TOTAL
a.m.								
p.m.								

🕐 daily planner

5 a.m. _____	2 p.m. _____
6 a.m. _____	3 p.m. _____
7 a.m. _____	4 p.m. _____
8 a.m _____	5 p.m. _____
9 a.m. _____	6 p.m. _____
10 a.m. _____	7 p.m. _____
11 a.m. _____	8 p.m. _____
12 p.m. _____	9 p.m. _____
1 p.m. _____	10 p.m. _____

✍ my training journal

my training log

SWIMMING WORKOUT:	*distance*
a.m.	
p.m.	
	total

BIKING WORKOUT:	*distance*
a.m.	
p.m.	
	total

RUNNING WORKOUT:	*distance*
a.m.	
p.m.	
	total

CROSS-TRAINING:	*time*
a.m.	
p.m.	
	total

TOMORROW'S TO DO

44

⩔RUNALOG® FOR TRIATHLETES

TODAY'S DATE _____

MY LONG-TERM GOAL(S) _____

_____

TODAY'S MEAL PLAN	BREAKFAST	SNACK	LUNCH	SNACK	DINNER
	_____	_____	_____	_____	_____
	_____	_____	_____	_____	_____

weekly planner

	SUNDAY	MONDAY	TUESDAY	WEDNESDAY	THURSDAY	FRIDAY	SATURDAY	TOTAL
a.m.								
p.m.								

🕐 daily planner

5 a.m. _____	2 p.m. _____
6 a.m. _____	3 p.m. _____
7 a.m. _____	4 p.m. _____
8 a.m _____	5 p.m. _____
9 a.m. _____	6 p.m. _____
10 a.m. _____	7 p.m. _____
11 a.m. _____	8 p.m. _____
12 p.m. _____	9 p.m. _____
1 p.m. _____	10 p.m. _____

✍ my training journal

(blank lined journal area)

my training log

SWIMMING WORKOUT:	*distance*
a.m.	
p.m.	
	total

🚴 BIKING WORKOUT:	*distance*
a.m.	
p.m.	
	total

🏃 RUNNING WORKOUT:	*distance*
a.m.	
p.m.	
	total

CROSS-TRAINING:	*time*
a.m.	
p.m.	
	total

TOMORROW'S TO DO

45

⅄RUNALOG® FOR TRIATHLETES

TODAY'S DATE _____

MY LONG-TERM GOAL(S) _____

_____

TODAY'S MEAL PLAN	BREAKFAST	SNACK	LUNCH	SNACK	DINNER
	_____	_____	_____	_____	_____
	_____	_____	_____	_____	_____

weekly planner

	SUNDAY	MONDAY	TUESDAY	WEDNESDAY	THURSDAY	FRIDAY	SATURDAY	TOTAL
a.m.								
p.m.								

🕐 *daily planner*

5 a.m. _____	2 p.m. _____
6 a.m. _____	3 p.m. _____
7 a.m. _____	4 p.m. _____
8 a.m _____	5 p.m. _____
9 a.m. _____	6 p.m. _____
10 a.m. _____	7 p.m. _____
11 a.m. _____	8 p.m. _____
12 p.m. _____	9 p.m. _____
1 p.m. _____	10 p.m. _____

✍ *my training journal*

my training log

🏊 SWIMMING WORKOUT:	*distance*
a.m.	
p.m.	
	total

🚴 BIKING WORKOUT:	*distance*
a.m.	
p.m.	
	total

🏃 RUNNING WORKOUT:	*distance*
a.m.	
p.m.	
	total

CROSS-TRAINING:	*time*
a.m.	
p.m.	
	total

TOMORROW'S To Do

√RUNALOG® FOR TRIATHLETES

TODAY'S DATE _____

MY LONG-TERM GOAL(S) _____

_____

TODAY'S MEAL PLAN	BREAKFAST	SNACK	LUNCH	SNACK	DINNER
	_____	_____	_____	_____	_____
	_____	_____	_____	_____	_____

weekly planner

	SUNDAY	MONDAY	TUESDAY	WEDNESDAY	THURSDAY	FRIDAY	SATURDAY	TOTAL
a.m.								
p.m.								

daily planner

5 a.m. _____	2 p.m. _____
6 a.m. _____	3 p.m. _____
7 a.m. _____	4 p.m. _____
8 a.m _____	5 p.m. _____
9 a.m. _____	6 p.m. _____
10 a.m. _____	7 p.m. _____
11 a.m. _____	8 p.m. _____
12 p.m. _____	9 p.m. _____
1 p.m. _____	10 p.m. _____

my training journal

my training log

SWIMMING WORKOUT:	distance
a.m.	
p.m.	
	total

BIKING WORKOUT:	distance
a.m.	
p.m.	
	total

RUNNING WORKOUT:	distance
a.m.	
p.m.	
	total

CROSS-TRAINING:	time
a.m.	
p.m.	
	total

TOMORROW'S TO DO

RUNALOG® *FOR TRIATHLETES*   *TODAY'S DATE* _____

MY LONG-TERM GOAL(S) _____
_____

TODAY'S MEAL PLAN	BREAKFAST	SNACK	LUNCH	SNACK	DINNER
	_____	_____	_____	_____	_____
	_____	_____	_____	_____	_____

weekly planner

	SUNDAY	MONDAY	TUESDAY	WEDNESDAY	THURSDAY	FRIDAY	SATURDAY	TOTAL
a.m.								
p.m.								

daily planner

5 a.m. _____	2 p.m. _____
6 a.m. _____	3 p.m. _____
7 a.m. _____	4 p.m. _____
8 a.m _____	5 p.m. _____
9 a.m. _____	6 p.m. _____
10 a.m. _____	7 p.m. _____
11 a.m. _____	8 p.m. _____
12 p.m. _____	9 p.m. _____
1 p.m. _____	10 p.m. _____

my training journal

my training log

SWIMMING WORKOUT:	*distance*
a.m.	
p.m.	
	total

BIKING WORKOUT:	*distance*
a.m.	
p.m.	
	total

RUNNING WORKOUT:	*distance*
a.m.	
p.m.	
	total

CROSS-TRAINING:	*time*
a.m.	
p.m.	
	total

TOMORROW'S TO DO

↟RUNALOG® FOR TRIATHLETES

TODAY'S DATE _____

MY LONG-TERM GOAL(S) _____

_____

TODAY'S MEAL PLAN	BREAKFAST	SNACK	LUNCH	SNACK	DINNER
	_____	_____	_____	_____	_____
	_____	_____	_____	_____	_____

weekly planner

	SUNDAY	MONDAY	TUESDAY	WEDNESDAY	THURSDAY	FRIDAY	SATURDAY	TOTAL
a.m.								
p.m.								

🕐 daily planner

5 a.m. _____	2 p.m. _____
6 a.m. _____	3 p.m. _____
7 a.m. _____	4 p.m. _____
8 a.m _____	5 p.m. _____
9 a.m. _____	6 p.m. _____
10 a.m. _____	7 p.m. _____
11 a.m. _____	8 p.m. _____
12 p.m. _____	9 p.m. _____
1 p.m. _____	10 p.m. _____

✍ my training journal

my training log

SWIMMING WORKOUT:	distance
a.m.	
p.m.	
	total

BIKING WORKOUT:	distance
a.m.	
p.m.	
	total

RUNNING WORKOUT:	distance
a.m.	
p.m.	
	total

CROSS-TRAINING:	time
a.m.	
p.m.	
	total

TOMORROW'S TO DO

49

ᛋRUNALOG® FOR TRIATHLETES

TODAY'S DATE _____

MY LONG-TERM GOAL(S) _____

_____

TODAY'S MEAL PLAN	BREAKFAST	SNACK	LUNCH	SNACK	DINNER
	_____	_____	_____	_____	_____
	_____	_____	_____	_____	_____

weekly planner

	SUNDAY	MONDAY	TUESDAY	WEDNESDAY	THURSDAY	FRIDAY	SATURDAY	TOTAL
a.m.								
p.m.								

daily planner

5 a.m. _____	2 p.m. _____
6 a.m. _____	3 p.m. _____
7 a.m. _____	4 p.m. _____
8 a.m _____	5 p.m. _____
9 a.m. _____	6 p.m. _____
10 a.m. _____	7 p.m. _____
11 a.m. _____	8 p.m. _____
12 p.m. _____	9 p.m. _____
1 p.m. _____	10 p.m. _____

my training journal

my training log

SWIMMING WORKOUT:	*distance*
a.m.	
p.m.	
	total

BIKING WORKOUT:	*distance*
a.m.	
p.m.	
	total

RUNNING WORKOUT:	*distance*
a.m.	
p.m.	
	total

CROSS-TRAINING:	*time*
a.m.	
p.m.	
	total

TOMORROW'S TO DO

√RUNALOG® FOR TRIATHLETES

TODAY'S DATE _____

MY LONG-TERM GOAL(S) _____

TODAY'S MEAL PLAN	BREAKFAST	SNACK	LUNCH	SNACK	DINNER
	_____	_____	_____	_____	_____
	_____	_____	_____	_____	_____

weekly planner

	SUNDAY	MONDAY	TUESDAY	WEDNESDAY	THURSDAY	FRIDAY	SATURDAY	TOTAL
a.m.								
p.m.								

daily planner

5 a.m. _____	2 p.m. _____
6 a.m. _____	3 p.m. _____
7 a.m. _____	4 p.m. _____
8 a.m _____	5 p.m. _____
9 a.m. _____	6 p.m. _____
10 a.m. _____	7 p.m. _____
11 a.m. _____	8 p.m. _____
12 p.m. _____	9 p.m. _____
1 p.m. _____	10 p.m. _____

my training journal

my training log

SWIMMING WORKOUT:	*distance*
a.m.	
p.m.	
	total

BIKING WORKOUT:	*distance*
a.m.	
p.m.	
	total

RUNNING WORKOUT:	*distance*
a.m.	
p.m.	
	total

CROSS-TRAINING:	*time*
a.m.	
p.m.	
	total

TOMORROW'S To Do

51

RUNALOG® For Triathletes

TODAY'S DATE _____

MY LONG-TERM GOAL(S) _____

_____

TODAY'S MEAL PLAN	BREAKFAST	SNACK	LUNCH	SNACK	DINNER
	_____	_____	_____	_____	_____
	_____	_____	_____	_____	_____

weekly planner

	SUNDAY	MONDAY	TUESDAY	WEDNESDAY	THURSDAY	FRIDAY	SATURDAY	TOTAL
a.m.								
p.m.								

daily planner

5 a.m.	_____	2 p.m.	_____
6 a.m.	_____	3 p.m.	_____
7 a.m.	_____	4 p.m.	_____
8 a.m	_____	5 p.m.	_____
9 a.m.	_____	6 p.m.	_____
10 a.m.	_____	7 p.m.	_____
11 a.m.	_____	8 p.m.	_____
12 p.m.	_____	9 p.m.	_____
1 p.m.	_____	10 p.m.	_____

my training journal

my training log

SWIMMING WORKOUT:	distance
a.m.	
p.m.	
	total

BIKING WORKOUT:	distance
a.m.	
p.m.	
	total

RUNNING WORKOUT:	distance
a.m.	
p.m.	
	total

CROSS-TRAINING:	time
a.m.	
p.m.	
	total

TOMORROW'S TO DO

52

RUNALOG® FOR TRIATHLETES

TODAY'S DATE _____

MY LONG-TERM GOAL(S) _____

TODAY'S MEAL PLAN	BREAKFAST	SNACK	LUNCH	SNACK	DINNER
	_____	_____	_____	_____	_____
	_____	_____	_____	_____	_____

weekly planner

	SUNDAY	MONDAY	TUESDAY	WEDNESDAY	THURSDAY	FRIDAY	SATURDAY	TOTAL
a.m.								
p.m.								

daily planner

5 a.m. _____	2 p.m. _____
6 a.m. _____	3 p.m. _____
7 a.m. _____	4 p.m. _____
8 a.m _____	5 p.m. _____
9 a.m. _____	6 p.m. _____
10 a.m. _____	7 p.m. _____
11 a.m. _____	8 p.m. _____
12 p.m. _____	9 p.m. _____
1 p.m. _____	10 p.m. _____

my training journal

my training log

SWIMMING WORKOUT:	distance
a.m.	
p.m.	
	total

BIKING WORKOUT:	distance
a.m.	
p.m.	
	total

RUNNING WORKOUT:	distance
a.m.	
p.m.	
	total

CROSS-TRAINING:	time
a.m.	
p.m.	
	total

TOMORROW'S TO DO

RUNALOG® FOR TRIATHLETES

TODAY'S DATE _____

MY LONG-TERM GOAL(S) _____

TODAY'S MEAL PLAN	BREAKFAST	SNACK	LUNCH	SNACK	DINNER
	_____	_____	_____	_____	_____
	_____	_____	_____	_____	_____

weekly planner

	SUNDAY	MONDAY	TUESDAY	WEDNESDAY	THURSDAY	FRIDAY	SATURDAY	TOTAL
a.m.								
p.m.								

daily planner

5 a.m.	_____	2 p.m.	_____
6 a.m.	_____	3 p.m.	_____
7 a.m.	_____	4 p.m.	_____
8 a.m	_____	5 p.m.	_____
9 a.m.	_____	6 p.m.	_____
10 a.m.	_____	7 p.m.	_____
11 a.m.	_____	8 p.m.	_____
12 p.m.	_____	9 p.m.	_____
1 p.m.	_____	10 p.m.	_____

my training journal

my training log

SWIMMING WORKOUT:	*distance*
a.m.	
p.m.	
	total

BIKING WORKOUT:	*distance*
a.m.	
p.m.	
	total

RUNNING WORKOUT:	*distance*
a.m.	
p.m.	
	total

CROSS-TRAINING:	*time*
a.m.	
p.m.	
	total

TOMORROW'S TO DO

√RUNALOG® *FOR TRIATHLETES*   *TODAY'S DATE* _____

MY LONG-TERM GOAL(S) _____
_____

TODAY'S MEAL PLAN	BREAKFAST	SNACK	LUNCH	SNACK	DINNER
	_____	_____	_____	_____	_____
	_____	_____	_____	_____	_____

weekly planner

	SUNDAY	MONDAY	TUESDAY	WEDNESDAY	THURSDAY	FRIDAY	SATURDAY	TOTAL
a.m.								
p.m.								

🕐 *daily planner*

5 a.m. _____	2 p.m. _____
6 a.m. _____	3 p.m. _____
7 a.m. _____	4 p.m. _____
8 a.m _____	5 p.m. _____
9 a.m. _____	6 p.m. _____
10 a.m. _____	7 p.m. _____
11 a.m. _____	8 p.m. _____
12 p.m. _____	9 p.m. _____
1 p.m. _____	10 p.m. _____

✎ *my training journal*

my training log

🏊 SWIMMING WORKOUT:	*distance*
a.m.	
p.m.	
	total

🚴 BIKING WORKOUT:	*distance*
a.m.	
p.m.	
	total

🏃 RUNNING WORKOUT:	*distance*
a.m.	
p.m.	
	total

CROSS-TRAINING:	*time*
a.m.	
p.m.	
	total

TOMORROW'S To Do

RUNALOG® *FOR TRIATHLETES*   *TODAY'S DATE* _____

MY LONG-TERM GOAL(S) _____
_____

TODAY'S MEAL PLAN	BREAKFAST	SNACK	LUNCH	SNACK	DINNER
	_____	_____	_____	_____	_____
	_____	_____	_____	_____	_____

weekly planner

	SUNDAY	MONDAY	TUESDAY	WEDNESDAY	THURSDAY	FRIDAY	SATURDAY	TOTAL
a.m.								
p.m.								

daily planner

5 a.m. _____	2 p.m. _____
6 a.m. _____	3 p.m. _____
7 a.m. _____	4 p.m. _____
8 a.m _____	5 p.m. _____
9 a.m. _____	6 p.m. _____
10 a.m. _____	7 p.m. _____
11 a.m. _____	8 p.m. _____
12 p.m. _____	9 p.m. _____
1 p.m. _____	10 p.m. _____

my training journal

my training log

SWIMMING WORKOUT:	*distance*
a.m.	
p.m.	
	total

BIKING WORKOUT:	*distance*
a.m.	
p.m.	
	total

RUNNING WORKOUT:	*distance*
a.m.	
p.m.	
	total

CROSS-TRAINING:	*time*
a.m.	
p.m.	
	total

TOMORROW'S To Do

⩗RUNALOG® FOR TRIATHLETES

TODAY'S DATE _____

MY LONG-TERM GOAL(S) _____

_____

TODAY'S MEAL PLAN	BREAKFAST	SNACK	LUNCH	SNACK	DINNER
	_____	_____	_____	_____	_____
	_____	_____	_____	_____	_____

weekly planner

	SUNDAY	MONDAY	TUESDAY	WEDNESDAY	THURSDAY	FRIDAY	SATURDAY	TOTAL
a.m.								
p.m.								

🕐 *daily planner*

5 a.m. _____	2 p.m. _____
6 a.m. _____	3 p.m. _____
7 a.m. _____	4 p.m. _____
8 a.m _____	5 p.m. _____
9 a.m. _____	6 p.m. _____
10 a.m. _____	7 p.m. _____
11 a.m. _____	8 p.m. _____
12 p.m. _____	9 p.m. _____
1 p.m. _____	10 p.m. _____

✍ *my training journal*

my training log

SWIMMING WORKOUT:	*distance*
a.m.	
p.m.	
	total

🚴 BIKING WORKOUT:	*distance*
a.m.	
p.m.	
	total

🏃 RUNNING WORKOUT:	*distance*
a.m.	
p.m.	
	total

CROSS-TRAINING:	*time*
a.m.	
p.m.	
	total

TOMORROW'S TO DO

57

⚘RUNALOG® FOR TRIATHLETES   *TODAY'S DATE* _____

MY LONG-TERM GOAL(S) _____

TODAY'S MEAL PLAN	BREAKFAST	SNACK	LUNCH	SNACK	DINNER
	_____	_____	_____	_____	_____
	_____	_____	_____	_____	_____

weekly planner

	SUNDAY	MONDAY	TUESDAY	WEDNESDAY	THURSDAY	FRIDAY	SATURDAY	TOTAL
a.m.								
p.m.								

daily planner

5 a.m. _____	2 p.m. _____
6 a.m. _____	3 p.m. _____
7 a.m. _____	4 p.m. _____
8 a.m _____	5 p.m. _____
9 a.m. _____	6 p.m. _____
10 a.m. _____	7 p.m. _____
11 a.m. _____	8 p.m. _____
12 p.m. _____	9 p.m. _____
1 p.m. _____	10 p.m. _____

my training journal

my training log

SWIMMING WORKOUT:	*distance*
a.m.	
p.m.	
	total

BIKING WORKOUT:	*distance*
a.m.	
p.m.	
	total

RUNNING WORKOUT:	*distance*
a.m.	
p.m.	
	total

CROSS-TRAINING:	*time*
a.m.	
p.m.	
	total

TOMORROW'S To Do

58

RUNALOG® FOR TRIATHLETES

TODAY'S DATE _____

MY LONG-TERM GOAL(S) _____

TODAY'S MEAL PLAN	BREAKFAST	SNACK	LUNCH	SNACK	DINNER
	_____	_____	_____	_____	_____

weekly planner

	SUNDAY	MONDAY	TUESDAY	WEDNESDAY	THURSDAY	FRIDAY	SATURDAY	TOTAL
a.m.								
p.m.								

daily planner

5 a.m. _____	2 p.m. _____
6 a.m. _____	3 p.m. _____
7 a.m. _____	4 p.m. _____
8 a.m _____	5 p.m. _____
9 a.m. _____	6 p.m. _____
10 a.m. _____	7 p.m. _____
11 a.m. _____	8 p.m. _____
12 p.m. _____	9 p.m. _____
1 p.m. _____	10 p.m. _____

my training journal

my training log

SWIMMING WORKOUT:	distance
a.m.	
p.m.	
	total

BIKING WORKOUT:	distance
a.m.	
p.m.	
	total

RUNNING WORKOUT:	distance
a.m.	
p.m.	
	total

CROSS-TRAINING:	time
a.m.	
p.m.	
	total

TOMORROW'S TO DO

59

√RUNALOG® For Triathletes

TODAY'S DATE _____

MY LONG-TERM GOAL(S) _____
_____

TODAY'S MEAL PLAN	BREAKFAST	SNACK	LUNCH	SNACK	DINNER
	_____	_____	_____	_____	_____
	_____	_____	_____	_____	_____

weekly planner

	SUNDAY	MONDAY	TUESDAY	WEDNESDAY	THURSDAY	FRIDAY	SATURDAY	TOTAL
a.m.								
p.m.								

daily planner

5 a.m. _____	2 p.m. _____
6 a.m. _____	3 p.m. _____
7 a.m. _____	4 p.m. _____
8 a.m _____	5 p.m. _____
9 a.m. _____	6 p.m. _____
10 a.m. _____	7 p.m. _____
11 a.m. _____	8 p.m. _____
12 p.m. _____	9 p.m. _____
1 p.m. _____	10 p.m. _____

my training journal

my training log

SWIMMING WORKOUT:	distance
a.m.	
p.m.	
	total

BIKING WORKOUT:	distance
a.m.	
p.m.	
	total

RUNNING WORKOUT:	distance
a.m.	
p.m.	
	total

CROSS-TRAINING:	time
a.m.	
p.m.	
	total

TOMORROW'S TO DO

RUNALOG® For Triathletes

TODAY'S DATE _____

MY LONG-TERM GOAL(S) _____

TODAY'S MEAL PLAN	BREAKFAST	SNACK	LUNCH	SNACK	DINNER

weekly planner

	SUNDAY	MONDAY	TUESDAY	WEDNESDAY	THURSDAY	FRIDAY	SATURDAY	TOTAL
a.m.								
p.m.								

daily planner

5 a.m. _____	2 p.m. _____
6 a.m. _____	3 p.m. _____
7 a.m. _____	4 p.m. _____
8 a.m _____	5 p.m. _____
9 a.m. _____	6 p.m. _____
10 a.m. _____	7 p.m. _____
11 a.m. _____	8 p.m. _____
12 p.m. _____	9 p.m. _____
1 p.m. _____	10 p.m. _____

my training journal

my training log

SWIMMING WORKOUT:	*distance*
a.m.	
p.m.	
	total

BIKING WORKOUT:	*distance*
a.m.	
p.m.	
	total

RUNNING WORKOUT:	*distance*
a.m.	
p.m.	
	total

CROSS-TRAINING:	*time*
a.m.	
p.m.	
	total

TOMORROW'S To Do

61

⚡ RUNALOG® FOR TRIATHLETES

TODAY'S DATE _____

MY LONG-TERM GOAL(S) _____

TODAY'S MEAL PLAN	BREAKFAST	SNACK	LUNCH	SNACK	DINNER
	_____	_____	_____	_____	_____
	_____	_____	_____	_____	_____

weekly planner

	SUNDAY	MONDAY	TUESDAY	WEDNESDAY	THURSDAY	FRIDAY	SATURDAY	TOTAL
a.m.								
p.m.								

🕐 daily planner

5 a.m. _____	2 p.m. _____
6 a.m. _____	3 p.m. _____
7 a.m. _____	4 p.m. _____
8 a.m _____	5 p.m. _____
9 a.m. _____	6 p.m. _____
10 a.m. _____	7 p.m. _____
11 a.m. _____	8 p.m. _____
12 p.m. _____	9 p.m. _____
1 p.m. _____	10 p.m. _____

✍ my training journal

my training log

🏊 SWIMMING WORKOUT: distance
a.m.

p.m.

total

🚴 BIKING WORKOUT: distance
a.m.

p.m.

total

🏃 RUNNING WORKOUT: distance
a.m.

p.m.

total

CROSS-TRAINING: time
a.m.

p.m.

total

TOMORROW'S TO DO

ᐱRUNALOG® FOR TRIATHLETES

TODAY'S DATE _____

MY LONG-TERM GOAL(S) _____

TODAY'S MEAL PLAN	BREAKFAST	SNACK	LUNCH	SNACK	DINNER

weekly planner

	SUNDAY	MONDAY	TUESDAY	WEDNESDAY	THURSDAY	FRIDAY	SATURDAY	TOTAL
a.m.								
p.m.								

🕐 *daily planner*

5 a.m. _____	2 p.m. _____
6 a.m. _____	3 p.m. _____
7 a.m. _____	4 p.m. _____
8 a.m _____	5 p.m. _____
9 a.m. _____	6 p.m. _____
10 a.m. _____	7 p.m. _____
11 a.m. _____	8 p.m. _____
12 p.m. _____	9 p.m. _____
1 p.m. _____	10 p.m. _____

✍ *my training journal*

my training log

SWIMMING WORKOUT:	*distance*
a.m.	
p.m.	
	total

BIKING WORKOUT:	*distance*
a.m.	
p.m.	
	total

RUNNING WORKOUT:	*distance*
a.m.	
p.m.	
	total

CROSS-TRAINING:	*time*
a.m.	
p.m.	
	total

TOMORROW'S TO DO

RUNALOG® FOR TRIATHLETES

TODAY'S DATE _____

MY LONG-TERM GOAL(S) _____

_____

TODAY'S MEAL PLAN	BREAKFAST	SNACK	LUNCH	SNACK	DINNER
	_____	_____	_____	_____	_____
	_____	_____	_____	_____	_____

weekly planner

	SUNDAY	MONDAY	TUESDAY	WEDNESDAY	THURSDAY	FRIDAY	SATURDAY	TOTAL
a.m.								
p.m.								

daily planner

5 a.m. _____	2 p.m. _____
6 a.m. _____	3 p.m. _____
7 a.m. _____	4 p.m. _____
8 a.m _____	5 p.m. _____
9 a.m. _____	6 p.m. _____
10 a.m. _____	7 p.m. _____
11 a.m. _____	8 p.m. _____
12 p.m. _____	9 p.m. _____
1 p.m. _____	10 p.m. _____

my training journal

my training log

SWIMMING WORKOUT:	distance
a.m.	
p.m.	
	total

BIKING WORKOUT:	distance
a.m.	
p.m.	
	total

RUNNING WORKOUT:	distance
a.m.	
p.m.	
	total

CROSS-TRAINING:	time
a.m.	
p.m.	
	total

TOMORROW'S TO DO

ᐯRUNALOG® FOR TRIATHLETES

TODAY'S DATE _____

MY LONG-TERM GOAL(S) _____

TODAY'S MEAL PLAN	BREAKFAST	SNACK	LUNCH	SNACK	DINNER
	_____	_____	_____	_____	_____

weekly planner

	SUNDAY	MONDAY	TUESDAY	WEDNESDAY	THURSDAY	FRIDAY	SATURDAY	TOTAL
a.m.								
p.m.								

daily planner

5 a.m. _____	2 p.m. _____
6 a.m. _____	3 p.m. _____
7 a.m. _____	4 p.m. _____
8 a.m _____	5 p.m. _____
9 a.m. _____	6 p.m. _____
10 a.m. _____	7 p.m. _____
11 a.m. _____	8 p.m. _____
12 p.m. _____	9 p.m. _____
1 p.m. _____	10 p.m. _____

my training journal

my training log

SWIMMING WORKOUT: *distance*

a.m.	
p.m.	
	total

BIKING WORKOUT: *distance*

a.m.	
p.m.	
	total

RUNNING WORKOUT: *distance*

a.m.	
p.m.	
	total

CROSS-TRAINING: *time*

a.m.	
p.m.	
	total

TOMORROW'S TO DO

√RUNALOG® FOR TRIATHLETES

TODAY'S DATE _____

MY LONG-TERM GOAL(S) _____

_____

TODAY'S MEAL PLAN	BREAKFAST	SNACK	LUNCH	SNACK	DINNER
	_____	_____	_____	_____	_____
	_____	_____	_____	_____	_____

weekly planner

	SUNDAY	MONDAY	TUESDAY	WEDNESDAY	THURSDAY	FRIDAY	SATURDAY	TOTAL
a.m.								
p.m.								

daily planner

5 a.m. _____	2 p.m. _____
6 a.m. _____	3 p.m. _____
7 a.m. _____	4 p.m. _____
8 a.m _____	5 p.m. _____
9 a.m. _____	6 p.m. _____
10 a.m. _____	7 p.m. _____
11 a.m. _____	8 p.m. _____
12 p.m. _____	9 p.m. _____
1 p.m. _____	10 p.m. _____

my training journal

my training log

SWIMMING WORKOUT:	*distance*
a.m.	
p.m.	
	total

BIKING WORKOUT:	*distance*
a.m.	
p.m.	
	total

RUNNING WORKOUT:	*distance*
a.m.	
p.m.	
	total

CROSS-TRAINING:	*time*
a.m.	
p.m.	
	total

TOMORROW'S To Do

66

ⱯRUNALOG® FOR TRIATHLETES

TODAY'S DATE _____

MY LONG-TERM GOAL(S) _____

TODAY'S MEAL PLAN	BREAKFAST	SNACK	LUNCH	SNACK	DINNER

weekly planner

	SUNDAY	MONDAY	TUESDAY	WEDNESDAY	THURSDAY	FRIDAY	SATURDAY	TOTAL
a.m.								
p.m.								

daily planner

5 a.m. _____	2 p.m. _____
6 a.m. _____	3 p.m. _____
7 a.m. _____	4 p.m. _____
8 a.m _____	5 p.m. _____
9 a.m. _____	6 p.m. _____
10 a.m. _____	7 p.m. _____
11 a.m. _____	8 p.m. _____
12 p.m. _____	9 p.m. _____
1 p.m. _____	10 p.m. _____

my training journal

my training log

SWIMMING WORKOUT:	distance
a.m.	
p.m.	
	total

BIKING WORKOUT:	distance
a.m.	
p.m.	
	total

RUNNING WORKOUT:	distance
a.m.	
p.m.	
	total

CROSS-TRAINING:	time
a.m.	
p.m.	
	total

TOMORROW'S To Do

67

⚕RUNALOG® FOR TRIATHLETES

TODAY'S DATE _____

MY LONG-TERM GOAL(S) _____

_____

TODAY'S MEAL PLAN	BREAKFAST	SNACK	LUNCH	SNACK	DINNER
	_____	_____	_____	_____	_____
	_____	_____	_____	_____	_____

weekly planner

	SUNDAY	MONDAY	TUESDAY	WEDNESDAY	THURSDAY	FRIDAY	SATURDAY	TOTAL
a.m.								
p.m.								

🕐 daily planner

5 a.m. _____	2 p.m. _____
6 a.m. _____	3 p.m. _____
7 a.m. _____	4 p.m. _____
8 a.m _____	5 p.m. _____
9 a.m. _____	6 p.m. _____
10 a.m. _____	7 p.m. _____
11 a.m. _____	8 p.m. _____
12 p.m. _____	9 p.m. _____
1 p.m. _____	10 p.m. _____

✍ my training journal

my training log

SWIMMING WORKOUT:	*distance*
a.m.	
p.m.	
	total

🚴 BIKING WORKOUT:	*distance*
a.m.	
p.m.	
	total

🏃 RUNNING WORKOUT:	*distance*
a.m.	
p.m.	
	total

CROSS-TRAINING:	*time*
a.m.	
p.m.	
	total

TOMORROW'S TO DO

ᐱRUNALOG® FOR TRIATHLETES

MY LONG-TERM GOAL(S) _____

TODAY'S MEAL PLAN	BREAKFAST	SNACK	LUNCH	SNACK	DINNER
	_____	_____	_____	_____	_____

weekly planner

	SUNDAY	MONDAY	TUESDAY	WEDNESDAY	THURSDAY	FRIDAY	SATURDAY	TOTAL
a.m.								
p.m.								

🕐 daily planner

5 a.m. _____	2 p.m. _____
6 a.m. _____	3 p.m. _____
7 a.m. _____	4 p.m. _____
8 a.m _____	5 p.m. _____
9 a.m. _____	6 p.m. _____
10 a.m. _____	7 p.m. _____
11 a.m. _____	8 p.m. _____
12 p.m. _____	9 p.m. _____
1 p.m. _____	10 p.m. _____

✍ my training journal

my training log

SWIMMING WORKOUT:	distance
a.m.	
p.m.	
	total

🚴 BIKING WORKOUT:	distance
a.m.	
p.m.	
	total

🏃 RUNNING WORKOUT:	distance
a.m.	
p.m.	
	total

CROSS-TRAINING:	time
a.m.	
p.m.	
	total

TOMORROW'S TO DO

MY LONG-TERM GOAL(S) _____

TODAY'S MEAL PLAN	BREAKFAST	SNACK	LUNCH	SNACK	DINNER
	____	____	____	____	____
	____	____	____	____	____

weekly planner

	SUNDAY	MONDAY	TUESDAY	WEDNESDAY	THURSDAY	FRIDAY	SATURDAY	TOTAL
a.m.								
p.m.								

daily planner

5 a.m. ____	2 p.m. ____
6 a.m. ____	3 p.m. ____
7 a.m. ____	4 p.m. ____
8 a.m ____	5 p.m. ____
9 a.m. ____	6 p.m. ____
10 a.m. ____	7 p.m. ____
11 a.m. ____	8 p.m. ____
12 p.m. ____	9 p.m. ____
1 p.m. ____	10 p.m. ____

my training journal

my training log

SWIMMING WORKOUT: *distance*

a.m.

p.m.

total

BIKING WORKOUT: *distance*

a.m.

p.m.

total

RUNNING WORKOUT: *distance*

a.m.

p.m.

total

CROSS-TRAINING: *time*

a.m.

p.m.

total

TOMORROW'S TO DO

ⱴRUNALOG® FOR TRIATHLETES

TODAY'S DATE _____

MY LONG-TERM GOAL(S) _____

TODAY'S MEAL PLAN	BREAKFAST	SNACK	LUNCH	SNACK	DINNER
	_____	_____	_____	_____	_____

weekly planner

	SUNDAY	MONDAY	TUESDAY	WEDNESDAY	THURSDAY	FRIDAY	SATURDAY	TOTAL
a.m.								
p.m.								

🕐 *daily planner*

5 a.m. _____	2 p.m. _____
6 a.m. _____	3 p.m. _____
7 a.m. _____	4 p.m. _____
8 a.m _____	5 p.m. _____
9 a.m. _____	6 p.m. _____
10 a.m. _____	7 p.m. _____
11 a.m. _____	8 p.m. _____
12 p.m. _____	9 p.m. _____
1 p.m. _____	10 p.m. _____

✍ *my training journal*

my training log

SWIMMING WORKOUT:	*distance*
a.m.	
p.m.	
	total

BIKING WORKOUT:	*distance*
a.m.	
p.m.	
	total

RUNNING WORKOUT:	*distance*
a.m.	
p.m.	
	total

CROSS-TRAINING:	*time*
a.m.	
p.m.	
	total

TOMORROW'S TO DO

RUNALOG® FOR TRIATHLETES

TODAY'S DATE _____

MY LONG-TERM GOAL(S) _____
_____

TODAY'S MEAL PLAN	BREAKFAST	SNACK	LUNCH	SNACK	DINNER
	_____	_____	_____	_____	_____
	_____	_____	_____	_____	_____

weekly planner

	SUNDAY	MONDAY	TUESDAY	WEDNESDAY	THURSDAY	FRIDAY	SATURDAY	TOTAL
a.m.								
p.m.								

daily planner

5 a.m. _____		2 p.m. _____	
6 a.m. _____		3 p.m. _____	
7 a.m. _____		4 p.m. _____	
8 a.m _____		5 p.m. _____	
9 a.m. _____		6 p.m. _____	
10 a.m. _____		7 p.m. _____	
11 a.m. _____		8 p.m. _____	
12 p.m. _____		9 p.m. _____	
1 p.m. _____		10 p.m. _____	

my training log

SWIMMING WORKOUT:	distance
a.m.	
p.m.	
	total

BIKING WORKOUT:	distance
a.m.	
p.m.	
	total

RUNNING WORKOUT:	distance
a.m.	
p.m.	
	total

CROSS-TRAINING:	time
a.m.	
p.m.	
	total

my training journal

TOMORROW'S TO DO

RUNALOG® FOR TRIATHLETES

TODAY'S DATE _____

MY LONG-TERM GOAL(S) _____

_____

TODAY'S MEAL PLAN	BREAKFAST	SNACK	LUNCH	SNACK	DINNER
	_____	_____	_____	_____	_____
	_____	_____	_____	_____	_____

weekly planner

	SUNDAY	MONDAY	TUESDAY	WEDNESDAY	THURSDAY	FRIDAY	SATURDAY	TOTAL
a.m.								
p.m.								

daily planner

5 a.m. _____	2 p.m. _____
6 a.m. _____	3 p.m. _____
7 a.m. _____	4 p.m. _____
8 a.m _____	5 p.m. _____
9 a.m. _____	6 p.m. _____
10 a.m. _____	7 p.m. _____
11 a.m. _____	8 p.m. _____
12 p.m. _____	9 p.m. _____
1 p.m. _____	10 p.m. _____

my training journal

my training log

SWIMMING WORKOUT:	distance
a.m.	
p.m.	
	total

BIKING WORKOUT:	distance
a.m.	
p.m.	
	total

RUNNING WORKOUT:	distance
a.m.	
p.m.	
	total

CROSS-TRAINING:	time
a.m.	
p.m.	
	total

TOMORROW'S TO DO

73

RUNALOG® FOR TRIATHLETES

TODAY'S DATE _____

MY LONG-TERM GOAL(S) _____

TODAY'S MEAL PLAN	BREAKFAST	SNACK	LUNCH	SNACK	DINNER
	_____	_____	_____	_____	_____
	_____	_____	_____	_____	_____

weekly planner

	SUNDAY	MONDAY	TUESDAY	WEDNESDAY	THURSDAY	FRIDAY	SATURDAY	TOTAL
a.m.								
p.m.								

daily planner

5 a.m. _____	2 p.m. _____
6 a.m. _____	3 p.m. _____
7 a.m. _____	4 p.m. _____
8 a.m _____	5 p.m. _____
9 a.m. _____	6 p.m. _____
10 a.m. _____	7 p.m. _____
11 a.m. _____	8 p.m. _____
12 p.m. _____	9 p.m. _____
1 p.m. _____	10 p.m. _____

my training journal

my training log

SWIMMING WORKOUT:	distance
a.m.	
p.m.	
	total

BIKING WORKOUT:	distance
a.m.	
p.m.	
	total

RUNNING WORKOUT:	distance
a.m.	
p.m.	
	total

CROSS-TRAINING:	time
a.m.	
p.m.	
	total

TOMORROW'S TO DO

⩗RUNALOG® FOR TRIATHLETES

TODAY'S DATE _____

MY LONG-TERM GOAL(S) _____ .

TODAY'S MEAL PLAN	BREAKFAST	SNACK	LUNCH	SNACK	DINNER
	_____	_____	_____	_____	_____
	_____	_____	_____	_____	_____

weekly planner

	SUNDAY	MONDAY	TUESDAY	WEDNESDAY	THURSDAY	FRIDAY	SATURDAY	TOTAL
a.m.								
p.m.								

🕐 daily planner

5 a.m. _____	2 p.m. _____
6 a.m. _____	3 p.m. _____
7 a.m. _____	4 p.m. _____
8 a.m _____	5 p.m. _____
9 a.m. _____	6 p.m. _____
10 a.m. _____	7 p.m. _____
11 a.m. _____	8 p.m. _____
12 p.m. _____	9 p.m. _____
1 p.m. _____	10 p.m. _____

✎ my training journal

my training log

🏊 SWIMMING WORKOUT:	*distance*
a.m.	
p.m.	
	total

🚴 BIKING WORKOUT:	*distance*
a.m.	
p.m.	
	total

🏃 RUNNING WORKOUT:	*distance*
a.m.	
p.m.	
	total

CROSS-TRAINING:	*time*
a.m.	
p.m.	
	total

TOMORROW'S To Do

75

√RUNALOG® FOR TRIATHLETES

TODAY'S DATE _____

MY LONG-TERM GOAL(S) _____

TODAY'S MEAL PLAN	BREAKFAST	SNACK	LUNCH	SNACK	DINNER
	_____	_____	_____	_____	_____
	_____	_____	_____	_____	_____

weekly planner

	SUNDAY	MONDAY	TUESDAY	WEDNESDAY	THURSDAY	FRIDAY	SATURDAY	TOTAL
a.m.								
p.m.								

daily planner

5 a.m. _____	2 p.m. _____
6 a.m. _____	3 p.m. _____
7 a.m. _____	4 p.m. _____
8 a.m _____	5 p.m. _____
9 a.m. _____	6 p.m. _____
10 a.m. _____	7 p.m. _____
11 a.m. _____	8 p.m. _____
12 p.m. _____	9 p.m. _____
1 p.m. _____	10 p.m. _____

my training journal

my training log

SWIMMING WORKOUT:	*distance*
a.m.	
p.m.	
	total

BIKING WORKOUT:	*distance*
a.m.	
p.m.	
	total

RUNNING WORKOUT:	*distance*
a.m.	
p.m.	
	total

CROSS-TRAINING:	*time*
a.m.	
p.m.	
	total

TOMORROW'S TO DO

RUNALOG® FOR TRIATHLETES

TODAY'S DATE _____

MY LONG-TERM GOAL(S) _____

TODAY'S MEAL PLAN	BREAKFAST	SNACK	LUNCH	SNACK	DINNER

weekly planner

	SUNDAY	MONDAY	TUESDAY	WEDNESDAY	THURSDAY	FRIDAY	SATURDAY	TOTAL
a.m.								
p.m.								

daily planner

5 a.m. _____	2 p.m. _____
6 a.m. _____	3 p.m. _____
7 a.m. _____	4 p.m. _____
8 a.m _____	5 p.m. _____
9 a.m. _____	6 p.m. _____
10 a.m. _____	7 p.m. _____
11 a.m. _____	8 p.m. _____
12 p.m. _____	9 p.m. _____
1 p.m. _____	10 p.m. _____

my training journal

my training log

SWIMMING WORKOUT:	distance
a.m.	
p.m.	
	total

BIKING WORKOUT:	distance
a.m.	
p.m.	
	total

RUNNING WORKOUT:	distance
a.m.	
p.m.	
	total

CROSS-TRAINING:	time
a.m.	
p.m.	
	total

TOMORROW'S TO DO

RUNALOG® FOR TRIATHLETES

TODAY'S DATE _____

MY LONG-TERM GOAL(S) _____

TODAY'S MEAL PLAN	BREAKFAST	SNACK	LUNCH	SNACK	DINNER
	_____	_____	_____	_____	_____
	_____	_____	_____	_____	_____

weekly planner

	SUNDAY	MONDAY	TUESDAY	WEDNESDAY	THURSDAY	FRIDAY	SATURDAY	TOTAL
a.m.								
p.m.								

daily planner

5 a.m. _____	2 p.m. _____
6 a.m. _____	3 p.m. _____
7 a.m. _____	4 p.m. _____
8 a.m _____	5 p.m. _____
9 a.m. _____	6 p.m. _____
10 a.m. _____	7 p.m. _____
11 a.m. _____	8 p.m. _____
12 p.m. _____	9 p.m. _____
1 p.m. _____	10 p.m. _____

my training journal

my training log

SWIMMING WORKOUT:	*distance*
a.m.	
p.m.	
	total

BIKING WORKOUT:	*distance*
a.m.	
p.m.	
	total

RUNNING WORKOUT:	*distance*
a.m.	
p.m.	
	total

CROSS-TRAINING:	*time*
a.m.	
p.m.	
	total

TOMORROW'S TO DO

∜RUNALOG® *FOR TRIATHLETES*　　**TODAY'S DATE** _____

MY LONG-TERM GOAL(S) _____

_____

TODAY'S MEAL PLAN	BREAKFAST	SNACK	LUNCH	SNACK	DINNER
	_____	_____	_____	_____	_____
	_____	_____	_____	_____	_____

weekly planner

	SUNDAY	MONDAY	TUESDAY	WEDNESDAY	THURSDAY	FRIDAY	SATURDAY	TOTAL
a.m.								
p.m.								

daily planner

5 a.m. _____	2 p.m. _____
6 a.m. _____	3 p.m. _____
7 a.m. _____	4 p.m. _____
8 a.m _____	5 p.m. _____
9 a.m. _____	6 p.m. _____
10 a.m. _____	7 p.m. _____
11 a.m. _____	8 p.m. _____
12 p.m. _____	9 p.m. _____
1 p.m. _____	10 p.m. _____

my training journal

my training log

SWIMMING WORKOUT:	*distance*
a.m.	
p.m.	
	total

BIKING WORKOUT:	*distance*
a.m.	
p.m.	
	total

RUNNING WORKOUT:	*distance*
a.m.	
p.m.	
	total

CROSS-TRAINING:	*time*
a.m.	
p.m.	
	total

TOMORROW'S TO DO

⚕ RUNALOG® FOR TRIATHLETES

TODAY'S DATE _____

MY LONG-TERM GOAL(S) _____

_____

TODAY'S MEAL PLAN	BREAKFAST	SNACK	LUNCH	SNACK	DINNER
	_____	_____	_____	_____	_____
	_____	_____	_____	_____	_____

weekly planner

	SUNDAY	MONDAY	TUESDAY	WEDNESDAY	THURSDAY	FRIDAY	SATURDAY	TOTAL
a.m.								
p.m.								

🕐 daily planner

5 a.m. _____	2 p.m. _____
6 a.m. _____	3 p.m. _____
7 a.m. _____	4 p.m. _____
8 a.m _____	5 p.m. _____
9 a.m. _____	6 p.m. _____
10 a.m. _____	7 p.m. _____
11 a.m. _____	8 p.m. _____
12 p.m. _____	9 p.m. _____
1 p.m. _____	10 p.m. _____

✍ my training journal

my training log

SWIMMING WORKOUT:	distance
a.m.	
p.m.	
	total

BIKING WORKOUT:	distance
a.m.	
p.m.	
	total

RUNNING WORKOUT:	distance
a.m.	
p.m.	
	total

CROSS-TRAINING:	time
a.m.	
p.m.	
	total

TOMORROW'S TO DO

⚡RUNALOG° *FOR TRIATHLETES*

TODAY'S DATE _____

MY LONG-TERM GOAL(S) _____
_____

TODAY'S MEAL PLAN	BREAKFAST	SNACK	LUNCH	SNACK	DINNER
	_____	_____	_____	_____	_____
	_____	_____	_____	_____	_____

weekly planner

	SUNDAY	MONDAY	TUESDAY	WEDNESDAY	THURSDAY	FRIDAY	SATURDAY	TOTAL
a.m.								
p.m.								

🕐 *daily planner*

5 a.m. _____	2 p.m. _____
6 a.m. _____	3 p.m. _____
7 a.m. _____	4 p.m. _____
8 a.m _____	5 p.m. _____
9 a.m. _____	6 p.m. _____
10 a.m. _____	7 p.m. _____
11 a.m. _____	8 p.m. _____
12 p.m. _____	9 p.m. _____
1 p.m. _____	10 p.m. _____

✍ *my training journal*

my training log

🏊 SWIMMING WORKOUT:	*distance*
a.m.	
p.m.	
	total

🚴 BIKING WORKOUT:	*distance*
a.m.	
p.m.	
	total

🏃 RUNNING WORKOUT:	*distance*
a.m.	
p.m.	
	total

CROSS-TRAINING:	*time*
a.m.	
p.m.	
	total

TOMORROW'S To Do

81

⚡RUNALOG® *FOR TRIATHLETES*

TODAY'S DATE _____

MY LONG-TERM GOAL(S) _____

_____

TODAY'S MEAL PLAN	BREAKFAST	SNACK	LUNCH	SNACK	DINNER
	_____	_____	_____	_____	_____
	_____	_____	_____	_____	_____

weekly planner

	SUNDAY	MONDAY	TUESDAY	WEDNESDAY	THURSDAY	FRIDAY	SATURDAY	TOTAL
a.m.								
p.m.								

🕐 *daily planner*

5 a.m. _____	2 p.m. _____
6 a.m. _____	3 p.m. _____
7 a.m. _____	4 p.m. _____
8 a.m _____	5 p.m. _____
9 a.m. _____	6 p.m. _____
10 a.m. _____	7 p.m. _____
11 a.m. _____	8 p.m. _____
12 p.m. _____	9 p.m. _____
1 p.m. _____	10 p.m. _____

✍ *my training journal*

my training log

SWIMMING WORKOUT: *distance*

a.m.		
p.m.		
		total

BIKING WORKOUT: *distance*

a.m.		
p.m.		
		total

RUNNING WORKOUT: *distance*

a.m.		
p.m.		
		total

CROSS-TRAINING: *time*

a.m.		
p.m.		
		total

TOMORROW'S TO DO

⩔RUNALOG® FOR TRIATHLETES   *TODAY'S DATE* _____

MY LONG-TERM GOAL(S) _____

TODAY'S MEAL PLAN	BREAKFAST	SNACK	LUNCH	SNACK	DINNER
	_____	_____	_____	_____	_____

weekly planner

	SUNDAY	MONDAY	TUESDAY	WEDNESDAY	THURSDAY	FRIDAY	SATURDAY	TOTAL
a.m.								
p.m.								

daily planner

5 a.m. _____	2 p.m. _____
6 a.m. _____	3 p.m. _____
7 a.m. _____	4 p.m. _____
8 a.m _____	5 p.m. _____
9 a.m. _____	6 p.m. _____
10 a.m. _____	7 p.m. _____
11 a.m. _____	8 p.m. _____
12 p.m. _____	9 p.m. _____
1 p.m. _____	10 p.m. _____

my training journal

my training log

SWIMMING WORKOUT:	distance
a.m.	
p.m.	
	total

BIKING WORKOUT:	distance
a.m.	
p.m.	
	total

RUNNING WORKOUT:	distance
a.m.	
p.m.	
	total

CROSS-TRAINING:	time
a.m.	
p.m.	
	total

TOMORROW'S To Do

83

© 2009 www.RUNALOGS.com

√RUNALOG® FOR TRIATHLETES

TODAY'S DATE _____

MY LONG-TERM GOAL(S) _____

_____

TODAY'S MEAL PLAN	BREAKFAST	SNACK	LUNCH	SNACK	DINNER
	_____	_____	_____	_____	_____
	_____	_____	_____	_____	_____

weekly planner

	SUNDAY	MONDAY	TUESDAY	WEDNESDAY	THURSDAY	FRIDAY	SATURDAY	TOTAL
a.m.								
p.m.								

daily planner

5 a.m. _____	2 p.m. _____
6 a.m. _____	3 p.m. _____
7 a.m. _____	4 p.m. _____
8 a.m _____	5 p.m. _____
9 a.m. _____	6 p.m. _____
10 a.m. _____	7 p.m. _____
11 a.m. _____	8 p.m. _____
12 p.m. _____	9 p.m. _____
1 p.m. _____	10 p.m. _____

my training journal

my training log

SWIMMING WORKOUT:	distance
a.m.	
p.m.	
	total

BIKING WORKOUT:	distance
a.m.	
p.m.	
	total

RUNNING WORKOUT:	distance
a.m.	
p.m.	
	total

CROSS-TRAINING:	time
a.m.	
p.m.	
	total

TOMORROW'S TO DO

ⱽRUNALOG® FOR TRIATHLETES

TODAY'S DATE _____

MY LONG-TERM GOAL(S)_____

TODAY'S MEAL PLAN	BREAKFAST	SNACK	LUNCH	SNACK	DINNER
	_____	_____	_____	_____	_____

weekly planner

	SUNDAY	MONDAY	TUESDAY	WEDNESDAY	THURSDAY	FRIDAY	SATURDAY	TOTAL
a.m.								
p.m.								

daily planner

5 a.m. _____	2 p.m. _____
6 a.m. _____	3 p.m. _____
7 a.m. _____	4 p.m. _____
8 a.m _____	5 p.m. _____
9 a.m. _____	6 p.m. _____
10 a.m. _____	7 p.m. _____
11 a.m. _____	8 p.m. _____
12 p.m. _____	9 p.m. _____
1 p.m. _____	10 p.m. _____

my training journal

my training log

SWIMMING WORKOUT:	*distance*
a.m.	
p.m.	
	total

BIKING WORKOUT:	*distance*
a.m.	
p.m.	
	total

RUNNING WORKOUT:	*distance*
a.m.	
p.m.	
	total

CROSS-TRAINING:	*time*
a.m.	
p.m.	
	total

TOMORROW'S To Do

85

ᐯRUNALOG® FOR TRIATHLETES

TODAY'S DATE _____

MY LONG-TERM GOAL(S) _____

TODAY'S MEAL PLAN	BREAKFAST	SNACK	LUNCH	SNACK	DINNER
	_____	_____	_____	_____	_____
	_____	_____	_____	_____	_____

weekly planner

	SUNDAY	MONDAY	TUESDAY	WEDNESDAY	THURSDAY	FRIDAY	SATURDAY	TOTAL
a.m.								
p.m.								

daily planner

5 a.m.	_____	2 p.m.	_____
6 a.m.	_____	3 p.m.	_____
7 a.m.	_____	4 p.m.	_____
8 a.m	_____	5 p.m.	_____
9 a.m.	_____	6 p.m.	_____
10 a.m.	_____	7 p.m.	_____
11 a.m.	_____	8 p.m.	_____
12 p.m.	_____	9 p.m.	_____
1 p.m.	_____	10 p.m.	_____

my training journal

my training log

SWIMMING WORKOUT:	*distance*
a.m.	
p.m.	
	total

BIKING WORKOUT:	*distance*
a.m.	
p.m.	
	total

RUNNING WORKOUT:	*distance*
a.m.	
p.m.	
	total

CROSS-TRAINING:	*time*
a.m.	
p.m.	
	total

TOMORROW'S TO DO

√RUNALOG® FOR TRIATHLETES   **TODAY'S DATE** _____

MY LONG-TERM GOAL(S) _____
_____

TODAY'S MEAL PLAN	BREAKFAST	SNACK	LUNCH	SNACK	DINNER
	_____	_____	_____	_____	_____
	_____	_____	_____	_____	_____

weekly planner

	SUNDAY	MONDAY	TUESDAY	WEDNESDAY	THURSDAY	FRIDAY	SATURDAY	TOTAL
a.m.								
p.m.								

🕐 *daily planner*

5 a.m. _____	2 p.m. _____
6 a.m. _____	3 p.m. _____
7 a.m. _____	4 p.m. _____
8 a.m _____	5 p.m. _____
9 a.m. _____	6 p.m. _____
10 a.m. _____	7 p.m. _____
11 a.m. _____	8 p.m. _____
12 p.m. _____	9 p.m. _____
1 p.m. _____	10 p.m. _____

✍ *my training journal*

my training log

SWIMMING WORKOUT:	*distance*
a.m.	
p.m.	
	total

🚴 BIKING WORKOUT:	*distance*
a.m.	
p.m.	
	total

🏃 RUNNING WORKOUT:	*distance*
a.m.	
p.m.	
	total

CROSS-TRAINING:	*time*
a.m.	
p.m.	
	total

TOMORROW'S To Do

TODAY'S DATE _____

MY LONG-TERM GOAL(S) _____
_____

TODAY'S MEAL PLAN	BREAKFAST	SNACK	LUNCH	SNACK	DINNER
	_____	_____	_____	_____	_____

weekly planner

	SUNDAY	MONDAY	TUESDAY	WEDNESDAY	THURSDAY	FRIDAY	SATURDAY	TOTAL
a.m.								
p.m.								

daily planner

5 a.m. _____	2 p.m. _____
6 a.m. _____	3 p.m. _____
7 a.m. _____	4 p.m. _____
8 a.m _____	5 p.m. _____
9 a.m. _____	6 p.m. _____
10 a.m. _____	7 p.m. _____
11 a.m. _____	8 p.m. _____
12 p.m. _____	9 p.m. _____
1 p.m. _____	10 p.m. _____

my training journal

my training log

SWIMMING WORKOUT:	*distance*
a.m.	
p.m.	
	total

BIKING WORKOUT:	*distance*
a.m.	
p.m.	
	total

RUNNING WORKOUT:	*distance*
a.m.	
p.m.	
	total

CROSS-TRAINING:	*time*
a.m.	
p.m.	
	total

TOMORROW'S TO DO

√RUNALOG® FOR TRIATHLETES

TODAY'S DATE _____

MY LONG-TERM GOAL(S) _____

TODAY'S MEAL PLAN	BREAKFAST	SNACK	LUNCH	SNACK	DINNER
	_____	_____	_____	_____	_____
	_____	_____	_____	_____	_____

weekly planner

	SUNDAY	MONDAY	TUESDAY	WEDNESDAY	THURSDAY	FRIDAY	SATURDAY	TOTAL
a.m.								
p.m.								

daily planner

5 a.m. _____	2 p.m. _____
6 a.m. _____	3 p.m. _____
7 a.m. _____	4 p.m. _____
8 a.m _____	5 p.m. _____
9 a.m. _____	6 p.m. _____
10 a.m. _____	7 p.m. _____
11 a.m. _____	8 p.m. _____
12 p.m. _____	9 p.m. _____
1 p.m. _____	10 p.m. _____

my training journal

my training log

SWIMMING WORKOUT: *distance*

a.m.	
p.m.	
	total

BIKING WORKOUT: *distance*

a.m.	
p.m.	
	total

RUNNING WORKOUT: *distance*

a.m.	
p.m.	
	total

CROSS-TRAINING: *time*

a.m.	
p.m.	
	total

Tomorrow's To Do

RUNALOG® FOR TRIATHLETES   *TODAY'S DATE* _____

MY LONG-TERM GOAL(S) _____

_____

TODAY'S MEAL PLAN	BREAKFAST	SNACK	LUNCH	SNACK	DINNER
	_____	_____	_____	_____	_____
	_____	_____	_____	_____	_____

weekly planner

	SUNDAY	MONDAY	TUESDAY	WEDNESDAY	THURSDAY	FRIDAY	SATURDAY	TOTAL
a.m.								
p.m.								

daily planner

5 a.m. _____	2 p.m. _____
6 a.m. _____	3 p.m. _____
7 a.m. _____	4 p.m. _____
8 a.m _____	5 p.m. _____
9 a.m. _____	6 p.m. _____
10 a.m. _____	7 p.m. _____
11 a.m. _____	8 p.m. _____
12 p.m. _____	9 p.m. _____
1 p.m. _____	10 p.m. _____

my training journal

my training log

SWIMMING WORKOUT:	*distance*
a.m.	
p.m.	
	total

BIKING WORKOUT:	*distance*
a.m.	
p.m.	
	total

RUNNING WORKOUT:	*distance*
a.m.	
p.m.	
	total

CROSS-TRAINING:	*time*
a.m.	
p.m.	
	total

TOMORROW'S To Do

90

√RUNALOG® FOR TRIATHLETES

TODAY'S DATE _____

MY LONG-TERM GOAL(S) _____

_____

TODAY'S MEAL PLAN	BREAKFAST	SNACK	LUNCH	SNACK	DINNER
	_____	_____	_____	_____	_____
	_____	_____	_____	_____	_____

weekly planner

	SUNDAY	MONDAY	TUESDAY	WEDNESDAY	THURSDAY	FRIDAY	SATURDAY	TOTAL
a.m.								
p.m.								

daily planner

5 a.m. _____	2 p.m. _____
6 a.m. _____	3 p.m. _____
7 a.m. _____	4 p.m. _____
8 a.m _____	5 p.m. _____
9 a.m. _____	6 p.m. _____
10 a.m. _____	7 p.m. _____
11 a.m. _____	8 p.m. _____
12 p.m. _____	9 p.m. _____
1 p.m. _____	10 p.m. _____

my training journal

my training log

SWIMMING WORKOUT:	*distance*
a.m.	
p.m.	
	total

BIKING WORKOUT:	*distance*
a.m.	
p.m.	
	total

RUNNING WORKOUT:	*distance*
a.m.	
p.m.	
	total

CROSS-TRAINING:	*time*
a.m.	
p.m.	
	total

TOMORROW'S To Do

91

⚡RUNALOG® *FOR TRIATHLETES*   *TODAY'S DATE* _____

MY LONG-TERM GOAL(S) _____
_____

TODAY'S MEAL PLAN	BREAKFAST	SNACK	LUNCH	SNACK	DINNER
	_____	_____	_____	_____	_____
	_____	_____	_____	_____	_____

weekly planner

	SUNDAY	MONDAY	TUESDAY	WEDNESDAY	THURSDAY	FRIDAY	SATURDAY	TOTAL
a.m.								
p.m.								

🕐 *daily planner*

5 a.m. _____	2 p.m. _____
6 a.m. _____	3 p.m. _____
7 a.m. _____	4 p.m. _____
8 a.m _____	5 p.m. _____
9 a.m. _____	6 p.m. _____
10 a.m. _____	7 p.m. _____
11 a.m. _____	8 p.m. _____
12 p.m. _____	9 p.m. _____
1 p.m. _____	10 p.m. _____

✍ *my training journal*

my training log

🏊 SWIMMING WORKOUT:	*distance*
a.m.	
p.m.	
	total

🚴 BIKING WORKOUT:	*distance*
a.m.	
p.m.	
	total

🏃 RUNNING WORKOUT:	*distance*
a.m.	
p.m.	
	total

CROSS-TRAINING:	*time*
a.m.	
p.m.	
	total

TOMORROW'S To Do

√RUNALOG® *FOR TRIATHLETES*   **TODAY'S DATE** _____

MY LONG-TERM GOAL(S) _____
_____

TODAY'S MEAL PLAN	BREAKFAST	SNACK	LUNCH	SNACK	DINNER
	_____	_____	_____	_____	_____
	_____	_____	_____	_____	_____

weekly planner

	SUNDAY	MONDAY	TUESDAY	WEDNESDAY	THURSDAY	FRIDAY	SATURDAY	TOTAL
a.m.								
p.m.								

daily planner

5 a.m. _____	2 p.m. _____
6 a.m. _____	3 p.m. _____
7 a.m. _____	4 p.m. _____
8 a.m _____	5 p.m. _____
9 a.m. _____	6 p.m. _____
10 a.m. _____	7 p.m. _____
11 a.m. _____	8 p.m. _____
12 p.m. _____	9 p.m. _____
1 p.m. _____	10 p.m. _____

my training journal

my training log

SWIMMING WORKOUT:	*distance*
a.m.	
p.m.	
	total

BIKING WORKOUT:	*distance*
a.m.	
p.m.	
	total

RUNNING WORKOUT:	*distance*
a.m.	
p.m.	
	total

CROSS-TRAINING:	*time*
a.m.	
p.m.	
	total

TOMORROW'S TO DO

RUNALOG® FOR TRIATHLETES

TODAY'S DATE _____

MY LONG-TERM GOAL(S) _____
_____

TODAY'S MEAL PLAN	BREAKFAST	SNACK	LUNCH	SNACK	DINNER
	_____	_____	_____	_____	_____
	_____	_____	_____	_____	_____

weekly planner

	SUNDAY	MONDAY	TUESDAY	WEDNESDAY	THURSDAY	FRIDAY	SATURDAY	TOTAL
a.m.								
p.m.								

daily planner

5 a.m. _____	2 p.m. _____
6 a.m. _____	3 p.m. _____
7 a.m. _____	4 p.m. _____
8 a.m _____	5 p.m. _____
9 a.m. _____	6 p.m. _____
10 a.m. _____	7 p.m. _____
11 a.m. _____	8 p.m. _____
12 p.m. _____	9 p.m. _____
1 p.m. _____	10 p.m. _____

my training journal

my training log

SWIMMING WORKOUT:	distance
a.m.	
p.m.	
	total

BIKING WORKOUT:	distance
a.m.	
p.m.	
	total

RUNNING WORKOUT:	distance
a.m.	
p.m.	
	total

CROSS-TRAINING:	time
a.m.	
p.m.	
	total

TOMORROW'S TO DO

ⱽRUNALOG® FOR TRIATHLETES

TODAY'S DATE _____

MY LONG-TERM GOAL(S) _____
_____

TODAY'S MEAL PLAN	BREAKFAST	SNACK	LUNCH	SNACK	DINNER
	_____	_____	_____	_____	_____
	_____	_____	_____	_____	_____

weekly planner

	SUNDAY	MONDAY	TUESDAY	WEDNESDAY	THURSDAY	FRIDAY	SATURDAY	TOTAL
a.m.								
p.m.								

🕐 daily planner

5 a.m. _____	2 p.m. _____
6 a.m. _____	3 p.m. _____
7 a.m. _____	4 p.m. _____
8 a.m _____	5 p.m. _____
9 a.m. _____	6 p.m. _____
10 a.m. _____	7 p.m. _____
11 a.m. _____	8 p.m. _____
12 p.m. _____	9 p.m. _____
1 p.m. _____	10 p.m. _____

✍ my training journal

my training log

SWIMMING WORKOUT:	distance
a.m.	
p.m.	
	total

BIKING WORKOUT:	distance
a.m.	
p.m.	
	total

RUNNING WORKOUT:	distance
a.m.	
p.m.	
	total

CROSS-TRAINING:	time
a.m.	
p.m.	
	total

TOMORROW'S To Do

95

ⱽRUNALOG° FOR TRIATHLETES   *TODAY'S DATE* _____

MY LONG-TERM GOAL(S) _____

_____

TODAY'S MEAL PLAN	BREAKFAST	SNACK	LUNCH	SNACK	DINNER
	_____	_____	_____	_____	_____
	_____	_____	_____	_____	_____

weekly planner

	SUNDAY	MONDAY	TUESDAY	WEDNESDAY	THURSDAY	FRIDAY	SATURDAY	TOTAL
a.m.								
p.m.								

🕐 *daily planner*

5 a.m. _____	2 p.m. _____
6 a.m. _____	3 p.m. _____
7 a.m. _____	4 p.m. _____
8 a.m _____	5 p.m. _____
9 a.m. _____	6 p.m. _____
10 a.m. _____	7 p.m. _____
11 a.m. _____	8 p.m. _____
12 p.m. _____	9 p.m. _____
1 p.m. _____	10 p.m. _____

✍ *my training journal*

my training log

🏊 SWIMMING WORKOUT:	*distance*
a.m.	
p.m.	
	total

🚴 BIKING WORKOUT:	*distance*
a.m.	
p.m.	
	total

🏃 RUNNING WORKOUT:	*distance*
a.m.	
p.m.	
	total

CROSS-TRAINING:	*time*
a.m.	
p.m.	
	total

TOMORROW'S TO DO

96

RUNALOG® **FOR TRIATHLETES**   **TODAY'S DATE** _____

MY LONG-TERM GOAL(S) _____

TODAY'S MEAL PLAN	BREAKFAST	SNACK	LUNCH	SNACK	DINNER
	_____	_____	_____	_____	_____

weekly planner

	SUNDAY	MONDAY	TUESDAY	WEDNESDAY	THURSDAY	FRIDAY	SATURDAY	TOTAL
a.m.								
p.m.								

daily planner

5 a.m. _____	2 p.m. _____
6 a.m. _____	3 p.m. _____
7 a.m. _____	4 p.m. _____
8 a.m _____	5 p.m. _____
9 a.m. _____	6 p.m. _____
10 a.m. _____	7 p.m. _____
11 a.m. _____	8 p.m. _____
12 p.m. _____	9 p.m. _____
1 p.m. _____	10 p.m. _____

my training journal

my training log

SWIMMING WORKOUT: *distance*

a.m.

p.m.

total

BIKING WORKOUT: *distance*

a.m.

p.m.

total

RUNNING WORKOUT: *distance*

a.m.

p.m.

total

CROSS-TRAINING: *time*

a.m.

p.m.

total

TOMORROW'S To Do

RUNALOG® FOR TRIATHLETES   TODAY'S DATE _____

MY LONG-TERM GOAL(S) _____
_____

TODAY'S MEAL PLAN	BREAKFAST	SNACK	LUNCH	SNACK	DINNER
	_____	_____	_____	_____	_____
	_____	_____	_____	_____	_____

weekly planner

	SUNDAY	MONDAY	TUESDAY	WEDNESDAY	THURSDAY	FRIDAY	SATURDAY	TOTAL
a.m.								
p.m.								

daily planner

5 a.m. _____	2 p.m. _____
6 a.m. _____	3 p.m. _____
7 a.m. _____	4 p.m. _____
8 a.m _____	5 p.m. _____
9 a.m. _____	6 p.m. _____
10 a.m. _____	7 p.m. _____
11 a.m. _____	8 p.m. _____
12 p.m. _____	9 p.m. _____
1 p.m. _____	10 p.m. _____

my training journal

my training log

SWIMMING WORKOUT:	*distance*
a.m.	
p.m.	
	total

BIKING WORKOUT:	*distance*
a.m.	
p.m.	
	total

RUNNING WORKOUT:	*distance*
a.m.	
p.m.	
	total

CROSS-TRAINING:	*time*
a.m.	
p.m.	
	total

TOMORROW'S TO DO

RUNALOG® FOR TRIATHLETES

TODAY'S DATE _____

MY LONG-TERM GOAL(S) _____
_____

TODAY'S MEAL PLAN	BREAKFAST	SNACK	LUNCH	SNACK	DINNER

weekly planner

	SUNDAY	MONDAY	TUESDAY	WEDNESDAY	THURSDAY	FRIDAY	SATURDAY	TOTAL
a.m.								
p.m.								

daily planner

5 a.m. _____	2 p.m. _____
6 a.m. _____	3 p.m. _____
7 a.m. _____	4 p.m. _____
8 a.m _____	5 p.m. _____
9 a.m. _____	6 p.m. _____
10 a.m. _____	7 p.m. _____
11 a.m. _____	8 p.m. _____
12 p.m. _____	9 p.m. _____
1 p.m. _____	10 p.m. _____

my training journal

my training log

SWIMMING WORKOUT:	distance
a.m.	
p.m.	
	total

BIKING WORKOUT:	distance
a.m.	
p.m.	
	total

RUNNING WORKOUT:	distance
a.m.	
p.m.	
	total

CROSS-TRAINING:	time
a.m.	
p.m.	
	total

Tomorrow's To Do

√RUNALOG® *FOR TRIATHLETES* **TODAY'S DATE** _____

MY LONG-TERM GOAL(S) _____

TODAY'S MEAL PLAN	BREAKFAST	SNACK	LUNCH	SNACK	DINNER
	_____	_____	_____	_____	_____
	_____	_____	_____	_____	_____

weekly planner

	SUNDAY	MONDAY	TUESDAY	WEDNESDAY	THURSDAY	FRIDAY	SATURDAY	TOTAL
a.m.								
p.m.								

daily planner

5 a.m. _____	2 p.m. _____
6 a.m. _____	3 p.m. _____
7 a.m. _____	4 p.m. _____
8 a.m _____	5 p.m. _____
9 a.m. _____	6 p.m. _____
10 a.m. _____	7 p.m. _____
11 a.m. _____	8 p.m. _____
12 p.m. _____	9 p.m. _____
1 p.m. _____	10 p.m. _____

my training journal

my training log

SWIMMING WORKOUT:	*distance*
a.m.	
p.m.	
	total

BIKING WORKOUT:	*distance*
a.m.	
p.m.	
	total

RUNNING WORKOUT:	*distance*
a.m.	
p.m.	
	total

CROSS-TRAINING:	*time*
a.m.	
p.m.	
	total

TOMORROW'S To Do

ᐁRUNALOG® FOR TRIATHLETES

TODAY'S DATE _____

MY LONG-TERM GOAL(S) _____

_____

TODAY'S MEAL PLAN	BREAKFAST	SNACK	LUNCH	SNACK	DINNER

weekly planner

	SUNDAY	MONDAY	TUESDAY	WEDNESDAY	THURSDAY	FRIDAY	SATURDAY	TOTAL
a.m.								
p.m.								

daily planner

5 a.m. _____	2 p.m. _____
6 a.m. _____	3 p.m. _____
7 a.m. _____	4 p.m. _____
8 a.m _____	5 p.m. _____
9 a.m. _____	6 p.m. _____
10 a.m. _____	7 p.m. _____
11 a.m. _____	8 p.m. _____
12 p.m. _____	9 p.m. _____
1 p.m. _____	10 p.m. _____

my training journal

my training log

SWIMMING WORKOUT: distance

a.m.	
p.m.	
	total

BIKING WORKOUT: distance

a.m.	
p.m.	
	total

RUNNING WORKOUT: distance

a.m.	
p.m.	
	total

CROSS-TRAINING: time

a.m.	
p.m.	
	total

TOMORROW'S To Do

√RUNALOG® FOR TRIATHLETES **TODAY'S DATE** _____

MY LONG-TERM GOAL(S) _____

TODAY'S MEAL PLAN	BREAKFAST	SNACK	LUNCH	SNACK	DINNER
	_____	_____	_____	_____	_____
	_____	_____	_____	_____	_____

weekly planner

	SUNDAY	MONDAY	TUESDAY	WEDNESDAY	THURSDAY	FRIDAY	SATURDAY	TOTAL
a.m.								
p.m.								

daily planner

5 a.m. _____	2 p.m. _____
6 a.m. _____	3 p.m. _____
7 a.m. _____	4 p.m. _____
8 a.m _____	5 p.m. _____
9 a.m. _____	6 p.m. _____
10 a.m. _____	7 p.m. _____
11 a.m. _____	8 p.m. _____
12 p.m. _____	9 p.m. _____
1 p.m. _____	10 p.m. _____

my training journal

my training log

SWIMMING WORKOUT:	*distance*
a.m.	
p.m.	
	total

BIKING WORKOUT:	*distance*
a.m.	
p.m.	
	total

RUNNING WORKOUT:	*distance*
a.m.	
p.m.	
	total

CROSS-TRAINING:	*time*
a.m.	
p.m.	
	total

Tomorrow's To Do

102

RUNALOG® FOR TRIATHLETES

TODAY'S DATE _____

MY LONG-TERM GOAL(S) _____

TODAY'S MEAL PLAN	BREAKFAST	SNACK	LUNCH	SNACK	DINNER

weekly planner

	SUNDAY	MONDAY	TUESDAY	WEDNESDAY	THURSDAY	FRIDAY	SATURDAY	TOTAL
a.m.								
p.m.								

daily planner

5 a.m.	_____	2 p.m.	_____
6 a.m.	_____	3 p.m.	_____
7 a.m.	_____	4 p.m.	_____
8 a.m	_____	5 p.m.	_____
9 a.m.	_____	6 p.m.	_____
10 a.m.	_____	7 p.m.	_____
11 a.m.	_____	8 p.m.	_____
12 p.m.	_____	9 p.m.	_____
1 p.m.	_____	10 p.m.	_____

my training journal

my training log

SWIMMING WORKOUT:	distance
a.m.	
p.m.	
	total

BIKING WORKOUT:	distance
a.m.	
p.m.	
	total

RUNNING WORKOUT:	distance
a.m.	
p.m.	
	total

CROSS-TRAINING:	time
a.m.	
p.m.	
	total

TOMORROW'S To Do

⚘RUNALOG® FOR TRIATHLETES

TODAY'S DATE _____

MY LONG-TERM GOAL(S) _____

_____

TODAY'S MEAL PLAN	BREAKFAST	SNACK	LUNCH	SNACK	DINNER
	_____	_____	_____	_____	_____
	_____	_____	_____	_____	_____

weekly planner

	SUNDAY	MONDAY	TUESDAY	WEDNESDAY	THURSDAY	FRIDAY	SATURDAY	TOTAL
a.m.								
p.m.								

🕐 daily planner

5 a.m. _____	2 p.m. _____
6 a.m. _____	3 p.m. _____
7 a.m. _____	4 p.m. _____
8 a.m _____	5 p.m. _____
9 a.m. _____	6 p.m. _____
10 a.m. _____	7 p.m. _____
11 a.m. _____	8 p.m. _____
12 p.m. _____	9 p.m. _____
1 p.m. _____	10 p.m. _____

✍ my training journal

my training log

SWIMMING WORKOUT:	*distance*
a.m.	
p.m.	
	total

BIKING WORKOUT:	*distance*
a.m.	
p.m.	
	total

RUNNING WORKOUT:	*distance*
a.m.	
p.m.	
	total

CROSS-TRAINING:	*time*
a.m.	
p.m.	
	total

TOMORROW'S TO DO

ⱽRUNALOG® FOR TRIATHLETES

TODAY'S DATE _____

MY LONG-TERM GOAL(S) _____

TODAY'S MEAL PLAN	BREAKFAST	SNACK	LUNCH	SNACK	DINNER
	_____	_____	_____	_____	_____

weekly planner

	SUNDAY	MONDAY	TUESDAY	WEDNESDAY	THURSDAY	FRIDAY	SATURDAY	TOTAL
a.m.								
p.m.								

🕐 *daily planner*

5 a.m. _____	2 p.m. _____
6 a.m. _____	3 p.m. _____
7 a.m. _____	4 p.m. _____
8 a.m _____	5 p.m. _____
9 a.m. _____	6 p.m. _____
10 a.m. _____	7 p.m. _____
11 a.m. _____	8 p.m. _____
12 p.m. _____	9 p.m. _____
1 p.m. _____	10 p.m. _____

✍ *my training journal*

my training log

SWIMMING WORKOUT:	*distance*
a.m.	
p.m.	
	total

🚴 BIKING WORKOUT:	*distance*
a.m.	
p.m.	
	total

🏃 RUNNING WORKOUT:	*distance*
a.m.	
p.m.	
	total

CROSS-TRAINING:	*time*
a.m.	
p.m.	
	total

TOMORROW'S TO DO

105

RUNALOG® FOR TRIATHLETES

TODAY'S DATE _____

MY LONG-TERM GOAL(S) _____
_____

TODAY'S MEAL PLAN	BREAKFAST	SNACK	LUNCH	SNACK	DINNER
	_____	_____	_____	_____	_____
	_____	_____	_____	_____	_____

weekly planner

	SUNDAY	MONDAY	TUESDAY	WEDNESDAY	THURSDAY	FRIDAY	SATURDAY	TOTAL
a.m.								
p.m.								

daily planner

5 a.m. _____	2 p.m. _____
6 a.m. _____	3 p.m. _____
7 a.m. _____	4 p.m. _____
8 a.m _____	5 p.m. _____
9 a.m. _____	6 p.m. _____
10 a.m. _____	7 p.m. _____
11 a.m. _____	8 p.m. _____
12 p.m. _____	9 p.m. _____
1 p.m. _____	10 p.m. _____

my training journal

my training log

SWIMMING WORKOUT: *distance*

a.m.	
p.m.	
	total

BIKING WORKOUT: *distance*

a.m.	
p.m.	
	total

RUNNING WORKOUT: *distance*

a.m.	
p.m.	
	total

CROSS-TRAINING: *time*

a.m.	
p.m.	
	total

TOMORROW'S TO DO

√RUNALOG® FOR TRIATHLETES

TODAY'S DATE _____

MY LONG-TERM GOAL(S) _____
_____

TODAY'S MEAL PLAN	BREAKFAST	SNACK	LUNCH	SNACK	DINNER
	_____	_____	_____	_____	_____
	_____	_____	_____	_____	_____

weekly planner

	SUNDAY	MONDAY	TUESDAY	WEDNESDAY	THURSDAY	FRIDAY	SATURDAY	TOTAL
a.m.								
p.m.								

daily planner

5 a.m. _____		2 p.m. _____
6 a.m. _____		3 p.m. _____
7 a.m. _____		4 p.m. _____
8 a.m _____		5 p.m. _____
9 a.m. _____		6 p.m. _____
10 a.m. _____		7 p.m. _____
11 a.m. _____		8 p.m. _____
12 p.m. _____		9 p.m. _____
1 p.m. _____		10 p.m. _____

my training journal

my training log

SWIMMING WORKOUT:	distance
a.m.	
p.m.	
	total

BIKING WORKOUT:	distance
a.m.	
p.m.	
	total

RUNNING WORKOUT:	distance
a.m.	
p.m.	
	total

CROSS-TRAINING:	time
a.m.	
p.m.	
	total

TOMORROW'S TO DO

107

RUNALOG® FOR TRIATHLETES

TODAY'S DATE _____

MY LONG-TERM GOAL(S) _____
_____

TODAY'S MEAL PLAN	BREAKFAST	SNACK	LUNCH	SNACK	DINNER
	_____	_____	_____	_____	_____
	_____	_____	_____	_____	_____

weekly planner

	SUNDAY	MONDAY	TUESDAY	WEDNESDAY	THURSDAY	FRIDAY	SATURDAY	TOTAL
a.m.								
p.m.								

daily planner

5 a.m. _____	2 p.m. _____
6 a.m. _____	3 p.m. _____
7 a.m. _____	4 p.m. _____
8 a.m _____	5 p.m. _____
9 a.m. _____	6 p.m. _____
10 a.m. _____	7 p.m. _____
11 a.m. _____	8 p.m. _____
12 p.m. _____	9 p.m. _____
1 p.m. _____	10 p.m. _____

my training journal

my training log

SWIMMING WORKOUT:	*distance*
a.m.	
p.m.	
	total

BIKING WORKOUT:	*distance*
a.m.	
p.m.	
	total

RUNNING WORKOUT:	*distance*
a.m.	
p.m.	
	total

CROSS-TRAINING:	*time*
a.m.	
p.m.	
	total

TOMORROW'S To Do

108

√RUNALOG® FOR TRIATHLETES

TODAY'S DATE _____

MY LONG-TERM GOAL(S) _____

TODAY'S MEAL PLAN	BREAKFAST	SNACK	LUNCH	SNACK	DINNER

weekly planner

	SUNDAY	MONDAY	TUESDAY	WEDNESDAY	THURSDAY	FRIDAY	SATURDAY	TOTAL
a.m.								
p.m.								

daily planner

5 a.m. _____	2 p.m. _____
6 a.m. _____	3 p.m. _____
7 a.m. _____	4 p.m. _____
8 a.m _____	5 p.m. _____
9 a.m. _____	6 p.m. _____
10 a.m. _____	7 p.m. _____
11 a.m. _____	8 p.m. _____
12 p.m. _____	9 p.m. _____
1 p.m. _____	10 p.m. _____

my training journal

my training log

SWIMMING WORKOUT:	distance
a.m.	
p.m.	
	total

BIKING WORKOUT:	distance
a.m.	
p.m.	
	total

RUNNING WORKOUT:	distance
a.m.	
p.m.	
	total

CROSS-TRAINING:	time
a.m.	
p.m.	
	total

TOMORROW'S TO DO

109

ⱽRUNALOG® FOR TRIATHLETES

TODAY'S DATE _____

MY LONG-TERM GOAL(S) _____
_____

TODAY'S MEAL PLAN	BREAKFAST	SNACK	LUNCH	SNACK	DINNER
	_____	_____	_____	_____	_____
	_____	_____	_____	_____	_____

weekly planner

	SUNDAY	MONDAY	TUESDAY	WEDNESDAY	THURSDAY	FRIDAY	SATURDAY	TOTAL
a.m.								
p.m.								

🕐 daily planner

5 a.m. _____	2 p.m. _____
6 a.m. _____	3 p.m. _____
7 a.m. _____	4 p.m. _____
8 a.m _____	5 p.m. _____
9 a.m. _____	6 p.m. _____
10 a.m. _____	7 p.m. _____
11 a.m. _____	8 p.m. _____
12 p.m. _____	9 p.m. _____
1 p.m. _____	10 p.m. _____

✍ my training journal

my training log

SWIMMING WORKOUT:	*distance*
a.m.	
p.m.	
	total

BIKING WORKOUT:	*distance*
a.m.	
p.m.	
	total

RUNNING WORKOUT:	*distance*
a.m.	
p.m.	
	total

CROSS-TRAINING:	*time*
a.m.	
p.m.	
	total

TOMORROW'S TO DO

110

RUNALOG® FOR TRIATHLETES

TODAY'S DATE _____

MY LONG-TERM GOAL(S) _____

TODAY'S MEAL PLAN	BREAKFAST	SNACK	LUNCH	SNACK	DINNER

weekly planner

	SUNDAY	MONDAY	TUESDAY	WEDNESDAY	THURSDAY	FRIDAY	SATURDAY	TOTAL
a.m.								
p.m.								

daily planner

5 a.m. _____	2 p.m. _____
6 a.m. _____	3 p.m. _____
7 a.m. _____	4 p.m. _____
8 a.m _____	5 p.m. _____
9 a.m. _____	6 p.m. _____
10 a.m. _____	7 p.m. _____
11 a.m. _____	8 p.m. _____
12 p.m. _____	9 p.m. _____
1 p.m. _____	10 p.m. _____

my training journal

my training log

SWIMMING WORKOUT:	distance
a.m.	
p.m.	
	total

BIKING WORKOUT:	distance
a.m.	
p.m.	
	total

RUNNING WORKOUT:	distance
a.m.	
p.m.	
	total

CROSS-TRAINING:	time
a.m.	
p.m.	
	total

TOMORROW'S To Do

RUNALOG® FOR TRIATHLETES

TODAY'S DATE _____

MY LONG-TERM GOAL(S) _____

_____

TODAY'S MEAL PLAN	BREAKFAST	SNACK	LUNCH	SNACK	DINNER
	_____	_____	_____	_____	_____
	_____	_____	_____	_____	_____

weekly planner

	SUNDAY	MONDAY	TUESDAY	WEDNESDAY	THURSDAY	FRIDAY	SATURDAY	TOTAL
a.m.								
p.m.								

daily planner

5 a.m. _____	2 p.m. _____
6 a.m. _____	3 p.m. _____
7 a.m. _____	4 p.m. _____
8 a.m _____	5 p.m. _____
9 a.m. _____	6 p.m. _____
10 a.m. _____	7 p.m. _____
11 a.m. _____	8 p.m. _____
12 p.m. _____	9 p.m. _____
1 p.m. _____	10 p.m. _____

my training journal

my training log

SWIMMING WORKOUT:	*distance*
a.m.	
p.m.	
	total

BIKING WORKOUT:	*distance*
a.m.	
p.m.	
	total

RUNNING WORKOUT:	*distance*
a.m.	
p.m.	
	total

CROSS-TRAINING:	*time*
a.m.	
p.m.	
	total

TOMORROW'S TO DO

TODAY'S DATE _____

MY LONG-TERM GOAL(S) _____

TODAY'S MEAL PLAN	BREAKFAST	SNACK	LUNCH	SNACK	DINNER
	_____	_____	_____	_____	_____

weekly planner

	SUNDAY	MONDAY	TUESDAY	WEDNESDAY	THURSDAY	FRIDAY	SATURDAY	TOTAL
a.m.								
p.m.								

daily planner

5 a.m. _____	2 p.m. _____
6 a.m. _____	3 p.m. _____
7 a.m. _____	4 p.m. _____
8 a.m _____	5 p.m. _____
9 a.m. _____	6 p.m. _____
10 a.m. _____	7 p.m. _____
11 a.m. _____	8 p.m. _____
12 p.m. _____	9 p.m. _____
1 p.m. _____	10 p.m. _____

my training journal

my training log

SWIMMING WORKOUT:	*distance*
a.m.	
p.m.	
	total

BIKING WORKOUT:	*distance*
a.m.	
p.m.	
	total

RUNNING WORKOUT:	*distance*
a.m.	
p.m.	
	total

CROSS-TRAINING:	*time*
a.m.	
p.m.	
	total

TOMORROW'S To Do

RUNALOG® *FOR TRIATHLETES*   *TODAY'S DATE* _____

MY LONG-TERM GOAL(S) _____

TODAY'S MEAL PLAN	BREAKFAST	SNACK	LUNCH	SNACK	DINNER
	____	____	____	____	____
	____	____	____	____	____

weekly planner

	SUNDAY	MONDAY	TUESDAY	WEDNESDAY	THURSDAY	FRIDAY	SATURDAY	TOTAL
a.m.								
p.m.								

daily planner

5 a.m. ____	2 p.m. ____		
6 a.m. ____	3 p.m. ____		
7 a.m. ____	4 p.m. ____		
8 a.m ____	5 p.m. ____		
9 a.m. ____	6 p.m. ____		
10 a.m. ____	7 p.m. ____		
11 a.m. ____	8 p.m. ____		
12 p.m. ____	9 p.m. ____		
1 p.m. ____	10 p.m. ____		

my training journal

my training log

SWIMMING WORKOUT: *distance*
a.m. / p.m. / total

BIKING WORKOUT: *distance*
a.m. / p.m. / total

RUNNING WORKOUT: *distance*
a.m. / p.m. / total

CROSS-TRAINING: *time*
a.m. / p.m. / total

TOMORROW'S To Do

114

MY LONG-TERM GOAL(S) _____
_____

TODAY'S MEAL PLAN	BREAKFAST	SNACK	LUNCH	SNACK	DINNER
	_____	_____	_____	_____	_____
	_____	_____	_____	_____	_____

weekly planner

	SUNDAY	MONDAY	TUESDAY	WEDNESDAY	THURSDAY	FRIDAY	SATURDAY	TOTAL
a.m.								
p.m.								

🕐 *daily planner*

5 a.m. _____	2 p.m. _____
6 a.m. _____	3 p.m. _____
7 a.m. _____	4 p.m. _____
8 a.m _____	5 p.m. _____
9 a.m. _____	6 p.m. _____
10 a.m. _____	7 p.m. _____
11 a.m. _____	8 p.m. _____
12 p.m. _____	9 p.m. _____
1 p.m. _____	10 p.m. _____

✍ *my training journal*

(blank lined journal area)

my training log

SWIMMING WORKOUT:	*distance*
a.m.	
p.m.	
	total

🚴 BIKING WORKOUT:	*distance*
a.m.	
p.m.	
	total

🏃 RUNNING WORKOUT:	*distance*
a.m.	
p.m.	
	total

CROSS-TRAINING:	*time*
a.m.	
p.m.	
	total

TOMORROW'S TO DO

ᐟᐯRUNALOG® FOR TRIATHLETES

TODAY'S DATE _____

MY LONG-TERM GOAL(S) _____
_____

TODAY'S MEAL PLAN	BREAKFAST	SNACK	LUNCH	SNACK	DINNER
	_____	_____	_____	_____	_____
	_____	_____	_____	_____	_____

weekly planner

	SUNDAY	MONDAY	TUESDAY	WEDNESDAY	THURSDAY	FRIDAY	SATURDAY	TOTAL
a.m.								
p.m.								

🕐 daily planner

5 a.m.	_____	2 p.m.	_____
6 a.m.	_____	3 p.m.	_____
7 a.m.	_____	4 p.m.	_____
8 a.m	_____	5 p.m.	_____
9 a.m.	_____	6 p.m.	_____
10 a.m.	_____	7 p.m.	_____
11 a.m.	_____	8 p.m.	_____
12 p.m.	_____	9 p.m.	_____
1 p.m.	_____	10 p.m.	_____

✍ my training journal

my training log

SWIMMING WORKOUT:	*distance*
a.m.	
p.m.	
	total

BIKING WORKOUT:	*distance*
a.m.	
p.m.	
	total

RUNNING WORKOUT:	*distance*
a.m.	
p.m.	
	total

CROSS-TRAINING:	*time*
a.m.	
p.m.	
	total

TOMORROW'S TO DO

116

ⱽRUNALOG® FOR TRIATHLETES

TODAY'S DATE _____

MY LONG-TERM GOAL(S) _____

_____

TODAY'S MEAL PLAN	BREAKFAST	SNACK	LUNCH	SNACK	DINNER
	_____	_____	_____	_____	_____
	_____	_____	_____	_____	_____

weekly planner

	SUNDAY	MONDAY	TUESDAY	WEDNESDAY	THURSDAY	FRIDAY	SATURDAY	TOTAL
a.m.								
p.m.								

🕐 daily planner

5 a.m.	_____	2 p.m.	_____
6 a.m.	_____	3 p.m.	_____
7 a.m.	_____	4 p.m.	_____
8 a.m	_____	5 p.m.	_____
9 a.m.	_____	6 p.m.	_____
10 a.m.	_____	7 p.m.	_____
11 a.m.	_____	8 p.m.	_____
12 p.m.	_____	9 p.m.	_____
1 p.m.	_____	10 p.m.	_____

✍ my training journal

my training log

SWIMMING WORKOUT:	*distance*
a.m.	
p.m.	
	total

BIKING WORKOUT:	*distance*
a.m.	
p.m.	
	total

RUNNING WORKOUT:	*distance*
a.m.	
p.m.	
	total

CROSS-TRAINING:	*time*
a.m.	
p.m.	
	total

TOMORROW'S TO DO

⛳ RUNALOG® FOR TRIATHLETES

TODAY'S DATE _____

MY LONG-TERM GOAL(S) _____
_____

TODAY'S MEAL PLAN	BREAKFAST	SNACK	LUNCH	SNACK	DINNER
	_____	_____	_____	_____	_____
	_____	_____	_____	_____	_____

weekly planner

	SUNDAY	MONDAY	TUESDAY	WEDNESDAY	THURSDAY	FRIDAY	SATURDAY	TOTAL
a.m.								
p.m.								

🕐 daily planner

5 a.m.	_____	2 p.m.	_____
6 a.m.	_____	3 p.m.	_____
7 a.m.	_____	4 p.m.	_____
8 a.m	_____	5 p.m.	_____
9 a.m.	_____	6 p.m.	_____
10 a.m.	_____	7 p.m.	_____
11 a.m.	_____	8 p.m.	_____
12 p.m.	_____	9 p.m.	_____
1 p.m.	_____	10 p.m.	_____

✍ my training journal

my training log

SWIMMING WORKOUT:	*distance*
a.m.	
p.m.	
	total

🚴 BIKING WORKOUT:	*distance*
a.m.	
p.m.	
	total

🏃 RUNNING WORKOUT:	*distance*
a.m.	
p.m.	
	total

CROSS-TRAINING:	*time*
a.m.	
p.m.	
	total

TOMORROW'S TO DO

118

RUNALOG® For Triathletes

TODAY'S DATE _____

MY LONG-TERM GOAL(S) _____

TODAY'S MEAL PLAN	BREAKFAST	SNACK	LUNCH	SNACK	DINNER
	_____	_____	_____	_____	_____
	_____	_____	_____	_____	_____

weekly planner

	SUNDAY	MONDAY	TUESDAY	WEDNESDAY	THURSDAY	FRIDAY	SATURDAY	TOTAL
a.m.								
p.m.								

daily planner

5 a.m. _____	2 p.m. _____
6 a.m. _____	3 p.m. _____
7 a.m. _____	4 p.m. _____
8 a.m _____	5 p.m. _____
9 a.m. _____	6 p.m. _____
10 a.m. _____	7 p.m. _____
11 a.m. _____	8 p.m. _____
12 p.m. _____	9 p.m. _____
1 p.m. _____	10 p.m. _____

my training journal

my training log

SWIMMING WORKOUT:	distance
a.m.	
p.m.	
	total

BIKING WORKOUT:	distance
a.m.	
p.m.	
	total

RUNNING WORKOUT:	distance
a.m.	
p.m.	
	total

CROSS-TRAINING:	time
a.m.	
p.m.	
	total

TOMORROW'S To Do

119

RUNALOG® FOR TRIATHLETES   *TODAY'S DATE* _____

MY LONG-TERM GOAL(S) _____
_____

TODAY'S MEAL PLAN	BREAKFAST	SNACK	LUNCH	SNACK	DINNER
	_____	_____	_____	_____	_____

weekly planner

	SUNDAY	MONDAY	TUESDAY	WEDNESDAY	THURSDAY	FRIDAY	SATURDAY	TOTAL
a.m.								
p.m.								

daily planner

5 a.m. _____	2 p.m. _____
6 a.m. _____	3 p.m. _____
7 a.m. _____	4 p.m. _____
8 a.m _____	5 p.m. _____
9 a.m. _____	6 p.m. _____
10 a.m. _____	7 p.m. _____
11 a.m. _____	8 p.m. _____
12 p.m. _____	9 p.m. _____
1 p.m. _____	10 p.m. _____

my training journal

my training log

SWIMMING WORKOUT:	*distance*
a.m.	
p.m.	
	total

BIKING WORKOUT:	*distance*
a.m.	
p.m.	
	total

RUNNING WORKOUT:	*distance*
a.m.	
p.m.	
	total

CROSS-TRAINING:	*time*
a.m.	
p.m.	
	total

TOMORROW'S TO DO

ᐯRUNALOG® FOR TRIATHLETES

TODAY'S DATE _____

MY LONG-TERM GOAL(S) _____

TODAY'S MEAL PLAN	BREAKFAST	SNACK	LUNCH	SNACK	DINNER
	_____	_____	_____	_____	_____

weekly planner

	SUNDAY	MONDAY	TUESDAY	WEDNESDAY	THURSDAY	FRIDAY	SATURDAY	TOTAL
a.m.								
p.m.								

daily planner

5 a.m. _____		2 p.m. _____
6 a.m. _____		3 p.m. _____
7 a.m. _____		4 p.m. _____
8 a.m _____		5 p.m. _____
9 a.m. _____		6 p.m. _____
10 a.m. _____		7 p.m. _____
11 a.m. _____		8 p.m. _____
12 p.m. _____		9 p.m. _____
1 p.m. _____		10 p.m. _____

my training journal

my training log

SWIMMING WORKOUT:	distance
a.m.	
p.m.	
	total

BIKING WORKOUT:	distance
a.m.	
p.m.	
	total

RUNNING WORKOUT:	distance
a.m.	
p.m.	
	total

CROSS-TRAINING:	time
a.m.	
p.m.	
	total

TOMORROW'S TO DO

121

RUNALOG® FOR TRIATHLETES

TODAY'S DATE _____

MY LONG-TERM GOAL(S) _____

TODAY'S MEAL PLAN	BREAKFAST	SNACK	LUNCH	SNACK	DINNER

weekly planner

	SUNDAY	MONDAY	TUESDAY	WEDNESDAY	THURSDAY	FRIDAY	SATURDAY	TOTAL
a.m.								
p.m.								

daily planner

5 a.m. _____	2 p.m. _____
6 a.m. _____	3 p.m. _____
7 a.m. _____	4 p.m. _____
8 a.m. _____	5 p.m. _____
9 a.m. _____	6 p.m. _____
10 a.m. _____	7 p.m. _____
11 a.m. _____	8 p.m. _____
12 p.m. _____	9 p.m. _____
1 p.m. _____	10 p.m. _____

my training journal

my training log

SWIMMING WORKOUT:	*distance*
a.m.	
p.m.	
	total

BIKING WORKOUT:	*distance*
a.m.	
p.m.	
	total

RUNNING WORKOUT:	*distance*
a.m.	
p.m.	
	total

CROSS-TRAINING:	*time*
a.m.	
p.m.	
	total

TOMORROW'S TO DO

⋎RUNALOG® FOR TRIATHLETES

TODAY'S DATE _____

MY LONG-TERM GOAL(S) _____

_____

TODAY'S MEAL PLAN	BREAKFAST	SNACK	LUNCH	SNACK	DINNER
	_____	_____	_____	_____	_____
	_____	_____	_____	_____	_____

weekly planner

	SUNDAY	MONDAY	TUESDAY	WEDNESDAY	THURSDAY	FRIDAY	SATURDAY	TOTAL
a.m.								
p.m.								

🕐 *daily planner*

5 a.m. _____		2 p.m. _____	
6 a.m. _____		3 p.m. _____	
7 a.m. _____		4 p.m. _____	
8 a.m _____		5 p.m. _____	
9 a.m. _____		6 p.m. _____	
10 a.m. _____		7 p.m. _____	
11 a.m. _____		8 p.m. _____	
12 p.m. _____		9 p.m. _____	
1 p.m. _____		10 p.m. _____	

✍ *my training journal*

my training log

SWIMMING WORKOUT:	*distance*
a.m.	
p.m.	
	total

🚴 BIKING WORKOUT:	*distance*
a.m.	
p.m.	
	total

🏃 RUNNING WORKOUT:	*distance*
a.m.	
p.m.	
	total

CROSS-TRAINING:	*time*
a.m.	
p.m.	
	total

TOMORROW'S To Do

RUNALOG® FOR TRIATHLETES

TODAY'S DATE _____

MY LONG-TERM GOAL(S) _____

TODAY'S MEAL PLAN	BREAKFAST	SNACK	LUNCH	SNACK	DINNER
	_____	_____	_____	_____	_____
	_____	_____	_____	_____	_____

weekly planner

	SUNDAY	MONDAY	TUESDAY	WEDNESDAY	THURSDAY	FRIDAY	SATURDAY	TOTAL
a.m.								
p.m.								

daily planner

5 a.m. _____	2 p.m. _____
6 a.m. _____	3 p.m. _____
7 a.m. _____	4 p.m. _____
8 a.m _____	5 p.m. _____
9 a.m. _____	6 p.m. _____
10 a.m. _____	7 p.m. _____
11 a.m. _____	8 p.m. _____
12 p.m. _____	9 p.m. _____
1 p.m. _____	10 p.m. _____

my training journal

my training log

SWIMMING WORKOUT: *distance*

a.m.	
p.m.	
	total

BIKING WORKOUT: *distance*

a.m.	
p.m.	
	total

RUNNING WORKOUT: *distance*

a.m.	
p.m.	
	total

CROSS-TRAINING: *time*

a.m.	
p.m.	
	total

TOMORROW'S TO DO

ⱽRUNALOG® FOR TRIATHLETES

TODAY'S DATE _____

MY LONG-TERM GOAL(S) _____
_____

TODAY'S MEAL PLAN	BREAKFAST	SNACK	LUNCH	SNACK	DINNER
	_____	_____	_____	_____	_____
	_____	_____	_____	_____	_____

weekly planner

	SUNDAY	MONDAY	TUESDAY	WEDNESDAY	THURSDAY	FRIDAY	SATURDAY	TOTAL
a.m.								
p.m.								

daily planner

5 a.m. _____	2 p.m. _____
6 a.m. _____	3 p.m. _____
7 a.m. _____	4 p.m. _____
8 a.m _____	5 p.m. _____
9 a.m. _____	6 p.m. _____
10 a.m. _____	7 p.m. _____
11 a.m. _____	8 p.m. _____
12 p.m. _____	9 p.m. _____
1 p.m. _____	10 p.m. _____

my training journal

my training log

SWIMMING WORKOUT: *distance*

a.m.	
p.m.	
	total

BIKING WORKOUT: *distance*

a.m.	
p.m.	
	total

RUNNING WORKOUT: *distance*

a.m.	
p.m.	
	total

CROSS-TRAINING: *time*

a.m.	
p.m.	
	total

TOMORROW'S To Do

MY LONG-TERM GOAL(S) _____
_____

TODAY'S MEAL PLAN	**BREAKFAST**	**SNACK**	**LUNCH**	**SNACK**	**DINNER**
	_____	_____	_____	_____	_____
	_____	_____	_____	_____	_____

weekly planner

	SUNDAY	MONDAY	TUESDAY	WEDNESDAY	THURSDAY	FRIDAY	SATURDAY	TOTAL
a.m.								
p.m.								

daily planner

5 a.m.	_____	2 p.m.	_____
6 a.m.	_____	3 p.m.	_____
7 a.m.	_____	4 p.m.	_____
8 a.m	_____	5 p.m.	_____
9 a.m.	_____	6 p.m.	_____
10 a.m.	_____	7 p.m.	_____
11 a.m.	_____	8 p.m.	_____
12 p.m.	_____	9 p.m.	_____
1 p.m.	_____	10 p.m.	_____

my training journal

my training log

SWIMMING WORKOUT:	*distance*
a.m.	
p.m.	
	total

BIKING WORKOUT:	*distance*
a.m.	
p.m.	
	total

RUNNING WORKOUT:	*distance*
a.m.	
p.m.	
	total

CROSS-TRAINING:	*time*
a.m.	
p.m.	
	total

TOMORROW'S TO DO

✔RUNALOG® *FOR TRIATHLETES*

TODAY'S DATE _____

MY LONG-TERM GOAL(S) _____

_____

TODAY'S MEAL PLAN	BREAKFAST	SNACK	LUNCH	SNACK	DINNER
	_____	_____	_____	_____	_____
	_____	_____	_____	_____	_____

weekly planner

	SUNDAY	MONDAY	TUESDAY	WEDNESDAY	THURSDAY	FRIDAY	SATURDAY	TOTAL
a.m.								
p.m.								

🕐 *daily planner*

5 a.m. _____	2 p.m. _____
6 a.m. _____	3 p.m. _____
7 a.m. _____	4 p.m. _____
8 a.m _____	5 p.m. _____
9 a.m. _____	6 p.m. _____
10 a.m. _____	7 p.m. _____
11 a.m. _____	8 p.m. _____
12 p.m. _____	9 p.m. _____
1 p.m. _____	10 p.m. _____

✍ *my training journal*

my training log

SWIMMING WORKOUT:	*distance*
a.m.	
p.m.	
	total

🚴 BIKING WORKOUT:	*distance*
a.m.	
p.m.	
	total

🏃 RUNNING WORKOUT:	*distance*
a.m.	
p.m.	
	total

CROSS-TRAINING:	*time*
a.m.	
p.m.	
	total

TOMORROW'S To Do

127

ᵛRUNALOG® FOR TRIATHLETES   TODAY'S DATE _____

MY LONG-TERM GOAL(S) _____
_____

TODAY'S MEAL PLAN	BREAKFAST	SNACK	LUNCH	SNACK	DINNER
	_____	_____	_____	_____	_____
	_____	_____	_____	_____	_____

weekly planner

	SUNDAY	MONDAY	TUESDAY	WEDNESDAY	THURSDAY	FRIDAY	SATURDAY	TOTAL
a.m.								
p.m.								

🕐 *daily planner*

5 a.m. _____	2 p.m. _____
6 a.m. _____	3 p.m. _____
7 a.m. _____	4 p.m. _____
8 a.m _____	5 p.m. _____
9 a.m. _____	6 p.m. _____
10 a.m. _____	7 p.m. _____
11 a.m. _____	8 p.m. _____
12 p.m. _____	9 p.m. _____
1 p.m. _____	10 p.m. _____

✒ *my training journal*

my training log

🏊 SWIMMING WORKOUT:	*distance*
a.m.	
p.m.	
	total

🚴 BIKING WORKOUT:	*distance*
a.m.	
p.m.	
	total

🏃 RUNNING WORKOUT:	*distance*
a.m.	
p.m.	
	total

CROSS-TRAINING:	*time*
a.m.	
p.m.	
	total

TOMORROW'S To Do

128

√RUNALOG° FOR TRIATHLETES

TODAY'S DATE _____

MY LONG-TERM GOAL(S) _____

TODAY'S MEAL PLAN	BREAKFAST	SNACK	LUNCH	SNACK	DINNER
	_____	_____	_____	_____	_____

weekly planner

	SUNDAY	MONDAY	TUESDAY	WEDNESDAY	THURSDAY	FRIDAY	SATURDAY	TOTAL
a.m.								
p.m.								

🕐 daily planner

5 a.m. _____	2 p.m. _____
6 a.m. _____	3 p.m. _____
7 a.m. _____	4 p.m. _____
8 a.m _____	5 p.m. _____
9 a.m. _____	6 p.m. _____
10 a.m. _____	7 p.m. _____
11 a.m. _____	8 p.m. _____
12 p.m. _____	9 p.m. _____
1 p.m. _____	10 p.m. _____

✍ my training journal

my training log

SWIMMING WORKOUT:	distance
a.m.	
p.m.	
	total

BIKING WORKOUT:	distance
a.m.	
p.m.	
	total

RUNNING WORKOUT:	distance
a.m.	
p.m.	
	total

CROSS-TRAINING:	time
a.m.	
p.m.	
	total

TOMORROW'S TO DO

RUNALOG® FOR TRIATHLETES

TODAY'S DATE _____

MY LONG-TERM GOAL(S) _____
_____

TODAY'S MEAL PLAN	BREAKFAST	SNACK	LUNCH	SNACK	DINNER
	_____	_____	_____	_____	_____
	_____	_____	_____	_____	_____

weekly planner

	SUNDAY	MONDAY	TUESDAY	WEDNESDAY	THURSDAY	FRIDAY	SATURDAY	TOTAL
a.m.								
p.m.								

daily planner

5 a.m.	_____	2 p.m.	_____
6 a.m.	_____	3 p.m.	_____
7 a.m.	_____	4 p.m.	_____
8 a.m	_____	5 p.m.	_____
9 a.m.	_____	6 p.m.	_____
10 a.m.	_____	7 p.m.	_____
11 a.m.	_____	8 p.m.	_____
12 p.m.	_____	9 p.m.	_____
1 p.m.	_____	10 p.m.	_____

my training journal

my training log

SWIMMING WORKOUT: distance

a.m.	
p.m.	
	total

BIKING WORKOUT: distance

a.m.	
p.m.	
	total

RUNNING WORKOUT: distance

a.m.	
p.m.	
	total

CROSS-TRAINING: time

a.m.	
p.m.	
	total

TOMORROW'S TO DO

✓RUNALOG® FOR TRIATHLETES

TODAY'S DATE _____

MY LONG-TERM GOAL(S) _____

TODAY'S MEAL PLAN	BREAKFAST	SNACK	LUNCH	SNACK	DINNER

weekly planner

	SUNDAY	MONDAY	TUESDAY	WEDNESDAY	THURSDAY	FRIDAY	SATURDAY	TOTAL
a.m.								
p.m.								

daily planner

5 a.m. _____	2 p.m. _____
6 a.m. _____	3 p.m. _____
7 a.m. _____	4 p.m. _____
8 a.m _____	5 p.m. _____
9 a.m. _____	6 p.m. _____
10 a.m. _____	7 p.m. _____
11 a.m. _____	8 p.m. _____
12 p.m. _____	9 p.m. _____
1 p.m. _____	10 p.m. _____

my training journal

my training log

SWIMMING WORKOUT: distance
a.m.
p.m.
total

BIKING WORKOUT: distance
a.m.
p.m.
total

RUNNING WORKOUT: distance
a.m.
p.m.
total

CROSS-TRAINING: time
a.m.
p.m.
total

TOMORROW'S TO DO

131

© 2009 www.RUNALOGS.com

RUNALOG® FOR TRIATHLETES

TODAY'S DATE _____

MY LONG-TERM GOAL(S) _____
_____

TODAY'S MEAL PLAN	BREAKFAST	SNACK	LUNCH	SNACK	DINNER
	_____	_____	_____	_____	_____
	_____	_____	_____	_____	_____

weekly planner

	SUNDAY	MONDAY	TUESDAY	WEDNESDAY	THURSDAY	FRIDAY	SATURDAY	TOTAL
a.m.								
p.m.								

daily planner

5 a.m. _____	2 p.m. _____
6 a.m. _____	3 p.m. _____
7 a.m. _____	4 p.m. _____
8 a.m _____	5 p.m. _____
9 a.m. _____	6 p.m. _____
10 a.m. _____	7 p.m. _____
11 a.m. _____	8 p.m. _____
12 p.m. _____	9 p.m. _____
1 p.m. _____	10 p.m. _____

my training journal

my training log

SWIMMING WORKOUT:	distance
a.m.	
p.m.	
	total

BIKING WORKOUT:	distance
a.m.	
p.m.	
	total

RUNNING WORKOUT:	distance
a.m.	
p.m.	
	total

CROSS-TRAINING:	time
a.m.	
p.m.	
	total

TOMORROW'S TO DO

RUNALOG® FOR TRIATHLETES

TODAY'S DATE _____

MY LONG-TERM GOAL(S) _____

TODAY'S MEAL PLAN	BREAKFAST	SNACK	LUNCH	SNACK	DINNER

weekly planner

	SUNDAY	MONDAY	TUESDAY	WEDNESDAY	THURSDAY	FRIDAY	SATURDAY	TOTAL
a.m.								
p.m.								

daily planner

5 a.m. _____	2 p.m. _____
6 a.m. _____	3 p.m. _____
7 a.m. _____	4 p.m. _____
8 a.m _____	5 p.m. _____
9 a.m. _____	6 p.m. _____
10 a.m. _____	7 p.m. _____
11 a.m. _____	8 p.m. _____
12 p.m. _____	9 p.m. _____
1 p.m. _____	10 p.m. _____

my training journal

my training log

SWIMMING WORKOUT:	distance
a.m.	
p.m.	
total	

BIKING WORKOUT:	distance
a.m.	
p.m.	
total	

RUNNING WORKOUT:	distance
a.m.	
p.m.	
total	

CROSS-TRAINING:	time
a.m.	
p.m.	
total	

TOMORROW'S TO DO

MY LONG-TERM GOAL(S) _____

TODAY'S MEAL PLAN	BREAKFAST	SNACK	LUNCH	SNACK	DINNER
	_____	_____	_____	_____	_____
	_____	_____	_____	_____	_____

weekly planner

	SUNDAY	MONDAY	TUESDAY	WEDNESDAY	THURSDAY	FRIDAY	SATURDAY	TOTAL
a.m.								
p.m.								

🕐 *daily planner*

5 a.m.	_____	2 p.m.	_____
6 a.m.	_____	3 p.m.	_____
7 a.m.	_____	4 p.m.	_____
8 a.m	_____	5 p.m.	_____
9 a.m.	_____	6 p.m.	_____
10 a.m.	_____	7 p.m.	_____
11 a.m.	_____	8 p.m.	_____
12 p.m.	_____	9 p.m.	_____
1 p.m.	_____	10 p.m.	_____

✍ *my training journal*

my training log

SWIMMING WORKOUT:	*distance*
a.m.	
p.m.	
	total

BIKING WORKOUT:	*distance*
a.m.	
p.m.	
	total

RUNNING WORKOUT:	*distance*
a.m.	
p.m.	
	total

CROSS-TRAINING:	*time*
a.m.	
p.m.	
	total

TOMORROW'S TO DO

ⱽRUNALOG® FOR TRIATHLETES

MY LONG-TERM GOAL(S) _____
_____

TODAY'S MEAL PLAN	BREAKFAST	SNACK	LUNCH	SNACK	DINNER
	_____	_____	_____	_____	_____
	_____	_____	_____	_____	_____

weekly planner

	SUNDAY	MONDAY	TUESDAY	WEDNESDAY	THURSDAY	FRIDAY	SATURDAY	TOTAL
a.m.								
p.m.								

daily planner

5 a.m. _____	2 p.m. _____
6 a.m. _____	3 p.m. _____
7 a.m. _____	4 p.m. _____
8 a.m _____	5 p.m. _____
9 a.m. _____	6 p.m. _____
10 a.m. _____	7 p.m. _____
11 a.m. _____	8 p.m. _____
12 p.m. _____	9 p.m. _____
1 p.m. _____	10 p.m. _____

my training journal

my training log

SWIMMING WORKOUT:	distance
a.m.	
p.m.	
	total

BIKING WORKOUT:	distance
a.m.	
p.m.	
	total

RUNNING WORKOUT:	distance
a.m.	
p.m.	
	total

CROSS-TRAINING:	time
a.m.	
p.m.	
	total

TOMORROW'S To Do

RUNALOG® FOR TRIATHLETES

TODAY'S DATE _____

MY LONG-TERM GOAL(S) _____

_____

TODAY'S MEAL PLAN	BREAKFAST	SNACK	LUNCH	SNACK	DINNER
	_____	_____	_____	_____	_____
	_____	_____	_____	_____	_____

weekly planner

	SUNDAY	MONDAY	TUESDAY	WEDNESDAY	THURSDAY	FRIDAY	SATURDAY	TOTAL
a.m.								
p.m.								

daily planner

5 a.m. _____	2 p.m. _____
6 a.m. _____	3 p.m. _____
7 a.m. _____	4 p.m. _____
8 a.m _____	5 p.m. _____
9 a.m. _____	6 p.m. _____
10 a.m. _____	7 p.m. _____
11 a.m. _____	8 p.m. _____
12 p.m. _____	9 p.m. _____
1 p.m. _____	10 p.m. _____

my training journal

my training log

SWIMMING WORKOUT:		*distance*
a.m.		
p.m.		
		total

BIKING WORKOUT:		*distance*
a.m.		
p.m.		
		total

RUNNING WORKOUT:		*distance*
a.m.		
p.m.		
		total

CROSS-TRAINING:		*time*
a.m.		
p.m.		
		total

TOMORROW'S TO DO

✓RUNALOG® FOR TRIATHLETES

MY LONG-TERM GOAL(S) _____
_____

TODAY'S MEAL PLAN	BREAKFAST	SNACK	LUNCH	SNACK	DINNER
	_____	_____	_____	_____	_____
	_____	_____	_____	_____	_____

weekly planner

	SUNDAY	MONDAY	TUESDAY	WEDNESDAY	THURSDAY	FRIDAY	SATURDAY	TOTAL
a.m.								
p.m.								

🕐 daily planner

5 a.m. _____	2 p.m. _____
6 a.m. _____	3 p.m. _____
7 a.m. _____	4 p.m. _____
8 a.m _____	5 p.m. _____
9 a.m. _____	6 p.m. _____
10 a.m. _____	7 p.m. _____
11 a.m. _____	8 p.m. _____
12 p.m. _____	9 p.m. _____
1 p.m. _____	10 p.m. _____

✎ my training journal

_____
_____
_____
_____
_____
_____
_____
_____
_____
_____
_____
_____
_____
_____
_____
_____
_____
_____
_____

my training log

SWIMMING WORKOUT:	distance
a.m.	
p.m.	
	total

🚴 BIKING WORKOUT:	distance
a.m.	
p.m.	
	total

🏃 RUNNING WORKOUT:	distance
a.m.	
p.m.	
	total

CROSS-TRAINING:	time
a.m.	
p.m.	
	total

TOMORROW'S TO DO

RUNALOG® FOR TRIATHLETES

TODAY'S DATE _____

MY LONG-TERM GOAL(S) _____

_____

TODAY'S MEAL PLAN	BREAKFAST	SNACK	LUNCH	SNACK	DINNER
	_____	_____	_____	_____	_____
	_____	_____	_____	_____	_____

weekly planner

	SUNDAY	MONDAY	TUESDAY	WEDNESDAY	THURSDAY	FRIDAY	SATURDAY	TOTAL
a.m.								
p.m.								

daily planner

5 a.m. _____	2 p.m. _____
6 a.m. _____	3 p.m. _____
7 a.m. _____	4 p.m. _____
8 a.m _____	5 p.m. _____
9 a.m. _____	6 p.m. _____
10 a.m. _____	7 p.m. _____
11 a.m. _____	8 p.m. _____
12 p.m. _____	9 p.m. _____
1 p.m. _____	10 p.m. _____

my training journal

my training log

SWIMMING WORKOUT:	*distance*
a.m.	
p.m.	
	total

BIKING WORKOUT:	*distance*
a.m.	
p.m.	
	total

RUNNING WORKOUT:	*distance*
a.m.	
p.m.	
	total

CROSS-TRAINING:	*time*
a.m.	
p.m.	
	total

TOMORROW'S TO DO

⚕RUNALOG® FOR TRIATHLETES

TODAY'S DATE _____

MY LONG-TERM GOAL(S) _____

TODAY'S MEAL PLAN	BREAKFAST	SNACK	LUNCH	SNACK	DINNER
	_____	_____	_____	_____	_____
	_____	_____	_____	_____	_____

weekly planner

	SUNDAY	MONDAY	TUESDAY	WEDNESDAY	THURSDAY	FRIDAY	SATURDAY	TOTAL
a.m.								
p.m.								

🕐 *daily planner*

5 a.m. _____	2 p.m. _____
6 a.m. _____	3 p.m. _____
7 a.m. _____	4 p.m. _____
8 a.m _____	5 p.m. _____
9 a.m. _____	6 p.m. _____
10 a.m. _____	7 p.m. _____
11 a.m. _____	8 p.m. _____
12 p.m. _____	9 p.m. _____
1 p.m. _____	10 p.m. _____

✍ *my training journal*

my training log

SWIMMING WORKOUT:	*distance*
a.m.	
p.m.	
	total

BIKING WORKOUT:	*distance*
a.m.	
p.m.	
	total

RUNNING WORKOUT:	*distance*
a.m.	
p.m.	
	total

CROSS-TRAINING:	*time*
a.m.	
p.m.	
	total

TOMORROW'S To Do

139

⩔ RUNALOG® FOR TRIATHLETES

TODAY'S DATE _____

MY LONG-TERM GOAL(S) _____

_____

TODAY'S MEAL PLAN	BREAKFAST	SNACK	LUNCH	SNACK	DINNER
	_____	_____	_____	_____	_____
	_____	_____	_____	_____	_____

weekly planner

	SUNDAY	MONDAY	TUESDAY	WEDNESDAY	THURSDAY	FRIDAY	SATURDAY	TOTAL
a.m.								
p.m.								

🕐 daily planner

5 a.m. _____	2 p.m. _____
6 a.m. _____	3 p.m. _____
7 a.m. _____	4 p.m. _____
8 a.m _____	5 p.m. _____
9 a.m. _____	6 p.m. _____
10 a.m. _____	7 p.m. _____
11 a.m. _____	8 p.m. _____
12 p.m. _____	9 p.m. _____
1 p.m. _____	10 p.m. _____

✍ my training journal

my training log

SWIMMING WORKOUT:	*distance*
a.m.	
p.m.	
	total

BIKING WORKOUT:	*distance*
a.m.	
p.m.	
	total

RUNNING WORKOUT:	*distance*
a.m.	
p.m.	
	total

CROSS-TRAINING:	*time*
a.m.	
p.m.	
	total

TOMORROW'S TO DO

√RUNALOG® FOR TRIATHLETES

TODAY'S DATE _____

MY LONG-TERM GOAL(S) _____
_____

TODAY'S MEAL PLAN	BREAKFAST	SNACK	LUNCH	SNACK	DINNER
	_____	_____	_____	_____	_____
	_____	_____	_____	_____	_____

weekly planner

	SUNDAY	MONDAY	TUESDAY	WEDNESDAY	THURSDAY	FRIDAY	SATURDAY	TOTAL
a.m.								
p.m.								

daily planner

5 a.m. _____	2 p.m. _____
6 a.m. _____	3 p.m. _____
7 a.m. _____	4 p.m. _____
8 a.m _____	5 p.m. _____
9 a.m. _____	6 p.m. _____
10 a.m. _____	7 p.m. _____
11 a.m. _____	8 p.m. _____
12 p.m. _____	9 p.m. _____
1 p.m. _____	10 p.m. _____

my training journal

my training log

SWIMMING WORKOUT: *distance*

a.m.	
p.m.	
	total

BIKING WORKOUT: *distance*

a.m.	
p.m.	
	total

RUNNING WORKOUT: *distance*

a.m.	
p.m.	
	total

CROSS-TRAINING: *time*

a.m.	
p.m.	
	total

TOMORROW'S TO DO

RUNALOG® FOR TRIATHLETES

TODAY'S DATE _____

MY LONG-TERM GOAL(S) _____

_____

TODAY'S MEAL PLAN	BREAKFAST	SNACK	LUNCH	SNACK	DINNER
	_____	_____	_____	_____	_____
	_____	_____	_____	_____	_____

weekly planner

	SUNDAY	MONDAY	TUESDAY	WEDNESDAY	THURSDAY	FRIDAY	SATURDAY	TOTAL
a.m.								
p.m.								

daily planner

5 a.m. _____	2 p.m. _____
6 a.m. _____	3 p.m. _____
7 a.m. _____	4 p.m. _____
8 a.m _____	5 p.m. _____
9 a.m. _____	6 p.m. _____
10 a.m. _____	7 p.m. _____
11 a.m. _____	8 p.m. _____
12 p.m. _____	9 p.m. _____
1 p.m. _____	10 p.m. _____

my training journal

my training log

SWIMMING WORKOUT:	distance
a.m.	
p.m.	
	total

BIKING WORKOUT:	distance
a.m.	
p.m.	
	total

RUNNING WORKOUT:	distance
a.m.	
p.m.	
	total

CROSS-TRAINING:	time
a.m.	
p.m.	
	total

Tomorrow's To Do

142

√RUNALOG® FOR TRIATHLETES   TODAY'S DATE _____

MY LONG-TERM GOAL(S) _____
_____

TODAY'S MEAL PLAN	BREAKFAST	SNACK	LUNCH	SNACK	DINNER
	_____	_____	_____	_____	_____
	_____	_____	_____	_____	_____

weekly planner

	SUNDAY	MONDAY	TUESDAY	WEDNESDAY	THURSDAY	FRIDAY	SATURDAY	TOTAL
a.m.								
p.m.								

daily planner

5 a.m. _____	2 p.m. _____
6 a.m. _____	3 p.m. _____
7 a.m. _____	4 p.m. _____
8 a.m _____	5 p.m. _____
9 a.m. _____	6 p.m. _____
10 a.m. _____	7 p.m. _____
11 a.m. _____	8 p.m. _____
12 p.m. _____	9 p.m. _____
1 p.m. _____	10 p.m. _____

my training journal

my training log

SWIMMING WORKOUT:	distance
a.m.	
p.m.	
	total

BIKING WORKOUT:	distance
a.m.	
p.m.	
	total

RUNNING WORKOUT:	distance
a.m.	
p.m.	
	total

CROSS-TRAINING:	time
a.m.	
p.m.	
	total

TOMORROW'S TO DO

143

RUNALOG *FOR TRIATHLETES*   *TODAY'S DATE* _____

MY LONG-TERM GOAL(S) _____

TODAY'S MEAL PLAN	BREAKFAST	SNACK	LUNCH	SNACK	DINNER
	_____	_____	_____	_____	_____
	_____	_____	_____	_____	_____

weekly planner

	SUNDAY	MONDAY	TUESDAY	WEDNESDAY	THURSDAY	FRIDAY	SATURDAY	TOTAL
a.m.								
p.m.								

daily planner

5 a.m. _____	2 p.m. _____
6 a.m. _____	3 p.m. _____
7 a.m. _____	4 p.m. _____
8 a.m _____	5 p.m. _____
9 a.m. _____	6 p.m. _____
10 a.m. _____	7 p.m. _____
11 a.m. _____	8 p.m. _____
12 p.m. _____	9 p.m. _____
1 p.m. _____	10 p.m. _____

my training journal

my training log

SWIMMING WORKOUT:	*distance*
a.m.	
p.m.	
	total

BIKING WORKOUT:	*distance*
a.m.	
p.m.	
	total

RUNNING WORKOUT:	*distance*
a.m.	
p.m.	
	total

CROSS-TRAINING:	*time*
a.m.	
p.m.	
	total

TOMORROW'S TO DO

144

√RUNALOG® FOR TRIATHLETES

TODAY'S DATE _____

MY LONG-TERM GOAL(S) _____
_____

TODAY'S MEAL PLAN	BREAKFAST	SNACK	LUNCH	SNACK	DINNER
	_____	_____	_____	_____	_____
	_____	_____	_____	_____	_____

weekly planner

	SUNDAY	MONDAY	TUESDAY	WEDNESDAY	THURSDAY	FRIDAY	SATURDAY	TOTAL
a.m.								
p.m.								

daily planner

5 a.m. _____	2 p.m. _____
6 a.m. _____	3 p.m. _____
7 a.m. _____	4 p.m. _____
8 a.m _____	5 p.m. _____
9 a.m. _____	6 p.m. _____
10 a.m. _____	7 p.m. _____
11 a.m. _____	8 p.m. _____
12 p.m. _____	9 p.m. _____
1 p.m. _____	10 p.m. _____

my training journal

my training log

SWIMMING WORKOUT:	*distance*
a.m.	
p.m.	
	total

BIKING WORKOUT:	*distance*
a.m.	
p.m.	
	total

RUNNING WORKOUT:	*distance*
a.m.	
p.m.	
	total

CROSS-TRAINING:	*time*
a.m.	
p.m.	
	total

TOMORROW'S To Do

RUNALOG® FOR TRIATHLETES

TODAY'S DATE _____

MY LONG-TERM GOAL(S) _____

TODAY'S MEAL PLAN	BREAKFAST	SNACK	LUNCH	SNACK	DINNER
	_____	_____	_____	_____	_____
	_____	_____	_____	_____	_____

weekly planner

	SUNDAY	MONDAY	TUESDAY	WEDNESDAY	THURSDAY	FRIDAY	SATURDAY	TOTAL
a.m.								
p.m.								

daily planner

5 a.m. _____	2 p.m. _____
6 a.m. _____	3 p.m. _____
7 a.m. _____	4 p.m. _____
8 a.m _____	5 p.m. _____
9 a.m. _____	6 p.m. _____
10 a.m. _____	7 p.m. _____
11 a.m. _____	8 p.m. _____
12 p.m. _____	9 p.m. _____
1 p.m. _____	10 p.m. _____

my training journal

my training log

SWIMMING WORKOUT:	distance
a.m.	
p.m.	
	total

BIKING WORKOUT:	distance
a.m.	
p.m.	
	total

RUNNING WORKOUT:	distance
a.m.	
p.m.	
	total

CROSS-TRAINING:	time
a.m.	
p.m.	
	total

TOMORROW'S To Do

RUNALOG® FOR TRIATHLETES

TODAY'S DATE _____

MY LONG-TERM GOAL(S) _____

TODAY'S MEAL PLAN	BREAKFAST	SNACK	LUNCH	SNACK	DINNER
	_____	_____	_____	_____	_____

weekly planner

	SUNDAY	MONDAY	TUESDAY	WEDNESDAY	THURSDAY	FRIDAY	SATURDAY	TOTAL
a.m.								
p.m.								

daily planner

5 a.m. _____	2 p.m. _____
6 a.m. _____	3 p.m. _____
7 a.m. _____	4 p.m. _____
8 a.m _____	5 p.m. _____
9 a.m. _____	6 p.m. _____
10 a.m. _____	7 p.m. _____
11 a.m. _____	8 p.m. _____
12 p.m. _____	9 p.m. _____
1 p.m. _____	10 p.m. _____

my training journal

my training log

SWIMMING WORKOUT:	distance
a.m.	
p.m.	
	total

BIKING WORKOUT:	distance
a.m.	
p.m.	
	total

RUNNING WORKOUT:	distance
a.m.	
p.m.	
	total

CROSS-TRAINING:	time
a.m.	
p.m.	
	total

TOMORROW'S To Do

√RUNALOG® For Triathletes

TODAY'S DATE _____

MY LONG-TERM GOAL(S) _____

TODAY'S MEAL PLAN	BREAKFAST	SNACK	LUNCH	SNACK	DINNER
	_____	_____	_____	_____	_____
	_____	_____	_____	_____	_____

weekly planner

	SUNDAY	MONDAY	TUESDAY	WEDNESDAY	THURSDAY	FRIDAY	SATURDAY	TOTAL
a.m.								
p.m.								

daily planner

5 a.m. _____	2 p.m. _____
6 a.m. _____	3 p.m. _____
7 a.m. _____	4 p.m. _____
8 a.m _____	5 p.m. _____
9 a.m. _____	6 p.m. _____
10 a.m. _____	7 p.m. _____
11 a.m. _____	8 p.m. _____
12 p.m. _____	9 p.m. _____
1 p.m. _____	10 p.m. _____

my training journal

my training log

SWIMMING WORKOUT:	*distance*
a.m.	
p.m.	
	total

BIKING WORKOUT:	*distance*
a.m.	
p.m.	
	total

RUNNING WORKOUT:	*distance*
a.m.	
p.m.	
	total

CROSS-TRAINING:	*time*
a.m.	
p.m.	
	total

TOMORROW'S TO DO

MY LONG-TERM GOAL(S) _____

_____

TODAY'S MEAL PLAN	BREAKFAST	SNACK	LUNCH	SNACK	DINNER
	_____	_____	_____	_____	_____
	_____	_____	_____	_____	_____

weekly planner

	SUNDAY	MONDAY	TUESDAY	WEDNESDAY	THURSDAY	FRIDAY	SATURDAY	TOTAL
a.m.								
p.m.								

🕐 *daily planner*

5 a.m. _____	2 p.m. _____
6 a.m. _____	3 p.m. _____
7 a.m. _____	4 p.m. _____
8 a.m _____	5 p.m. _____
9 a.m. _____	6 p.m. _____
10 a.m. _____	7 p.m. _____
11 a.m. _____	8 p.m. _____
12 p.m. _____	9 p.m. _____
1 p.m. _____	10 p.m. _____

✎ *my training journal*

my training log

SWIMMING WORKOUT:	*distance*
a.m.	
p.m.	
	total

🚴 BIKING WORKOUT:	*distance*
a.m.	
p.m.	
	total

🏃 RUNNING WORKOUT:	*distance*
a.m.	
p.m.	
	total

CROSS-TRAINING:	*time*
a.m.	
p.m.	
	total

TOMORROW'S To Do

RUNALOG® FOR TRIATHLETES

TODAY'S DATE _____

MY LONG-TERM GOAL(S) _____

TODAY'S MEAL PLAN	BREAKFAST	SNACK	LUNCH	SNACK	DINNER
	_____	_____	_____	_____	_____
	_____	_____	_____	_____	_____

weekly planner

	SUNDAY	MONDAY	TUESDAY	WEDNESDAY	THURSDAY	FRIDAY	SATURDAY	TOTAL
a.m.								
p.m.								

daily planner

5 a.m.	_____	2 p.m.	_____
6 a.m.	_____	3 p.m.	_____
7 a.m.	_____	4 p.m.	_____
8 a.m	_____	5 p.m.	_____
9 a.m.	_____	6 p.m.	_____
10 a.m.	_____	7 p.m.	_____
11 a.m.	_____	8 p.m.	_____
12 p.m.	_____	9 p.m.	_____
1 p.m.	_____	10 p.m.	_____

my training journal

my training log

SWIMMING WORKOUT:	*distance*
a.m.	
p.m.	
	total

BIKING WORKOUT:	*distance*
a.m.	
p.m.	
	total

RUNNING WORKOUT:	*distance*
a.m.	
p.m.	
	total

CROSS-TRAINING:	*time*
a.m.	
p.m.	
	total

TOMORROW'S TO DO

ᐯRUNALOG® FOR TRIATHLETES

TODAY'S DATE _____

MY LONG-TERM GOAL(S) _____

_____

TODAY'S MEAL PLAN	BREAKFAST	SNACK	LUNCH	SNACK	DINNER
	_____	_____	_____	_____	_____
	_____	_____	_____	_____	_____

weekly planner

	SUNDAY	MONDAY	TUESDAY	WEDNESDAY	THURSDAY	FRIDAY	SATURDAY	TOTAL
a.m.								
p.m.								

🕐 daily planner

5 a.m. _____	2 p.m. _____
6 a.m. _____	3 p.m. _____
7 a.m. _____	4 p.m. _____
8 a.m _____	5 p.m. _____
9 a.m. _____	6 p.m. _____
10 a.m. _____	7 p.m. _____
11 a.m. _____	8 p.m. _____
12 p.m. _____	9 p.m. _____
1 p.m. _____	10 p.m. _____

✍ my training journal

my training log

SWIMMING WORKOUT:	*distance*
a.m.	
p.m.	
	total

🚴 BIKING WORKOUT:	*distance*
a.m.	
p.m.	
	total

🏃 RUNNING WORKOUT:	*distance*
a.m.	
p.m.	
	total

CROSS-TRAINING:	*time*
a.m.	
p.m.	
	total

TOMORROW'S TO DO

151

RUNALOG® FOR TRIATHLETES

TODAY'S DATE _____

MY LONG-TERM GOAL(S) _____

_____

TODAY'S MEAL PLAN	BREAKFAST	SNACK	LUNCH	SNACK	DINNER
	_____	_____	_____	_____	_____
	_____	_____	_____	_____	_____

weekly planner

	SUNDAY	MONDAY	TUESDAY	WEDNESDAY	THURSDAY	FRIDAY	SATURDAY	TOTAL
a.m.								
p.m.								

daily planner

5 a.m. _____	2 p.m. _____
6 a.m. _____	3 p.m. _____
7 a.m. _____	4 p.m. _____
8 a.m _____	5 p.m. _____
9 a.m. _____	6 p.m. _____
10 a.m. _____	7 p.m. _____
11 a.m. _____	8 p.m. _____
12 p.m. _____	9 p.m. _____
1 p.m. _____	10 p.m. _____

my training journal

my training log

SWIMMING WORKOUT:	distance
a.m.	
p.m.	
	total

BIKING WORKOUT:	distance
a.m.	
p.m.	
	total

RUNNING WORKOUT:	distance
a.m.	
p.m.	
	total

CROSS-TRAINING:	time
a.m.	
p.m.	
	total

TOMORROW'S TO DO

✓RUNALOG® FOR TRIATHLETES

TODAY'S DATE _____

MY LONG-TERM GOAL(S) _____

TODAY'S MEAL PLAN	BREAKFAST	SNACK	LUNCH	SNACK	DINNER
	_____	_____	_____	_____	_____

weekly planner

	SUNDAY	MONDAY	TUESDAY	WEDNESDAY	THURSDAY	FRIDAY	SATURDAY	TOTAL
a.m.								
p.m.								

🕐 *daily planner*

5 a.m. _____	2 p.m. _____
6 a.m. _____	3 p.m. _____
7 a.m. _____	4 p.m. _____
8 a.m _____	5 p.m. _____
9 a.m. _____	6 p.m. _____
10 a.m. _____	7 p.m. _____
11 a.m. _____	8 p.m. _____
12 p.m. _____	9 p.m. _____
1 p.m. _____	10 p.m. _____

✍ *my training journal*

my training log

🏊 SWIMMING WORKOUT:	*distance*
a.m.	
p.m.	
	total

🚴 BIKING WORKOUT:	*distance*
a.m.	
p.m.	
	total

🏃 RUNNING WORKOUT:	*distance*
a.m.	
p.m.	
	total

CROSS-TRAINING:	*time*
a.m.	
p.m.	
	total

TOMORROW'S TO DO

153

© 2009 www.RUNALOGS.com

ϒRUNALOG® FOR TRIATHLETES

TODAY'S DATE _____

MY LONG-TERM GOAL(S) _____

_____

TODAY'S MEAL PLAN	BREAKFAST	SNACK	LUNCH	SNACK	DINNER
	_____	_____	_____	_____	_____
	_____	_____	_____	_____	_____

weekly planner

	SUNDAY	MONDAY	TUESDAY	WEDNESDAY	THURSDAY	FRIDAY	SATURDAY	TOTAL
a.m.								
p.m.								

daily planner

5 a.m. _____	2 p.m. _____
6 a.m. _____	3 p.m. _____
7 a.m. _____	4 p.m. _____
8 a.m _____	5 p.m. _____
9 a.m. _____	6 p.m. _____
10 a.m. _____	7 p.m. _____
11 a.m. _____	8 p.m. _____
12 p.m. _____	9 p.m. _____
1 p.m. _____	10 p.m. _____

my training journal

my training log

SWIMMING WORKOUT:	*distance*
a.m.	
p.m.	
	total

BIKING WORKOUT:	*distance*
a.m.	
p.m.	
	total

RUNNING WORKOUT:	*distance*
a.m.	
p.m.	
	total

CROSS-TRAINING:	*time*
a.m.	
p.m.	
	total

TOMORROW'S To Do

154

⊽RUNALOG® FOR TRIATHLETES

TODAY'S DATE _____

MY LONG-TERM GOAL(S) _____

TODAY'S MEAL PLAN	BREAKFAST	SNACK	LUNCH	SNACK	DINNER
	_____	_____	_____	_____	_____
	_____	_____	_____	_____	_____
	_____	_____	_____	_____	_____

weekly planner

	SUNDAY	MONDAY	TUESDAY	WEDNESDAY	THURSDAY	FRIDAY	SATURDAY	TOTAL
a.m.								
p.m.								

daily planner

5 a.m. _____	2 p.m. _____
6 a.m. _____	3 p.m. _____
7 a.m. _____	4 p.m. _____
8 a.m _____	5 p.m. _____
9 a.m. _____	6 p.m. _____
10 a.m. _____	7 p.m. _____
11 a.m. _____	8 p.m. _____
12 p.m. _____	9 p.m. _____
1 p.m. _____	10 p.m. _____

my training journal

my training log

SWIMMING WORKOUT:	distance
a.m.	
p.m.	
	total

BIKING WORKOUT:	distance
a.m.	
p.m.	
	total

RUNNING WORKOUT:	distance
a.m.	
p.m.	
	total

CROSS-TRAINING:	time
a.m.	
p.m.	
	total

TOMORROW'S To Do

155

⅋RUNALOG® FOR TRIATHLETES

TODAY'S DATE _____

MY LONG-TERM GOAL(S) _____

_____

TODAY'S MEAL PLAN	BREAKFAST	SNACK	LUNCH	SNACK	DINNER
	_____	_____	_____	_____	_____
	_____	_____	_____	_____	_____

weekly planner

	SUNDAY	MONDAY	TUESDAY	WEDNESDAY	THURSDAY	FRIDAY	SATURDAY	TOTAL
a.m.								
p.m.								

daily planner

5 a.m. _____	2 p.m. _____
6 a.m. _____	3 p.m. _____
7 a.m. _____	4 p.m. _____
8 a.m _____	5 p.m. _____
9 a.m. _____	6 p.m. _____
10 a.m. _____	7 p.m. _____
11 a.m. _____	8 p.m. _____
12 p.m. _____	9 p.m. _____
1 p.m. _____	10 p.m. _____

my training journal

my training log

SWIMMING WORKOUT:	*distance*
a.m.	
p.m.	
	total

BIKING WORKOUT:	*distance*
a.m.	
p.m.	
	total

RUNNING WORKOUT:	*distance*
a.m.	
p.m.	
	total

CROSS-TRAINING:	*time*
a.m.	
p.m.	
	total

TOMORROW'S TO DO

RUNALOG® FOR TRIATHLETES

TODAY'S DATE _____

MY LONG-TERM GOAL(S) _____

TODAY'S MEAL PLAN	BREAKFAST	SNACK	LUNCH	SNACK	DINNER

weekly planner

	SUNDAY	MONDAY	TUESDAY	WEDNESDAY	THURSDAY	FRIDAY	SATURDAY	TOTAL
a.m.								
p.m.								

daily planner

5 a.m. _____	2 p.m. _____
6 a.m. _____	3 p.m. _____
7 a.m. _____	4 p.m. _____
8 a.m _____	5 p.m. _____
9 a.m. _____	6 p.m. _____
10 a.m. _____	7 p.m. _____
11 a.m. _____	8 p.m. _____
12 p.m. _____	9 p.m. _____
1 p.m. _____	10 p.m. _____

my training journal

my training log

SWIMMING WORKOUT:	*distance*
a.m.	
p.m.	
	total

BIKING WORKOUT:	*distance*
a.m.	
p.m.	
	total

RUNNING WORKOUT:	*distance*
a.m.	
p.m.	
	total

CROSS-TRAINING:	*time*
a.m.	
p.m.	
	total

TOMORROW'S TO DO

RUNALOG® *FOR TRIATHLETES*

TODAY'S DATE _____

MY LONG-TERM GOAL(S) _____

_____

TODAY'S MEAL PLAN	BREAKFAST	SNACK	LUNCH	SNACK	DINNER
	_____	_____	_____	_____	_____
	_____	_____	_____	_____	_____

weekly planner

	SUNDAY	MONDAY	TUESDAY	WEDNESDAY	THURSDAY	FRIDAY	SATURDAY	TOTAL
a.m.								
p.m.								

daily planner

5 a.m. _____	2 p.m. _____
6 a.m. _____	3 p.m. _____
7 a.m. _____	4 p.m. _____
8 a.m _____	5 p.m. _____
9 a.m. _____	6 p.m. _____
10 a.m. _____	7 p.m. _____
11 a.m. _____	8 p.m. _____
12 p.m. _____	9 p.m. _____
1 p.m. _____	10 p.m. _____

my training journal

my training log

SWIMMING WORKOUT:	*distance*
a.m.	
p.m.	
	total

BIKING WORKOUT:	*distance*
a.m.	
p.m.	
	total

RUNNING WORKOUT:	*distance*
a.m.	
p.m.	
	total

CROSS-TRAINING:	*time*
a.m.	
p.m.	
	total

TOMORROW'S TO DO

MY LONG-TERM GOAL(S) _____
_____

TODAY'S MEAL PLAN	BREAKFAST	SNACK	LUNCH	SNACK	DINNER
	_____	_____	_____	_____	_____
	_____	_____	_____	_____	_____

weekly planner

	SUNDAY	MONDAY	TUESDAY	WEDNESDAY	THURSDAY	FRIDAY	SATURDAY	TOTAL
a.m.								
p.m.								

🕐 *daily planner*

5 a.m. _____	2 p.m. _____
6 a.m. _____	3 p.m. _____
7 a.m. _____	4 p.m. _____
8 a.m _____	5 p.m. _____
9 a.m. _____	6 p.m. _____
10 a.m. _____	7 p.m. _____
11 a.m. _____	8 p.m. _____
12 p.m. _____	9 p.m. _____
1 p.m. _____	10 p.m. _____

✍ *my training journal*

my training log

SWIMMING WORKOUT:	*distance*
a.m.	
p.m.	
	total

BIKING WORKOUT:	*distance*
a.m.	
p.m.	
	total

RUNNING WORKOUT:	*distance*
a.m.	
p.m.	
	total

CROSS-TRAINING:	*time*
a.m.	
p.m.	
	total

TOMORROW'S TO DO

MY LONG-TERM GOAL(S) _____

TODAY'S MEAL PLAN	BREAKFAST	SNACK	LUNCH	SNACK	DINNER
	_____	_____	_____	_____	_____
	_____	_____	_____	_____	_____

weekly planner

	SUNDAY	MONDAY	TUESDAY	WEDNESDAY	THURSDAY	FRIDAY	SATURDAY	TOTAL
a.m.								
p.m.								

daily planner

5 a.m. _____	2 p.m. _____
6 a.m. _____	3 p.m. _____
7 a.m. _____	4 p.m. _____
8 a.m _____	5 p.m. _____
9 a.m. _____	6 p.m. _____
10 a.m. _____	7 p.m. _____
11 a.m. _____	8 p.m. _____
12 p.m. _____	9 p.m. _____
1 p.m. _____	10 p.m. _____

my training journal

my training log

SWIMMING WORKOUT:	*distance*
a.m.	
p.m.	
	total

BIKING WORKOUT:	*distance*
a.m.	
p.m.	
	total

RUNNING WORKOUT:	*distance*
a.m.	
p.m.	
	total

CROSS-TRAINING:	*time*
a.m.	
p.m.	
	total

TOMORROW'S To Do

RUNALOG® FOR TRIATHLETES

TODAY'S DATE _____

MY LONG-TERM GOAL(S) _____

_____

TODAY'S MEAL PLAN	BREAKFAST	SNACK	LUNCH	SNACK	DINNER

weekly planner

	SUNDAY	MONDAY	TUESDAY	WEDNESDAY	THURSDAY	FRIDAY	SATURDAY	TOTAL
a.m.								
p.m.								

daily planner

5 a.m. _____	2 p.m. _____
6 a.m. _____	3 p.m. _____
7 a.m. _____	4 p.m. _____
8 a.m _____	5 p.m. _____
9 a.m. _____	6 p.m. _____
10 a.m. _____	7 p.m. _____
11 a.m. _____	8 p.m. _____
12 p.m. _____	9 p.m. _____
1 p.m. _____	10 p.m. _____

my training log

SWIMMING WORKOUT:	*distance*
a.m.	
p.m.	
	total

BIKING WORKOUT:	*distance*
a.m.	
p.m.	
	total

RUNNING WORKOUT:	*distance*
a.m.	
p.m.	
	total

CROSS-TRAINING:	*time*
a.m.	
p.m.	
	total

TOMORROW'S To Do

my training journal

⚜RUNALOG® FOR TRIATHLETES

TODAY'S DATE _____

MY LONG-TERM GOAL(S) _____

TODAY'S MEAL PLAN	BREAKFAST	SNACK	LUNCH	SNACK	DINNER
	_____	_____	_____	_____	_____
	_____	_____	_____	_____	_____

weekly planner

	SUNDAY	MONDAY	TUESDAY	WEDNESDAY	THURSDAY	FRIDAY	SATURDAY	TOTAL
a.m.								
p.m.								

daily planner

5 a.m. _____	2 p.m. _____
6 a.m. _____	3 p.m. _____
7 a.m. _____	4 p.m. _____
8 a.m _____	5 p.m. _____
9 a.m. _____	6 p.m. _____
10 a.m. _____	7 p.m. _____
11 a.m. _____	8 p.m. _____
12 p.m. _____	9 p.m. _____
1 p.m. _____	10 p.m. _____

my training journal

my training log

SWIMMING WORKOUT: distance

a.m.		
p.m.		
		total

BIKING WORKOUT: distance

a.m.		
p.m.		
		total

RUNNING WORKOUT: distance

a.m.		
p.m.		
		total

CROSS-TRAINING: time

a.m.		
p.m.		
		total

TOMORROW'S TO DO

✓RUNALOG® FOR TRIATHLETES

TODAY'S DATE _____

MY LONG-TERM GOAL(S) _____
_____

TODAY'S MEAL PLAN	BREAKFAST	SNACK	LUNCH	SNACK	DINNER
	_____	_____	_____	_____	_____
	_____	_____	_____	_____	_____

weekly planner

	SUNDAY	MONDAY	TUESDAY	WEDNESDAY	THURSDAY	FRIDAY	SATURDAY	TOTAL
a.m.								
p.m.								

🕐 daily planner

5 a.m. _____	2 p.m. _____
6 a.m. _____	3 p.m. _____
7 a.m. _____	4 p.m. _____
8 a.m _____	5 p.m. _____
9 a.m. _____	6 p.m. _____
10 a.m. _____	7 p.m. _____
11 a.m. _____	8 p.m. _____
12 p.m. _____	9 p.m. _____
1 p.m. _____	10 p.m. _____

✍ my training journal

my training log

SWIMMING WORKOUT:	distance
a.m.	
p.m.	
	total

BIKING WORKOUT:	distance
a.m.	
p.m.	
	total

RUNNING WORKOUT:	distance
a.m.	
p.m.	
	total

CROSS-TRAINING:	time
a.m.	
p.m.	
	total

TOMORROW'S TO DO

163

⚐RUNALOG® FOR TRIATHLETES

TODAY'S DATE _____

MY LONG-TERM GOAL(S) _____

_____

TODAY'S MEAL PLAN	BREAKFAST	SNACK	LUNCH	SNACK	DINNER
	_____	_____	_____	_____	_____
	_____	_____	_____	_____	_____

weekly planner

	SUNDAY	MONDAY	TUESDAY	WEDNESDAY	THURSDAY	FRIDAY	SATURDAY	TOTAL
a.m.								
p.m.								

🕐 daily planner

5 a.m. _____	2 p.m. _____
6 a.m. _____	3 p.m. _____
7 a.m. _____	4 p.m. _____
8 a.m _____	5 p.m. _____
9 a.m. _____	6 p.m. _____
10 a.m. _____	7 p.m. _____
11 a.m. _____	8 p.m. _____
12 p.m. _____	9 p.m. _____
1 p.m. _____	10 p.m. _____

✍ my training journal

my training log

SWIMMING WORKOUT:	*distance*
a.m.	
p.m.	
	total

BIKING WORKOUT:	*distance*
a.m.	
p.m.	
	total

RUNNING WORKOUT:	*distance*
a.m.	
p.m.	
	total

CROSS-TRAINING:	*time*
a.m.	
p.m.	
	total

TOMORROW'S TO DO

Today's Meal Plan	Breakfast	Snack	Lunch	Snack	Dinner
	_____	_____	_____	_____	_____
	_____	_____	_____	_____	_____

weekly planner

	SUNDAY	MONDAY	TUESDAY	WEDNESDAY	THURSDAY	FRIDAY	SATURDAY	TOTAL
a.m.								
p.m.								

daily planner

5 a.m. _____	2 p.m. _____
6 a.m. _____	3 p.m. _____
7 a.m. _____	4 p.m. _____
8 a.m _____	5 p.m. _____
9 a.m. _____	6 p.m. _____
10 a.m. _____	7 p.m. _____
11 a.m. _____	8 p.m. _____
12 p.m. _____	9 p.m. _____
1 p.m. _____	10 p.m. _____

my training journal

my training log

SWIMMING WORKOUT: *distance*

a.m.	
p.m.	
	total

BIKING WORKOUT: *distance*

a.m.	
p.m.	
	total

RUNNING WORKOUT: *distance*

a.m.	
p.m.	
	total

CROSS-TRAINING: *time*

a.m.	
p.m.	
	total

Tomorrow's To Do

ᵛ͚RUNALOG® FOR TRIATHLETES

TODAY'S DATE _____

MY LONG-TERM GOAL(S) _____
_____

TODAY'S MEAL PLAN	BREAKFAST	SNACK	LUNCH	SNACK	DINNER
	_____	_____	_____	_____	_____
	_____	_____	_____	_____	_____

weekly planner

	SUNDAY	MONDAY	TUESDAY	WEDNESDAY	THURSDAY	FRIDAY	SATURDAY	TOTAL
a.m.								
p.m.								

daily planner

5 a.m. _____	2 p.m. _____
6 a.m. _____	3 p.m. _____
7 a.m. _____	4 p.m. _____
8 a.m _____	5 p.m. _____
9 a.m. _____	6 p.m. _____
10 a.m. _____	7 p.m. _____
11 a.m. _____	8 p.m. _____
12 p.m. _____	9 p.m. _____
1 p.m. _____	10 p.m. _____

my training journal

my training log

SWIMMING WORKOUT:	*distance*
a.m.	
p.m.	
	total

BIKING WORKOUT:	*distance*
a.m.	
p.m.	
	total

RUNNING WORKOUT:	*distance*
a.m.	
p.m.	
	total

CROSS-TRAINING:	*time*
a.m.	
p.m.	
	total

TOMORROW'S To Do

166

RUNALOG® FOR TRIATHLETES

TODAY'S DATE _____

MY LONG-TERM GOAL(S) _____

TODAY'S MEAL PLAN	BREAKFAST	SNACK	LUNCH	SNACK	DINNER
	_____	_____	_____	_____	_____
	_____	_____	_____	_____	_____

weekly planner

	SUNDAY	MONDAY	TUESDAY	WEDNESDAY	THURSDAY	FRIDAY	SATURDAY	TOTAL
a.m.								
p.m.								

daily planner

5 a.m. _____	2 p.m. _____
6 a.m. _____	3 p.m. _____
7 a.m. _____	4 p.m. _____
8 a.m _____	5 p.m. _____
9 a.m. _____	6 p.m. _____
10 a.m. _____	7 p.m. _____
11 a.m. _____	8 p.m. _____
12 p.m. _____	9 p.m. _____
1 p.m. _____	10 p.m. _____

my training journal

my training log

SWIMMING WORKOUT:	*distance*
a.m.	
p.m.	
	total

BIKING WORKOUT:	*distance*
a.m.	
p.m.	
	total

RUNNING WORKOUT:	*distance*
a.m.	
p.m.	
	total

CROSS-TRAINING:	*time*
a.m.	
p.m.	
	total

TOMORROW'S TO DO

⩔RUNALOG® FOR TRIATHLETES

TODAY'S DATE _____

MY LONG-TERM GOAL(S) _____

_____

TODAY'S MEAL PLAN	BREAKFAST	SNACK	LUNCH	SNACK	DINNER
	_____	_____	_____	_____	_____
	_____	_____	_____	_____	_____

weekly planner

	SUNDAY	MONDAY	TUESDAY	WEDNESDAY	THURSDAY	FRIDAY	SATURDAY	TOTAL
a.m.								
p.m.								

🕐 daily planner

5 a.m. _____	2 p.m. _____
6 a.m. _____	3 p.m. _____
7 a.m. _____	4 p.m. _____
8 a.m _____	5 p.m. _____
9 a.m. _____	6 p.m. _____
10 a.m. _____	7 p.m. _____
11 a.m. _____	8 p.m. _____
12 p.m. _____	9 p.m. _____
1 p.m. _____	10 p.m. _____

✍ my training journal

my training log

SWIMMING WORKOUT:	*distance*
a.m.	
p.m.	
	total

BIKING WORKOUT:	*distance*
a.m.	
p.m.	
	total

RUNNING WORKOUT:	*distance*
a.m.	
p.m.	
	total

CROSS-TRAINING:	*time*
a.m.	
p.m.	
	total

TOMORROW'S TO DO

ᐱRUNALOG® FOR TRIATHLETES

TODAY'S DATE _____

MY LONG-TERM GOAL(S) _____
_____

TODAY'S MEAL PLAN	BREAKFAST	SNACK	LUNCH	SNACK	DINNER
	_____	_____	_____	_____	_____
	_____	_____	_____	_____	_____

weekly planner

	SUNDAY	MONDAY	TUESDAY	WEDNESDAY	THURSDAY	FRIDAY	SATURDAY	TOTAL
a.m.								
p.m.								

daily planner

5 a.m. _____	2 p.m. _____
6 a.m. _____	3 p.m. _____
7 a.m. _____	4 p.m. _____
8 a.m _____	5 p.m. _____
9 a.m. _____	6 p.m. _____
10 a.m. _____	7 p.m. _____
11 a.m. _____	8 p.m. _____
12 p.m. _____	9 p.m. _____
1 p.m. _____	10 p.m. _____

my training journal

my training log

SWIMMING WORKOUT:	distance
a.m.	
p.m.	
	total

BIKING WORKOUT:	distance
a.m.	
p.m.	
	total

RUNNING WORKOUT:	distance
a.m.	
p.m.	
	total

CROSS-TRAINING:	time
a.m.	
p.m.	
	total

TOMORROW'S TO DO

169

ᐯRUNALOG® FOR TRIATHLETES

TODAY'S DATE _____

MY LONG-TERM GOAL(S) _____

_____

TODAY'S MEAL PLAN	BREAKFAST	SNACK	LUNCH	SNACK	DINNER
	_____	_____	_____	_____	_____
	_____	_____	_____	_____	_____

weekly planner

	SUNDAY	MONDAY	TUESDAY	WEDNESDAY	THURSDAY	FRIDAY	SATURDAY	TOTAL
a.m.								
p.m.								

🕐 daily planner

5 a.m.	_____	2 p.m.	_____
6 a.m.	_____	3 p.m.	_____
7 a.m.	_____	4 p.m.	_____
8 a.m	_____	5 p.m.	_____
9 a.m.	_____	6 p.m.	_____
10 a.m.	_____	7 p.m.	_____
11 a.m.	_____	8 p.m.	_____
12 p.m.	_____	9 p.m.	_____
1 p.m.	_____	10 p.m.	_____

✍ my training journal

my training log

SWIMMING WORKOUT:	*distance*
a.m.	
p.m.	
	total

🚴 BIKING WORKOUT:	*distance*
a.m.	
p.m.	
	total

🏃 RUNNING WORKOUT:	*distance*
a.m.	
p.m.	
	total

CROSS-TRAINING:	*time*
a.m.	
p.m.	
	total

TOMORROW'S TO DO

RUNALOG® FOR TRIATHLETES

TODAY'S DATE _____

MY LONG-TERM GOAL(S) _____

TODAY'S MEAL PLAN	BREAKFAST	SNACK	LUNCH	SNACK	DINNER
	_____	_____	_____	_____	_____

weekly planner

	SUNDAY	MONDAY	TUESDAY	WEDNESDAY	THURSDAY	FRIDAY	SATURDAY	TOTAL
a.m.								
p.m.								

daily planner

5 a.m. _____	2 p.m. _____
6 a.m. _____	3 p.m. _____
7 a.m. _____	4 p.m. _____
8 a.m _____	5 p.m. _____
9 a.m. _____	6 p.m. _____
10 a.m. _____	7 p.m. _____
11 a.m. _____	8 p.m. _____
12 p.m. _____	9 p.m. _____
1 p.m. _____	10 p.m. _____

my training journal

my training log

SWIMMING WORKOUT: distance

a.m.		
p.m.		
		total

BIKING WORKOUT: distance

a.m.		
p.m.		
		total

RUNNING WORKOUT: distance

a.m.		
p.m.		
		total

CROSS-TRAINING: time

a.m.		
p.m.		
		total

TOMORROW'S To Do

RUNALOG® FOR TRIATHLETES

TODAY'S DATE _____

MY LONG-TERM GOAL(S) _____

TODAY'S MEAL PLAN	BREAKFAST	SNACK	LUNCH	SNACK	DINNER

weekly planner

	SUNDAY	MONDAY	TUESDAY	WEDNESDAY	THURSDAY	FRIDAY	SATURDAY	TOTAL
a.m.								
p.m.								

daily planner

5 a.m. _____	2 p.m. _____
6 a.m. _____	3 p.m. _____
7 a.m. _____	4 p.m. _____
8 a.m _____	5 p.m. _____
9 a.m. _____	6 p.m. _____
10 a.m. _____	7 p.m. _____
11 a.m. _____	8 p.m. _____
12 p.m. _____	9 p.m. _____
1 p.m. _____	10 p.m. _____

my training journal

my training log

SWIMMING WORKOUT:	distance
a.m.	
p.m.	
	total

BIKING WORKOUT:	distance
a.m.	
p.m.	
	total

RUNNING WORKOUT:	distance
a.m.	
p.m.	
	total

CROSS-TRAINING:	time
a.m.	
p.m.	
	total

TOMORROW'S TO DO

⚡RUNALOG® FOR TRIATHLETES

TODAY'S DATE _____

MY LONG-TERM GOAL(S) _____
_____

TODAY'S MEAL PLAN	BREAKFAST	SNACK	LUNCH	SNACK	DINNER
	_____	_____	_____	_____	_____
	_____	_____	_____	_____	_____

weekly planner

	SUNDAY	MONDAY	TUESDAY	WEDNESDAY	THURSDAY	FRIDAY	SATURDAY	TOTAL
a.m.								
p.m.								

🕐 daily planner

5 a.m. _____	2 p.m. _____
6 a.m. _____	3 p.m. _____
7 a.m. _____	4 p.m. _____
8 a.m _____	5 p.m. _____
9 a.m. _____	6 p.m. _____
10 a.m. _____	7 p.m. _____
11 a.m. _____	8 p.m. _____
12 p.m. _____	9 p.m. _____
1 p.m. _____	10 p.m. _____

✍ my training journal

my training log

SWIMMING WORKOUT:	distance
a.m.	
p.m.	
	total

BIKING WORKOUT:	distance
a.m.	
p.m.	
	total

RUNNING WORKOUT:	distance
a.m.	
p.m.	
	total

CROSS-TRAINING:	time
a.m.	
p.m.	
	total

TOMORROW'S TO DO

RUNALOG® FOR TRIATHLETES   TODAY'S DATE _____

MY LONG-TERM GOAL(S) _____
_____

TODAY'S MEAL PLAN	BREAKFAST	SNACK	LUNCH	SNACK	DINNER
	_____	_____	_____	_____	_____
	_____	_____	_____	_____	_____

weekly planner

	SUNDAY	MONDAY	TUESDAY	WEDNESDAY	THURSDAY	FRIDAY	SATURDAY	TOTAL
a.m.								
p.m.								

daily planner

5 a.m. _____	2 p.m. _____
6 a.m. _____	3 p.m. _____
7 a.m. _____	4 p.m. _____
8 a.m _____	5 p.m. _____
9 a.m. _____	6 p.m. _____
10 a.m. _____	7 p.m. _____
11 a.m. _____	8 p.m. _____
12 p.m. _____	9 p.m. _____
1 p.m. _____	10 p.m. _____

my training journal

my training log

SWIMMING WORKOUT:	*distance*
a.m.	
p.m.	
	total

BIKING WORKOUT:	*distance*
a.m.	
p.m.	
	total

RUNNING WORKOUT:	*distance*
a.m.	
p.m.	
	total

CROSS-TRAINING:	*time*
a.m.	
p.m.	
	total

Tomorrow's To Do

√RUNALOG® FOR TRIATHLETES

TODAY'S DATE _____

MY LONG-TERM GOAL(S) _____

_____

TODAY'S MEAL PLAN	BREAKFAST	SNACK	LUNCH	SNACK	DINNER
	_____	_____	_____	_____	_____
	_____	_____	_____	_____	_____
	_____	_____	_____	_____	_____

weekly planner

	SUNDAY	MONDAY	TUESDAY	WEDNESDAY	THURSDAY	FRIDAY	SATURDAY	TOTAL
a.m.								
p.m.								

daily planner

5 a.m. _____	2 p.m. _____
6 a.m. _____	3 p.m. _____
7 a.m. _____	4 p.m. _____
8 a.m _____	5 p.m. _____
9 a.m. _____	6 p.m. _____
10 a.m. _____	7 p.m. _____
11 a.m. _____	8 p.m. _____
12 p.m. _____	9 p.m. _____
1 p.m. _____	10 p.m. _____

my training journal

my training log

SWIMMING WORKOUT:	distance
a.m.	
p.m.	
	total

BIKING WORKOUT:	distance
a.m.	
p.m.	
	total

RUNNING WORKOUT:	distance
a.m.	
p.m.	
	total

CROSS-TRAINING:	time
a.m.	
p.m.	
	total

TOMORROW'S TO DO

175

⚡RUNALOG® FOR TRIATHLETES

TODAY'S DATE _____

MY LONG-TERM GOAL(S) _____

TODAY'S MEAL PLAN	BREAKFAST	SNACK	LUNCH	SNACK	DINNER
	_____	_____	_____	_____	_____
	_____	_____	_____	_____	_____

weekly planner

	SUNDAY	MONDAY	TUESDAY	WEDNESDAY	THURSDAY	FRIDAY	SATURDAY	TOTAL
a.m.								
p.m.								

🕐 daily planner

5 a.m. _____	2 p.m. _____
6 a.m. _____	3 p.m. _____
7 a.m. _____	4 p.m. _____
8 a.m _____	5 p.m. _____
9 a.m. _____	6 p.m. _____
10 a.m. _____	7 p.m. _____
11 a.m. _____	8 p.m. _____
12 p.m. _____	9 p.m. _____
1 p.m. _____	10 p.m. _____

✍ my training journal

my training log

SWIMMING WORKOUT:	*distance*
a.m.	
p.m.	
	total

BIKING WORKOUT:	*distance*
a.m.	
p.m.	
	total

RUNNING WORKOUT:	*distance*
a.m.	
p.m.	
	total

CROSS-TRAINING:	*time*
a.m.	
p.m.	
	total

TOMORROW'S To Do

176

⩔RUNALOG® FOR TRIATHLETES

TODAY'S DATE _____

MY LONG-TERM GOAL(S) _____

TODAY'S MEAL PLAN	BREAKFAST	SNACK	LUNCH	SNACK	DINNER
	_____	_____	_____	_____	_____

weekly planner

	SUNDAY	MONDAY	TUESDAY	WEDNESDAY	THURSDAY	FRIDAY	SATURDAY	TOTAL
a.m.								
p.m.								

🕐 *daily planner*

5 a.m. _____	2 p.m. _____
6 a.m. _____	3 p.m. _____
7 a.m. _____	4 p.m. _____
8 a.m _____	5 p.m. _____
9 a.m. _____	6 p.m. _____
10 a.m. _____	7 p.m. _____
11 a.m. _____	8 p.m. _____
12 p.m. _____	9 p.m. _____
1 p.m. _____	10 p.m. _____

✍ *my training journal*

my training log

SWIMMING WORKOUT:	*distance*
a.m.	
p.m.	
	total

🚴 BIKING WORKOUT:	*distance*
a.m.	
p.m.	
	total

🏃 RUNNING WORKOUT:	*distance*
a.m.	
p.m.	
	total

CROSS-TRAINING:	*time*
a.m.	
p.m.	
	total

TOMORROW'S To Do

177

RUNALOG® FOR TRIATHLETES

TODAY'S DATE _____

MY LONG-TERM GOAL(S) _____

TODAY'S MEAL PLAN	BREAKFAST	SNACK	LUNCH	SNACK	DINNER
	_____	_____	_____	_____	_____
	_____	_____	_____	_____	_____

weekly planner

	SUNDAY	MONDAY	TUESDAY	WEDNESDAY	THURSDAY	FRIDAY	SATURDAY	TOTAL
a.m.								
p.m.								

daily planner

5 a.m. _____	2 p.m. _____
6 a.m. _____	3 p.m. _____
7 a.m. _____	4 p.m. _____
8 a.m _____	5 p.m. _____
9 a.m. _____	6 p.m. _____
10 a.m. _____	7 p.m. _____
11 a.m. _____	8 p.m. _____
12 p.m. _____	9 p.m. _____
1 p.m. _____	10 p.m. _____

my training journal

my training log

SWIMMING WORKOUT:	*distance*
a.m.	
p.m.	
	total

BIKING WORKOUT:	*distance*
a.m.	
p.m.	
	total

RUNNING WORKOUT:	*distance*
a.m.	
p.m.	
	total

CROSS-TRAINING:	*time*
a.m.	
p.m.	
	total

TOMORROW'S TO DO

√RUNALOG® FOR TRIATHLETES

TODAY'S DATE _____

MY LONG-TERM GOAL(S) _____

_____

TODAY'S MEAL PLAN	BREAKFAST	SNACK	LUNCH	SNACK	DINNER
	_____	_____	_____	_____	_____
	_____	_____	_____	_____	_____

weekly planner

	SUNDAY	MONDAY	TUESDAY	WEDNESDAY	THURSDAY	FRIDAY	SATURDAY	TOTAL
a.m.								
p.m.								

daily planner

5 a.m. _____	2 p.m. _____
6 a.m. _____	3 p.m. _____
7 a.m. _____	4 p.m. _____
8 a.m _____	5 p.m. _____
9 a.m. _____	6 p.m. _____
10 a.m. _____	7 p.m. _____
11 a.m. _____	8 p.m. _____
12 p.m. _____	9 p.m. _____
1 p.m. _____	10 p.m. _____

my training journal

my training log

SWIMMING WORKOUT:	*distance*
a.m.	
p.m.	
	total

BIKING WORKOUT:	*distance*
a.m.	
p.m.	
	total

RUNNING WORKOUT:	*distance*
a.m.	
p.m.	
	total

CROSS-TRAINING:	*time*
a.m.	
p.m.	
	total

TOMORROW'S TO DO

179

✓RUNALOG® For Triathletes

Today's Date _____

MY LONG-TERM GOAL(S) _____

_____

Today's Meal Plan	Breakfast	Snack	Lunch	Snack	Dinner
	_____	_____	_____	_____	_____
	_____	_____	_____	_____	_____

weekly planner

	SUNDAY	MONDAY	TUESDAY	WEDNESDAY	THURSDAY	FRIDAY	SATURDAY	TOTAL
a.m.								
p.m.								

daily planner

5 a.m.	_____	2 p.m.	_____
6 a.m.	_____	3 p.m.	_____
7 a.m.	_____	4 p.m.	_____
8 a.m	_____	5 p.m.	_____
9 a.m.	_____	6 p.m.	_____
10 a.m.	_____	7 p.m.	_____
11 a.m.	_____	8 p.m.	_____
12 p.m.	_____	9 p.m.	_____
1 p.m.	_____	10 p.m.	_____

my training journal

my training log

SWIMMING WORKOUT:	*distance*
a.m.	
p.m.	
	total

BIKING WORKOUT:	*distance*
a.m.	
p.m.	
	total

RUNNING WORKOUT:	*distance*
a.m.	
p.m.	
	total

CROSS-TRAINING:	*time*
a.m.	
p.m.	
	total

Tomorrow's To Do

✔RUNALOG® FOR TRIATHLETES

TODAY'S DATE _____

MY LONG-TERM GOAL(S) _____
_____

TODAY'S MEAL PLAN	BREAKFAST	SNACK	LUNCH	SNACK	DINNER
	_____	_____	_____	_____	_____
	_____	_____	_____	_____	_____

weekly planner

	SUNDAY	MONDAY	TUESDAY	WEDNESDAY	THURSDAY	FRIDAY	SATURDAY	TOTAL
a.m.								
p.m.								

daily planner

5 a.m. _____	2 p.m. _____
6 a.m. _____	3 p.m. _____
7 a.m. _____	4 p.m. _____
8 a.m _____	5 p.m. _____
9 a.m. _____	6 p.m. _____
10 a.m. _____	7 p.m. _____
11 a.m. _____	8 p.m. _____
12 p.m. _____	9 p.m. _____
1 p.m. _____	10 p.m. _____

my training journal

my training log

SWIMMING WORKOUT:	distance
a.m.	
p.m.	
	total

BIKING WORKOUT:	distance
a.m.	
p.m.	
	total

RUNNING WORKOUT:	distance
a.m.	
p.m.	
	total

CROSS-TRAINING:	time
a.m.	
p.m.	
	total

TOMORROW'S TO DO

RUNALOG® FOR TRIATHLETES   TODAY'S DATE _____

MY LONG-TERM GOAL(S) _____

TODAY'S MEAL PLAN	BREAKFAST	SNACK	LUNCH	SNACK	DINNER
	_____	_____	_____	_____	_____
	_____	_____	_____	_____	_____

weekly planner

	SUNDAY	MONDAY	TUESDAY	WEDNESDAY	THURSDAY	FRIDAY	SATURDAY	TOTAL
a.m.								
p.m.								

daily planner

5 a.m. _____	2 p.m. _____
6 a.m. _____	3 p.m. _____
7 a.m. _____	4 p.m. _____
8 a.m _____	5 p.m. _____
9 a.m. _____	6 p.m. _____
10 a.m. _____	7 p.m. _____
11 a.m. _____	8 p.m. _____
12 p.m. _____	9 p.m. _____
1 p.m. _____	10 p.m. _____

my training journal

my training log

SWIMMING WORKOUT:	*distance*
a.m.	
p.m.	
	total

BIKING WORKOUT:	*distance*
a.m.	
p.m.	
	total

RUNNING WORKOUT:	*distance*
a.m.	
p.m.	
	total

CROSS-TRAINING:	*time*
a.m.	
p.m.	
	total

TOMORROW'S TO DO

⚘RUNALOG® FOR TRIATHLETES

TODAY'S DATE _____

MY LONG-TERM GOAL(S) _____
_____

TODAY'S MEAL PLAN	BREAKFAST	SNACK	LUNCH	SNACK	DINNER
	_____	_____	_____	_____	_____

weekly planner

SUNDAY	MONDAY	TUESDAY	WEDNESDAY	THURSDAY	FRIDAY	SATURDAY	TOTAL
a.m.							
p.m.							

🕐 daily planner

5 a.m. _____	2 p.m. _____
6 a.m. _____	3 p.m. _____
7 a.m. _____	4 p.m. _____
8 a.m _____	5 p.m. _____
9 a.m. _____	6 p.m. _____
10 a.m. _____	7 p.m. _____
11 a.m. _____	8 p.m. _____
12 p.m. _____	9 p.m. _____
1 p.m. _____	10 p.m. _____

✍ my training journal

my training log

SWIMMING WORKOUT:	*distance*
a.m.	
p.m.	
	total

BIKING WORKOUT:	*distance*
a.m.	
p.m.	
	total

RUNNING WORKOUT:	*distance*
a.m.	
p.m.	
	total

CROSS-TRAINING:	*time*
a.m.	
p.m.	
	total

TOMORROW'S To Do

183

√RUNALOG® FOR TRIATHLETES

TODAY'S DATE _____

MY LONG-TERM GOAL(S) _____

_____

TODAY'S MEAL PLAN	BREAKFAST	SNACK	LUNCH	SNACK	DINNER
	_____	_____	_____	_____	_____
	_____	_____	_____	_____	_____

weekly planner

	SUNDAY	MONDAY	TUESDAY	WEDNESDAY	THURSDAY	FRIDAY	SATURDAY	TOTAL
a.m.								
p.m.								

daily planner

5 a.m. _____	2 p.m. _____
6 a.m. _____	3 p.m. _____
7 a.m. _____	4 p.m. _____
8 a.m _____	5 p.m. _____
9 a.m. _____	6 p.m. _____
10 a.m. _____	7 p.m. _____
11 a.m. _____	8 p.m. _____
12 p.m. _____	9 p.m. _____
1 p.m. _____	10 p.m. _____

my training journal

my training log

SWIMMING WORKOUT:	*distance*
a.m.	
p.m.	
	total

BIKING WORKOUT:	*distance*
a.m.	
p.m.	
	total

RUNNING WORKOUT:	*distance*
a.m.	
p.m.	
	total

CROSS-TRAINING:	*time*
a.m.	
p.m.	
	total

TOMORROW'S To Do

RUNALOG® FOR TRIATHLETES

TODAY'S DATE _____

MY LONG-TERM GOAL(S) _____
_____

TODAY'S MEAL PLAN	BREAKFAST	SNACK	LUNCH	SNACK	DINNER
	_____	_____	_____	_____	_____

weekly planner

	SUNDAY	MONDAY	TUESDAY	WEDNESDAY	THURSDAY	FRIDAY	SATURDAY	TOTAL
a.m.								
p.m.								

daily planner

5 a.m. _____	2 p.m. _____
6 a.m. _____	3 p.m. _____
7 a.m. _____	4 p.m. _____
8 a.m _____	5 p.m. _____
9 a.m. _____	6 p.m. _____
10 a.m. _____	7 p.m. _____
11 a.m. _____	8 p.m. _____
12 p.m. _____	9 p.m. _____
1 p.m. _____	10 p.m. _____

my training journal

my training log

SWIMMING WORKOUT:	distance
a.m.	
p.m.	
	total

BIKING WORKOUT:	distance
a.m.	
p.m.	
	total

RUNNING WORKOUT:	distance
a.m.	
p.m.	
	total

CROSS-TRAINING:	time
a.m.	
p.m.	
	total

TOMORROW'S To Do

185

RUNALOG® FOR TRIATHLETES

TODAY'S DATE _____

MY LONG-TERM GOAL(S) _____
_____

TODAY'S MEAL PLAN	BREAKFAST	SNACK	LUNCH	SNACK	DINNER
	_____	_____	_____	_____	_____
	_____	_____	_____	_____	_____

weekly planner

	SUNDAY	MONDAY	TUESDAY	WEDNESDAY	THURSDAY	FRIDAY	SATURDAY	TOTAL
a.m.								
p.m.								

daily planner

5 a.m. _____	2 p.m. _____
6 a.m. _____	3 p.m. _____
7 a.m. _____	4 p.m. _____
8 a.m _____	5 p.m. _____
9 a.m. _____	6 p.m. _____
10 a.m. _____	7 p.m. _____
11 a.m. _____	8 p.m. _____
12 p.m. _____	9 p.m. _____
1 p.m. _____	10 p.m. _____

my training journal

my training log

SWIMMING WORKOUT:	*distance*
a.m.	
p.m.	
	total

BIKING WORKOUT:	*distance*
a.m.	
p.m.	
	total

RUNNING WORKOUT:	*distance*
a.m.	
p.m.	
	total

CROSS-TRAINING:	*time*
a.m.	
p.m.	
	total

TOMORROW'S TO DO

√RUNALOG® FOR TRIATHLETES

TODAY'S DATE _____

MY LONG-TERM GOAL(S) _____

_____

TODAY'S MEAL PLAN	BREAKFAST	SNACK	LUNCH	SNACK	DINNER
	_____	_____	_____	_____	_____
	_____	_____	_____	_____	_____

weekly planner

	SUNDAY	MONDAY	TUESDAY	WEDNESDAY	THURSDAY	FRIDAY	SATURDAY	TOTAL
a.m.								
p.m.								

🕐 *daily planner*

5 a.m. _____	2 p.m. _____
6 a.m. _____	3 p.m. _____
7 a.m. _____	4 p.m. _____
8 a.m _____	5 p.m. _____
9 a.m. _____	6 p.m. _____
10 a.m. _____	7 p.m. _____
11 a.m. _____	8 p.m. _____
12 p.m. _____	9 p.m. _____
1 p.m. _____	10 p.m. _____

✍ *my training journal*

my training log

SWIMMING WORKOUT:	*distance*
a.m.	
p.m.	
	total

BIKING WORKOUT:	*distance*
a.m.	
p.m.	
	total

RUNNING WORKOUT:	*distance*
a.m.	
p.m.	
	total

CROSS-TRAINING:	*time*
a.m.	
p.m.	
	total

TOMORROW'S To Do

ᐯRUNALOG® FOR TRIATHLETES
TODAY'S DATE _____

MY LONG-TERM GOAL(S) _____
_____

TODAY'S MEAL PLAN	BREAKFAST	SNACK	LUNCH	SNACK	DINNER
	_____	_____	_____	_____	_____
	_____	_____	_____	_____	_____

weekly planner

	SUNDAY	MONDAY	TUESDAY	WEDNESDAY	THURSDAY	FRIDAY	SATURDAY	TOTAL
a.m.								
p.m.								

daily planner

5 a.m.	_____	2 p.m.	_____
6 a.m.	_____	3 p.m.	_____
7 a.m.	_____	4 p.m.	_____
8 a.m	_____	5 p.m.	_____
9 a.m.	_____	6 p.m.	_____
10 a.m.	_____	7 p.m.	_____
11 a.m.	_____	8 p.m.	_____
12 p.m.	_____	9 p.m.	_____
1 p.m.	_____	10 p.m.	_____

my training journal

my training log

SWIMMING WORKOUT:	*distance*
a.m.	
p.m.	
	total

BIKING WORKOUT:	*distance*
a.m.	
p.m.	
	total

RUNNING WORKOUT:	*distance*
a.m.	
p.m.	
	total

CROSS-TRAINING:	*time*
a.m.	
p.m.	
	total

TOMORROW'S TO DO

RUNALOG® FOR TRIATHLETES

TODAY'S DATE _____

MY LONG-TERM GOAL(S) _____

TODAY'S MEAL PLAN	BREAKFAST	SNACK	LUNCH	SNACK	DINNER
	_____	_____	_____	_____	_____

weekly planner

	SUNDAY	MONDAY	TUESDAY	WEDNESDAY	THURSDAY	FRIDAY	SATURDAY	TOTAL
a.m.								
p.m.								

daily planner

5 a.m. _____	2 p.m. _____
6 a.m. _____	3 p.m. _____
7 a.m. _____	4 p.m. _____
8 a.m _____	5 p.m. _____
9 a.m. _____	6 p.m. _____
10 a.m. _____	7 p.m. _____
11 a.m. _____	8 p.m. _____
12 p.m. _____	9 p.m. _____
1 p.m. _____	10 p.m. _____

my training journal

my training log

SWIMMING WORKOUT:	distance
a.m.	
p.m.	
	total

BIKING WORKOUT:	distance
a.m.	
p.m.	
	total

RUNNING WORKOUT:	distance
a.m.	
p.m.	
	total

CROSS-TRAINING:	time
a.m.	
p.m.	
	total

TOMORROW'S TO DO

189

RUNALOG® FOR TRIATHLETES

TODAY'S DATE _____

MY LONG-TERM GOAL(S) _____

TODAY'S MEAL PLAN	BREAKFAST	SNACK	LUNCH	SNACK	DINNER
	_____	_____	_____	_____	_____
	_____	_____	_____	_____	_____

weekly planner

	SUNDAY	MONDAY	TUESDAY	WEDNESDAY	THURSDAY	FRIDAY	SATURDAY	TOTAL
a.m.								
p.m.								

daily planner

5 a.m. _____	2 p.m. _____
6 a.m. _____	3 p.m. _____
7 a.m. _____	4 p.m. _____
8 a.m _____	5 p.m. _____
9 a.m. _____	6 p.m. _____
10 a.m. _____	7 p.m. _____
11 a.m. _____	8 p.m. _____
12 p.m. _____	9 p.m. _____
1 p.m. _____	10 p.m. _____

my training journal

my training log

SWIMMING WORKOUT:	*distance*
a.m.	
p.m.	
	total

BIKING WORKOUT:	*distance*
a.m.	
p.m.	
	total

RUNNING WORKOUT:	*distance*
a.m.	
p.m.	
	total

CROSS-TRAINING:	*time*
a.m.	
p.m.	
	total

TOMORROW'S TO DO

√RUNALOG® FOR TRIATHLETES

TODAY'S DATE _____

MY LONG-TERM GOAL(S) _____

TODAY'S MEAL PLAN	BREAKFAST	SNACK	LUNCH	SNACK	DINNER

weekly planner

	SUNDAY	MONDAY	TUESDAY	WEDNESDAY	THURSDAY	FRIDAY	SATURDAY	TOTAL
a.m.								
p.m.								

daily planner

5 a.m. _____	2 p.m. _____
6 a.m. _____	3 p.m. _____
7 a.m. _____	4 p.m. _____
8 a.m _____	5 p.m. _____
9 a.m. _____	6 p.m. _____
10 a.m. _____	7 p.m. _____
11 a.m. _____	8 p.m. _____
12 p.m. _____	9 p.m. _____
1 p.m. _____	10 p.m. _____

my training journal

my training log

SWIMMING WORKOUT:	*distance*
a.m.	
p.m.	
	total

BIKING WORKOUT:	*distance*
a.m.	
p.m.	
	total

RUNNING WORKOUT:	*distance*
a.m.	
p.m.	
	total

CROSS-TRAINING:	*time*
a.m.	
p.m.	
	total

TOMORROW'S To Do

RUNALOG® FOR TRIATHLETES

TODAY'S DATE _____

MY LONG-TERM GOAL(S) _____

TODAY'S MEAL PLAN	BREAKFAST	SNACK	LUNCH	SNACK	DINNER
	_____	_____	_____	_____	_____
	_____	_____	_____	_____	_____

weekly planner

	SUNDAY	MONDAY	TUESDAY	WEDNESDAY	THURSDAY	FRIDAY	SATURDAY	TOTAL
a.m.								
p.m.								

daily planner

5 a.m. _____	2 p.m. _____
6 a.m. _____	3 p.m. _____
7 a.m. _____	4 p.m. _____
8 a.m _____	5 p.m. _____
9 a.m. _____	6 p.m. _____
10 a.m. _____	7 p.m. _____
11 a.m. _____	8 p.m. _____
12 p.m. _____	9 p.m. _____
1 p.m. _____	10 p.m. _____

my training journal

my training log

SWIMMING WORKOUT:	*distance*
a.m.	
p.m.	
	total

BIKING WORKOUT:	*distance*
a.m.	
p.m.	
	total

RUNNING WORKOUT:	*distance*
a.m.	
p.m.	
	total

CROSS-TRAINING:	*time*
a.m.	
p.m.	
	total

TOMORROW'S TO DO

RUNALOG® FOR TRIATHLETES

TODAY'S DATE _____

MY LONG-TERM GOAL(S) _____

TODAY'S MEAL PLAN	BREAKFAST	SNACK	LUNCH	SNACK	DINNER
	_____	_____	_____	_____	_____

weekly planner

	SUNDAY	MONDAY	TUESDAY	WEDNESDAY	THURSDAY	FRIDAY	SATURDAY	TOTAL
a.m.								
p.m.								

daily planner

5 a.m. _____	2 p.m. _____
6 a.m. _____	3 p.m. _____
7 a.m. _____	4 p.m. _____
8 a.m _____	5 p.m. _____
9 a.m. _____	6 p.m. _____
10 a.m. _____	7 p.m. _____
11 a.m. _____	8 p.m. _____
12 p.m. _____	9 p.m. _____
1 p.m. _____	10 p.m. _____

my training journal

my training log

SWIMMING WORKOUT:	distance
a.m.	
p.m.	
	total

BIKING WORKOUT:	distance
a.m.	
p.m.	
	total

RUNNING WORKOUT:	distance
a.m.	
p.m.	
	total

CROSS-TRAINING:	time
a.m.	
p.m.	
	total

TOMORROW'S To Do

193

MY LONG-TERM GOAL(S) _____

TODAY'S MEAL PLAN	**BREAKFAST**	**SNACK**	**LUNCH**	**SNACK**	**DINNER**
	_____	_____	_____	_____	_____
	_____	_____	_____	_____	_____

weekly planner

SUNDAY	MONDAY	TUESDAY	WEDNESDAY	THURSDAY	FRIDAY	SATURDAY	TOTAL
a.m.							
p.m.							

daily planner

5 a.m.	_____	2 p.m.	_____
6 a.m.	_____	3 p.m.	_____
7 a.m.	_____	4 p.m.	_____
8 a.m	_____	5 p.m.	_____
9 a.m.	_____	6 p.m.	_____
10 a.m.	_____	7 p.m.	_____
11 a.m.	_____	8 p.m.	_____
12 p.m.	_____	9 p.m.	_____
1 p.m.	_____	10 p.m.	_____

my training journal

my training log

SWIMMING WORKOUT:	*distance*
a.m.	
p.m.	
	total

BIKING WORKOUT:	*distance*
a.m.	
p.m.	
	total

RUNNING WORKOUT:	*distance*
a.m.	
p.m.	
	total

CROSS-TRAINING:	*time*
a.m.	
p.m.	
	total

TOMORROW'S To Do

⚐ RUNALOG® FOR TRIATHLETES   TODAY'S DATE _____

MY LONG-TERM GOAL(S) _____

_____

TODAY'S	BREAKFAST	SNACK	LUNCH	SNACK	DINNER
MEAL	_____	_____	_____	_____	_____
PLAN	_____	_____	_____	_____	_____

weekly planner

	SUNDAY	MONDAY	TUESDAY	WEDNESDAY	THURSDAY	FRIDAY	SATURDAY	TOTAL
a.m.								
p.m.								

🕐 daily planner

5 a.m. _____	2 p.m. _____
6 a.m. _____	3 p.m. _____
7 a.m. _____	4 p.m. _____
8 a.m _____	5 p.m. _____
9 a.m. _____	6 p.m. _____
10 a.m. _____	7 p.m. _____
11 a.m. _____	8 p.m. _____
12 p.m. _____	9 p.m. _____
1 p.m. _____	10 p.m. _____

✍ my training journal

my training log

SWIMMING WORKOUT:	distance
a.m.	
p.m.	
	total

BIKING WORKOUT:	distance
a.m.	
p.m.	
	total

RUNNING WORKOUT:	distance
a.m.	
p.m.	
	total

CROSS-TRAINING:	time
a.m.	
p.m.	
	total

TOMORROW'S TO DO

ᐯRUNALOG® FOR TRIATHLETES

TODAY'S DATE _____

MY LONG-TERM GOAL(S) _____
_____

TODAY'S MEAL PLAN	BREAKFAST	SNACK	LUNCH	SNACK	DINNER
	_____	_____	_____	_____	_____
	_____	_____	_____	_____	_____

weekly planner

	SUNDAY	MONDAY	TUESDAY	WEDNESDAY	THURSDAY	FRIDAY	SATURDAY	TOTAL
a.m.								
p.m.								

🕐 daily planner

5 a.m. _____	2 p.m. _____
6 a.m. _____	3 p.m. _____
7 a.m. _____	4 p.m. _____
8 a.m _____	5 p.m. _____
9 a.m. _____	6 p.m. _____
10 a.m. _____	7 p.m. _____
11 a.m. _____	8 p.m. _____
12 p.m. _____	9 p.m. _____
1 p.m. _____	10 p.m. _____

✍ my training journal

my training log

SWIMMING WORKOUT:	*distance*
a.m.	
p.m.	
	total

BIKING WORKOUT:	*distance*
a.m.	
p.m.	
	total

RUNNING WORKOUT:	*distance*
a.m.	
p.m.	
	total

CROSS-TRAINING:	*time*
a.m.	
p.m.	
	total

TOMORROW'S TO DO

196

ᐁRUNALOG® FOR TRIATHLETES

TODAY'S DATE _____

MY LONG-TERM GOAL(S) _____

_____

TODAY'S MEAL PLAN	BREAKFAST	SNACK	LUNCH	SNACK	DINNER
	_____	_____	_____	_____	_____
	_____	_____	_____	_____	_____

weekly planner

	SUNDAY	MONDAY	TUESDAY	WEDNESDAY	THURSDAY	FRIDAY	SATURDAY	TOTAL
a.m.								
p.m.								

🕐 daily planner

5 a.m. _____		2 p.m. _____	
6 a.m. _____		3 p.m. _____	
7 a.m. _____		4 p.m. _____	
8 a.m _____		5 p.m. _____	
9 a.m. _____		6 p.m. _____	
10 a.m. _____		7 p.m. _____	
11 a.m. _____		8 p.m. _____	
12 p.m. _____		9 p.m. _____	
1 p.m. _____		10 p.m. _____	

✍ my training journal

my training log

SWIMMING WORKOUT:	*distance*
a.m.	
p.m.	
	total

🚴 BIKING WORKOUT:	*distance*
a.m.	
p.m.	
	total

🏃 RUNNING WORKOUT:	*distance*
a.m.	
p.m.	
	total

CROSS-TRAINING:	*time*
a.m.	
p.m.	
	total

TOMORROW'S TO DO

RUNALOG® FOR TRIATHLETES

TODAY'S DATE _____

MY LONG-TERM GOAL(S) _____
_____

TODAY'S MEAL PLAN	BREAKFAST	SNACK	LUNCH	SNACK	DINNER
	_____	_____	_____	_____	_____
	_____	_____	_____	_____	_____

weekly planner

	SUNDAY	MONDAY	TUESDAY	WEDNESDAY	THURSDAY	FRIDAY	SATURDAY	TOTAL
a.m.								
p.m.								

daily planner

5 a.m. _____	2 p.m. _____
6 a.m. _____	3 p.m. _____
7 a.m. _____	4 p.m. _____
8 a.m _____	5 p.m. _____
9 a.m. _____	6 p.m. _____
10 a.m. _____	7 p.m. _____
11 a.m. _____	8 p.m. _____
12 p.m. _____	9 p.m. _____
1 p.m. _____	10 p.m. _____

my training journal

my training log

SWIMMING WORKOUT:	*distance*
a.m.	
p.m.	
	total

BIKING WORKOUT:	*distance*
a.m.	
p.m.	
	total

RUNNING WORKOUT:	*distance*
a.m.	
p.m.	
	total

CROSS-TRAINING:	*time*
a.m.	
p.m.	
	total

TOMORROW'S TO DO

RUNALOG® FOR TRIATHLETES

TODAY'S DATE _____

MY LONG-TERM GOAL(S) _____

_____

TODAY'S MEAL PLAN	BREAKFAST	SNACK	LUNCH	SNACK	DINNER
	_____	_____	_____	_____	_____

weekly planner

	SUNDAY	MONDAY	TUESDAY	WEDNESDAY	THURSDAY	FRIDAY	SATURDAY	TOTAL
a.m.								
p.m.								

daily planner

5 a.m. _____	2 p.m. _____
6 a.m. _____	3 p.m. _____
7 a.m. _____	4 p.m. _____
8 a.m _____	5 p.m. _____
9 a.m. _____	6 p.m. _____
10 a.m. _____	7 p.m. _____
11 a.m. _____	8 p.m. _____
12 p.m. _____	9 p.m. _____
1 p.m. _____	10 p.m. _____

my training journal

my training log

SWIMMING WORKOUT:	distance
a.m.	
p.m.	
	total

BIKING WORKOUT:	distance
a.m.	
p.m.	
	total

RUNNING WORKOUT:	distance
a.m.	
p.m.	
	total

CROSS-TRAINING:	time
a.m.	
p.m.	
	total

TOMORROW'S TO DO

ᐛRUNALOG® FOR TRIATHLETES

TODAY'S DATE _____

MY LONG-TERM GOAL(S) _____

_____

TODAY'S MEAL PLAN	BREAKFAST	SNACK	LUNCH	SNACK	DINNER
	_____	_____	_____	_____	_____
	_____	_____	_____	_____	_____

weekly planner

	SUNDAY	MONDAY	TUESDAY	WEDNESDAY	THURSDAY	FRIDAY	SATURDAY	TOTAL
a.m.								
p.m.								

🕐 daily planner

5 a.m. _____	2 p.m. _____
6 a.m. _____	3 p.m. _____
7 a.m. _____	4 p.m. _____
8 a.m _____	5 p.m. _____
9 a.m. _____	6 p.m. _____
10 a.m. _____	7 p.m. _____
11 a.m. _____	8 p.m. _____
12 p.m. _____	9 p.m. _____
1 p.m. _____	10 p.m. _____

✎ my training journal

my training log

🏊 SWIMMING WORKOUT:	*distance*
a.m.	
p.m.	
	total

🚴 BIKING WORKOUT:	*distance*
a.m.	
p.m.	
	total

🏃 RUNNING WORKOUT:	*distance*
a.m.	
p.m.	
	total

CROSS-TRAINING:	*time*
a.m.	
p.m.	
	total

TOMORROW'S TO DO

✓RUNALOG® FOR TRIATHLETES

TODAY'S DATE _____

MY LONG-TERM GOAL(S) _____
_____

TODAY'S MEAL PLAN	BREAKFAST	SNACK	LUNCH	SNACK	DINNER
	_____	_____	_____	_____	_____

weekly planner

	SUNDAY	MONDAY	TUESDAY	WEDNESDAY	THURSDAY	FRIDAY	SATURDAY	TOTAL
a.m.								
p.m.								

🕐 daily planner

5 a.m. _____	2 p.m. _____
6 a.m. _____	3 p.m. _____
7 a.m. _____	4 p.m. _____
8 a.m _____	5 p.m. _____
9 a.m. _____	6 p.m. _____
10 a.m. _____	7 p.m. _____
11 a.m. _____	8 p.m. _____
12 p.m. _____	9 p.m. _____
1 p.m. _____	10 p.m. _____

✍ my training journal

my training log

SWIMMING WORKOUT: *distance*

a.m.		
p.m.		
		total

BIKING WORKOUT: *distance*

a.m.		
p.m.		
		total

RUNNING WORKOUT: *distance*

a.m.		
p.m.		
		total

CROSS-TRAINING: *time*

a.m.		
p.m.		
		total

TOMORROW'S To Do

MY LONG-TERM GOAL(S) _____

_____

TODAY'S MEAL PLAN	BREAKFAST	SNACK	LUNCH	SNACK	DINNER
	_____	_____	_____	_____	_____
	_____	_____	_____	_____	_____

weekly planner

	SUNDAY	MONDAY	TUESDAY	WEDNESDAY	THURSDAY	FRIDAY	SATURDAY	TOTAL
a.m.								
p.m.								

daily planner

5 a.m. _____	2 p.m. _____
6 a.m. _____	3 p.m. _____
7 a.m. _____	4 p.m. _____
8 a.m _____	5 p.m. _____
9 a.m. _____	6 p.m. _____
10 a.m. _____	7 p.m. _____
11 a.m. _____	8 p.m. _____
12 p.m. _____	9 p.m. _____
1 p.m. _____	10 p.m. _____

my training journal

my training log

SWIMMING WORKOUT:	*distance*
a.m.	
p.m.	
	total

BIKING WORKOUT:	*distance*
a.m.	
p.m.	
	total

RUNNING WORKOUT:	*distance*
a.m.	
p.m.	
	total

CROSS-TRAINING:	*time*
a.m.	
p.m.	
	total

TOMORROW'S TO DO

√RUNALOG® FOR TRIATHLETES

TODAY'S DATE _____

MY LONG-TERM GOAL(S) _____
_____

TODAY'S MEAL PLAN	BREAKFAST	SNACK	LUNCH	SNACK	DINNER
	_____	_____	_____	_____	_____
	_____	_____	_____	_____	_____

weekly planner

	SUNDAY	MONDAY	TUESDAY	WEDNESDAY	THURSDAY	FRIDAY	SATURDAY	TOTAL
a.m.								
p.m.								

🕐 *daily planner*

5 a.m. _____	2 p.m. _____
6 a.m. _____	3 p.m. _____
7 a.m. _____	4 p.m. _____
8 a.m _____	5 p.m. _____
9 a.m. _____	6 p.m. _____
10 a.m. _____	7 p.m. _____
11 a.m. _____	8 p.m. _____
12 p.m. _____	9 p.m. _____
1 p.m. _____	10 p.m. _____

☞ *my training journal*

my training log

SWIMMING WORKOUT:	*distance*
a.m.	
p.m.	
	total

BIKING WORKOUT:	*distance*
a.m.	
p.m.	
	total

RUNNING WORKOUT:	*distance*
a.m.	
p.m.	
	total

CROSS-TRAINING:	*time*
a.m.	
p.m.	
	total

TOMORROW'S TO DO

203

© 2009 www.RUNALOGS.com

✓

√RUNALOG® FOR TRIATHLETES

TODAY'S DATE _____

MY LONG-TERM GOAL(S) _____

_____

TODAY'S MEAL PLAN	BREAKFAST	SNACK	LUNCH	SNACK	DINNER
	_____	_____	_____	_____	_____
	_____	_____	_____	_____	_____

weekly planner

	SUNDAY	MONDAY	TUESDAY	WEDNESDAY	THURSDAY	FRIDAY	SATURDAY	TOTAL
a.m.								
p.m.								

daily planner

5 a.m. _____	2 p.m. _____
6 a.m. _____	3 p.m. _____
7 a.m. _____	4 p.m. _____
8 a.m _____	5 p.m. _____
9 a.m. _____	6 p.m. _____
10 a.m. _____	7 p.m. _____
11 a.m. _____	8 p.m. _____
12 p.m. _____	9 p.m. _____
1 p.m. _____	10 p.m. _____

my training journal

my training log

SWIMMING WORKOUT: *distance*
a.m.
p.m.
total

BIKING WORKOUT: *distance*
a.m.
p.m.
total

RUNNING WORKOUT: *distance*
a.m.
p.m.
total

CROSS-TRAINING: *time*
a.m.
p.m.
total

TOMORROW'S TO DO

√RUNALOG® FOR TRIATHLETES TODAY'S DATE _____

MY LONG-TERM GOAL(S) _____

TODAY'S MEAL PLAN	BREAKFAST	SNACK	LUNCH	SNACK	DINNER
	_____	_____	_____	_____	_____
	_____	_____	_____	_____	_____

weekly planner

	SUNDAY	MONDAY	TUESDAY	WEDNESDAY	THURSDAY	FRIDAY	SATURDAY	TOTAL
a.m.								
p.m.								

daily planner

5 a.m. _____	2 p.m. _____
6 a.m. _____	3 p.m. _____
7 a.m. _____	4 p.m. _____
8 a.m _____	5 p.m. _____
9 a.m. _____	6 p.m. _____
10 a.m. _____	7 p.m. _____
11 a.m. _____	8 p.m. _____
12 p.m. _____	9 p.m. _____
1 p.m. _____	10 p.m. _____

my training journal

my training log

SWIMMING WORKOUT:	*distance*
a.m.	
p.m.	
	total

BIKING WORKOUT:	*distance*
a.m.	
p.m.	
	total

RUNNING WORKOUT:	*distance*
a.m.	
p.m.	
	total

CROSS-TRAINING:	*time*
a.m.	
p.m.	
	total

TOMORROW'S TO DO

√ RUNALOG® FOR TRIATHLETES   TODAY'S DATE _____

MY LONG-TERM GOAL(S) _____
_____

TODAY'S MEAL PLAN	BREAKFAST	SNACK	LUNCH	SNACK	DINNER
	_____	_____	_____	_____	_____
	_____	_____	_____	_____	_____

weekly planner

	SUNDAY	MONDAY	TUESDAY	WEDNESDAY	THURSDAY	FRIDAY	SATURDAY	TOTAL
a.m.								
p.m.								

daily planner

5 a.m. _____	2 p.m. _____
6 a.m. _____	3 p.m. _____
7 a.m. _____	4 p.m. _____
8 a.m _____	5 p.m. _____
9 a.m. _____	6 p.m. _____
10 a.m. _____	7 p.m. _____
11 a.m. _____	8 p.m. _____
12 p.m. _____	9 p.m. _____
1 p.m. _____	10 p.m. _____

my training journal

my training log

SWIMMING WORKOUT:	*distance*
a.m.	
p.m.	
	total

BIKING WORKOUT:	*distance*
a.m.	
p.m.	
	total

RUNNING WORKOUT:	*distance*
a.m.	
p.m.	
	total

CROSS-TRAINING:	*time*
a.m.	
p.m.	
	total

TOMORROW'S TO DO

✔RUNALOG® FOR TRIATHLETES

TODAY'S DATE _____

MY LONG-TERM GOAL(S) _____
_____

	BREAKFAST	SNACK	LUNCH	SNACK	DINNER
TODAY'S MEAL PLAN	_____ _____	_____ _____	_____ _____	_____ _____	_____ _____

weekly planner

	SUNDAY	MONDAY	TUESDAY	WEDNESDAY	THURSDAY	FRIDAY	SATURDAY	TOTAL
a.m.								
p.m.								

🕐 *daily planner*

5 a.m. _____	2 p.m. _____
6 a.m. _____	3 p.m. _____
7 a.m. _____	4 p.m. _____
8 a.m _____	5 p.m. _____
9 a.m. _____	6 p.m. _____
10 a.m. _____	7 p.m. _____
11 a.m. _____	8 p.m. _____
12 p.m. _____	9 p.m. _____
1 p.m. _____	10 p.m. _____

✍ *my training journal*

my training log

SWIMMING WORKOUT: *distance*

a.m.	
p.m.	
	total

BIKING WORKOUT: *distance*

a.m.	
p.m.	
	total

RUNNING WORKOUT: *distance*

a.m.	
p.m.	
	total

CROSS-TRAINING: *time*

a.m.	
p.m.	
	total

TOMORROW'S TO DO

TODAY'S DATE _____

MY LONG-TERM GOAL(S) _____

	BREAKFAST	SNACK	LUNCH	SNACK	DINNER
TODAY'S MEAL PLAN	_____	_____	_____	_____	_____
	_____	_____	_____	_____	_____

weekly planner

	SUNDAY	MONDAY	TUESDAY	WEDNESDAY	THURSDAY	FRIDAY	SATURDAY	TOTAL
a.m.								
p.m.								

daily planner

5 a.m. _____	2 p.m. _____
6 a.m. _____	3 p.m. _____
7 a.m. _____	4 p.m. _____
8 a.m _____	5 p.m. _____
9 a.m. _____	6 p.m. _____
10 a.m. _____	7 p.m. _____
11 a.m. _____	8 p.m. _____
12 p.m. _____	9 p.m. _____
1 p.m. _____	10 p.m. _____

my training journal

my training log

SWIMMING WORKOUT: *distance*

a.m.		
p.m.		
		total

BIKING WORKOUT: *distance*

a.m.		
p.m.		
		total

RUNNING WORKOUT: *distance*

a.m.		
p.m.		
		total

CROSS-TRAINING: *time*

a.m.		
p.m.		
		total

TOMORROW'S TO DO

ᐁRUNALOG® FOR TRIATHLETES

TODAY'S DATE _____

MY LONG-TERM GOAL(S) _____

TODAY'S MEAL PLAN	BREAKFAST	SNACK	LUNCH	SNACK	DINNER
	_____	_____	_____	_____	_____
	_____	_____	_____	_____	_____

weekly planner

	SUNDAY	MONDAY	TUESDAY	WEDNESDAY	THURSDAY	FRIDAY	SATURDAY	TOTAL
a.m.								
p.m.								

🕐 daily planner

5 a.m. _____	2 p.m. _____
6 a.m. _____	3 p.m. _____
7 a.m. _____	4 p.m. _____
8 a.m _____	5 p.m. _____
9 a.m. _____	6 p.m. _____
10 a.m. _____	7 p.m. _____
11 a.m. _____	8 p.m. _____
12 p.m. _____	9 p.m. _____
1 p.m. _____	10 p.m. _____

✍ my training journal

my training log

SWIMMING WORKOUT:	distance
a.m.	
p.m.	
	total

🚴 BIKING WORKOUT:	distance
a.m.	
p.m.	
	total

🏃 RUNNING WORKOUT:	distance
a.m.	
p.m.	
	total

CROSS-TRAINING:	time
a.m.	
p.m.	
	total

TOMORROW'S TO DO

✔RUNALOG® FOR TRIATHLETES

TODAY'S DATE _____

MY LONG-TERM GOAL(S) _____

TODAY'S MEAL PLAN	BREAKFAST	SNACK	LUNCH	SNACK	DINNER

weekly planner

SUNDAY	MONDAY	TUESDAY	WEDNESDAY	THURSDAY	FRIDAY	SATURDAY	TOTAL
a.m.							
p.m.							

daily planner

5 a.m.	_____	2 p.m.	_____
6 a.m.	_____	3 p.m.	_____
7 a.m.	_____	4 p.m.	_____
8 a.m	_____	5 p.m.	_____
9 a.m.	_____	6 p.m.	_____
10 a.m.	_____	7 p.m.	_____
11 a.m.	_____	8 p.m.	_____
12 p.m.	_____	9 p.m.	_____
1 p.m.	_____	10 p.m.	_____

my training journal

my training log

SWIMMING WORKOUT:	*distance*
a.m.	
p.m.	
	total

BIKING WORKOUT:	*distance*
a.m.	
p.m.	
	total

RUNNING WORKOUT:	*distance*
a.m.	
p.m.	
	total

CROSS-TRAINING:	*time*
a.m.	
p.m.	
	total

TOMORROW'S To Do

210

√RUNALOG° FOR TRIATHLETES

TODAY'S DATE _____

MY LONG-TERM GOAL(S) _____
_____

TODAY'S MEAL PLAN	BREAKFAST	SNACK	LUNCH	SNACK	DINNER
	_____	_____	_____	_____	_____
	_____	_____	_____	_____	_____

weekly planner

	SUNDAY	MONDAY	TUESDAY	WEDNESDAY	THURSDAY	FRIDAY	SATURDAY	TOTAL
a.m.								
p.m.								

daily planner

5 a.m. _____	2 p.m. _____
6 a.m. _____	3 p.m. _____
7 a.m. _____	4 p.m. _____
8 a.m. _____	5 p.m. _____
9 a.m. _____	6 p.m. _____
10 a.m. _____	7 p.m. _____
11 a.m. _____	8 p.m. _____
12 p.m. _____	9 p.m. _____
1 p.m. _____	10 p.m. _____

my training journal

my training log

SWIMMING WORKOUT:	distance
a.m.	
p.m.	
	total

BIKING WORKOUT:	distance
a.m.	
p.m.	
	total

RUNNING WORKOUT:	distance
a.m.	
p.m.	
	total

CROSS-TRAINING:	time
a.m.	
p.m.	
	total

TOMORROW'S TO DO

211

√RUNALOG® FOR TRIATHLETES

TODAY'S DATE _____

MY LONG-TERM GOAL(S) _____

TODAY'S MEAL PLAN	BREAKFAST	SNACK	LUNCH	SNACK	DINNER
	_____	_____	_____	_____	_____
	_____	_____	_____	_____	_____

weekly planner

	SUNDAY	MONDAY	TUESDAY	WEDNESDAY	THURSDAY	FRIDAY	SATURDAY	TOTAL
a.m.								
p.m.								

daily planner

5 a.m. _____	2 p.m. _____
6 a.m. _____	3 p.m. _____
7 a.m. _____	4 p.m. _____
8 a.m _____	5 p.m. _____
9 a.m. _____	6 p.m. _____
10 a.m. _____	7 p.m. _____
11 a.m. _____	8 p.m. _____
12 p.m. _____	9 p.m. _____
1 p.m. _____	10 p.m. _____

my training journal

my training log

SWIMMING WORKOUT: *distance*

a.m.	
p.m.	
	total

BIKING WORKOUT: *distance*

a.m.	
p.m.	
	total

RUNNING WORKOUT: *distance*

a.m.	
p.m.	
	total

CROSS-TRAINING: *time*

a.m.	
p.m.	
	total

TOMORROW'S To Do

⚘RUNALOG® *FOR TRIATHLETES*

TODAY'S DATE _____

MY LONG-TERM GOAL(S) _____
_____

TODAY'S MEAL PLAN	**BREAKFAST**	**SNACK**	**LUNCH**	**SNACK**	**DINNER**
	_____	_____	_____	_____	_____
	_____	_____	_____	_____	_____

weekly planner

	SUNDAY	MONDAY	TUESDAY	WEDNESDAY	THURSDAY	FRIDAY	SATURDAY	TOTAL
a.m.								
p.m.								

🕐 *daily planner*

5 a.m. _____		2 p.m. _____
6 a.m. _____		3 p.m. _____
7 a.m. _____		4 p.m. _____
8 a.m _____		5 p.m. _____
9 a.m. _____		6 p.m. _____
10 a.m. _____		7 p.m. _____
11 a.m. _____		8 p.m. _____
12 p.m. _____		9 p.m. _____
1 p.m. _____		10 p.m. _____

✍ *my training journal*

my training log

SWIMMING WORKOUT: *distance*

a.m.	
p.m.	
	total

BIKING WORKOUT: *distance*

a.m.	
p.m.	
	total

RUNNING WORKOUT: *distance*

a.m.	
p.m.	
	total

CROSS-TRAINING: *time*

a.m.	
p.m.	
	total

TOMORROW'S TO DO

√RUNALOG® FOR TRIATHLETES   TODAY'S DATE _____

MY LONG-TERM GOAL(S) _____
_____

TODAY'S MEAL PLAN	BREAKFAST	SNACK	LUNCH	SNACK	DINNER
	_____	_____	_____	_____	_____
	_____	_____	_____	_____	_____

weekly planner

	SUNDAY	MONDAY	TUESDAY	WEDNESDAY	THURSDAY	FRIDAY	SATURDAY	TOTAL
a.m.								
p.m.								

daily planner

5 a.m. _____	2 p.m. _____
6 a.m. _____	3 p.m. _____
7 a.m. _____	4 p.m. _____
8 a.m _____	5 p.m. _____
9 a.m. _____	6 p.m. _____
10 a.m. _____	7 p.m. _____
11 a.m. _____	8 p.m. _____
12 p.m. _____	9 p.m. _____
1 p.m. _____	10 p.m. _____

my training journal

my training log

SWIMMING WORKOUT:	*distance*
a.m.	
p.m.	
	total

BIKING WORKOUT:	*distance*
a.m.	
p.m.	
	total

RUNNING WORKOUT:	*distance*
a.m.	
p.m.	
	total

CROSS-TRAINING:	*time*
a.m.	
p.m.	
	total

TOMORROW'S To Do

RUNALOG® FOR TRIATHLETES

TODAY'S DATE _____

MY LONG-TERM GOAL(S) _____

_____

TODAY'S MEAL PLAN	BREAKFAST	SNACK	LUNCH	SNACK	DINNER
	_____	_____	_____	_____	_____
	_____	_____	_____	_____	_____

weekly planner

	SUNDAY	MONDAY	TUESDAY	WEDNESDAY	THURSDAY	FRIDAY	SATURDAY	TOTAL
a.m.								
p.m.								

daily planner

5 a.m. _____	2 p.m. _____
6 a.m. _____	3 p.m. _____
7 a.m. _____	4 p.m. _____
8 a.m _____	5 p.m. _____
9 a.m. _____	6 p.m. _____
10 a.m. _____	7 p.m. _____
11 a.m. _____	8 p.m. _____
12 p.m. _____	9 p.m. _____
1 p.m. _____	10 p.m. _____

my training journal

my training log

SWIMMING WORKOUT:	distance
a.m.	
p.m.	
	total

BIKING WORKOUT:	distance
a.m.	
p.m.	
	total

RUNNING WORKOUT:	distance
a.m.	
p.m.	
	total

CROSS-TRAINING:	time
a.m.	
p.m.	
	total

TOMORROW'S To Do

ᐱRUNALOG® *FOR TRIATHLETES*

TODAY'S DATE _____

MY LONG-TERM GOAL(S) _____
_____

TODAY'S MEAL PLAN	BREAKFAST	SNACK	LUNCH	SNACK	DINNER
	_____	_____	_____	_____	_____
	_____	_____	_____	_____	_____

weekly planner

SUNDAY	MONDAY	TUESDAY	WEDNESDAY	THURSDAY	FRIDAY	SATURDAY	TOTAL
a.m.							
p.m.							

daily planner

5 a.m.	_____	2 p.m.	_____
6 a.m.	_____	3 p.m.	_____
7 a.m.	_____	4 p.m.	_____
8 a.m	_____	5 p.m.	_____
9 a.m.	_____	6 p.m.	_____
10 a.m.	_____	7 p.m.	_____
11 a.m.	_____	8 p.m.	_____
12 p.m.	_____	9 p.m.	_____
1 p.m.	_____	10 p.m.	_____

my training journal

my training log

SWIMMING WORKOUT:	*distance*
a.m.	
p.m.	
	total

BIKING WORKOUT:	*distance*
a.m.	
p.m.	
	total

RUNNING WORKOUT:	*distance*
a.m.	
p.m.	
	total

CROSS-TRAINING:	*time*
a.m.	
p.m.	
	total

TOMORROW'S TO DO

TODAY'S MEAL PLAN	BREAKFAST	SNACK	LUNCH	SNACK	DINNER
	_____	_____	_____	_____	_____
	_____	_____	_____	_____	_____

weekly planner

	SUNDAY	MONDAY	TUESDAY	WEDNESDAY	THURSDAY	FRIDAY	SATURDAY	TOTAL
a.m.								
p.m.								

daily planner

5 a.m. _____	2 p.m. _____
6 a.m. _____	3 p.m. _____
7 a.m. _____	4 p.m. _____
8 a.m _____	5 p.m. _____
9 a.m. _____	6 p.m. _____
10 a.m. _____	7 p.m. _____
11 a.m. _____	8 p.m. _____
12 p.m. _____	9 p.m. _____
1 p.m. _____	10 p.m. _____

my training journal

my training log

SWIMMING WORKOUT:	*distance*
a.m.	
p.m.	
	total

BIKING WORKOUT:	*distance*
a.m.	
p.m.	
	total

RUNNING WORKOUT:	*distance*
a.m.	
p.m.	
	total

CROSS-TRAINING:	*time*
a.m.	
p.m.	
	total

TOMORROW'S TO DO

217

RUNALOG® *For Triathletes*

TODAY'S DATE _____

MY LONG-TERM GOAL(S) _____

TODAY'S MEAL PLAN	BREAKFAST	SNACK	LUNCH	SNACK	DINNER

weekly planner

	SUNDAY	MONDAY	TUESDAY	WEDNESDAY	THURSDAY	FRIDAY	SATURDAY	TOTAL
a.m.								
p.m.								

daily planner

5 a.m.	_____	2 p.m.	_____
6 a.m.	_____	3 p.m.	_____
7 a.m.	_____	4 p.m.	_____
8 a.m	_____	5 p.m.	_____
9 a.m.	_____	6 p.m.	_____
10 a.m.	_____	7 p.m.	_____
11 a.m.	_____	8 p.m.	_____
12 p.m.	_____	9 p.m.	_____
1 p.m.	_____	10 p.m.	_____

my training journal

my training log

SWIMMING WORKOUT: *distance*

a.m.		
p.m.		
		total

BIKING WORKOUT: *distance*

a.m.		
p.m.		
		total

RUNNING WORKOUT: *distance*

a.m.		
p.m.		
		total

CROSS-TRAINING: *time*

a.m.		
p.m.		
		total

Tomorrow's To Do

MY LONG-TERM GOAL(S) _____

TODAY'S DATE _____

TODAY'S MEAL PLAN	BREAKFAST	SNACK	LUNCH	SNACK	DINNER

weekly planner

	SUNDAY	MONDAY	TUESDAY	WEDNESDAY	THURSDAY	FRIDAY	SATURDAY	TOTAL
a.m.								
p.m.								

daily planner

5 a.m. _____	2 p.m. _____
6 a.m. _____	3 p.m. _____
7 a.m. _____	4 p.m. _____
8 a.m _____	5 p.m. _____
9 a.m. _____	6 p.m. _____
10 a.m. _____	7 p.m. _____
11 a.m. _____	8 p.m. _____
12 p.m. _____	9 p.m. _____
1 p.m. _____	10 p.m. _____

my training journal

my training log

SWIMMING WORKOUT:	*distance*
a.m.	
p.m.	
	total

BIKING WORKOUT:	*distance*
a.m.	
p.m.	
	total

RUNNING WORKOUT:	*distance*
a.m.	
p.m.	
	total

CROSS-TRAINING:	*time*
a.m.	
p.m.	
	total

TOMORROW'S TO DO

RUNALOG® FOR TRIATHLETES

TODAY'S DATE _____

MY LONG-TERM GOAL(S) _____

Today's Meal Plan	BREAKFAST	SNACK	LUNCH	SNACK	DINNER
	_____	_____	_____	_____	_____
	_____	_____	_____	_____	_____

weekly planner

	SUNDAY	MONDAY	TUESDAY	WEDNESDAY	THURSDAY	FRIDAY	SATURDAY	TOTAL
a.m.								
p.m.								

daily planner

5 a.m.	_____	2 p.m.	_____
6 a.m.	_____	3 p.m.	_____
7 a.m.	_____	4 p.m.	_____
8 a.m	_____	5 p.m.	_____
9 a.m.	_____	6 p.m.	_____
10 a.m.	_____	7 p.m.	_____
11 a.m.	_____	8 p.m.	_____
12 p.m.	_____	9 p.m.	_____
1 p.m.	_____	10 p.m.	_____

my training journal

my training log

SWIMMING WORKOUT: *distance*

a.m.	
p.m.	
	total

BIKING WORKOUT: *distance*

a.m.	
p.m.	
	total

RUNNING WORKOUT: *distance*

a.m.	
p.m.	
	total

CROSS-TRAINING: *time*

a.m.	
p.m.	
	total

TOMORROW'S TO DO

√RUNALOG® FOR TRIATHLETES

TODAY'S DATE _____

MY LONG-TERM GOAL(S) _____

_____

TODAY'S MEAL PLAN	BREAKFAST	SNACK	LUNCH	SNACK	DINNER
	_____	_____	_____	_____	_____
	_____	_____	_____	_____	_____

weekly planner

	SUNDAY	MONDAY	TUESDAY	WEDNESDAY	THURSDAY	FRIDAY	SATURDAY	TOTAL
a.m.								
p.m.								

daily planner

5 a.m. _____	2 p.m. _____
6 a.m. _____	3 p.m. _____
7 a.m. _____	4 p.m. _____
8 a.m _____	5 p.m. _____
9 a.m. _____	6 p.m. _____
10 a.m. _____	7 p.m. _____
11 a.m. _____	8 p.m. _____
12 p.m. _____	9 p.m. _____
1 p.m. _____	10 p.m. _____

my training log

SWIMMING WORKOUT: distance

a.m.	
p.m.	
	total

BIKING WORKOUT: distance

a.m.	
p.m.	
	total

RUNNING WORKOUT: distance

a.m.	
p.m.	
	total

CROSS-TRAINING: time

a.m.	
p.m.	
	total

TOMORROW'S To Do

my training journal

221

✓RUNALOG® FOR TRIATHLETES

TODAY'S DATE _____

MY LONG-TERM GOAL(S) _____

_____

TODAY'S MEAL PLAN	BREAKFAST	SNACK	LUNCH	SNACK	DINNER
	_____	_____	_____	_____	_____
	_____	_____	_____	_____	_____

weekly planner

	SUNDAY	MONDAY	TUESDAY	WEDNESDAY	THURSDAY	FRIDAY	SATURDAY	TOTAL
a.m.								
p.m.								

🕐 *daily planner*

5 a.m. _____	2 p.m. _____
6 a.m. _____	3 p.m. _____
7 a.m. _____	4 p.m. _____
8 a.m _____	5 p.m. _____
9 a.m. _____	6 p.m. _____
10 a.m. _____	7 p.m. _____
11 a.m. _____	8 p.m. _____
12 p.m. _____	9 p.m. _____
1 p.m. _____	10 p.m. _____

✍ *my training journal*

my training log

SWIMMING WORKOUT:	*distance*
a.m.	
p.m.	
	total

BIKING WORKOUT:	*distance*
a.m.	
p.m.	
	total

RUNNING WORKOUT:	*distance*
a.m.	
p.m.	
	total

CROSS-TRAINING:	*time*
a.m.	
p.m.	
	total

TOMORROW'S To Do

RUNALOG® FOR TRIATHLETES

TODAY'S DATE _____

MY LONG-TERM GOAL(S) _____

TODAY'S MEAL PLAN	BREAKFAST	SNACK	LUNCH	SNACK	DINNER
	_____	_____	_____	_____	_____
	_____	_____	_____	_____	_____

weekly planner

	SUNDAY	MONDAY	TUESDAY	WEDNESDAY	THURSDAY	FRIDAY	SATURDAY	TOTAL
a.m.								
p.m.								

daily planner

5 a.m. _____		2 p.m. _____
6 a.m. _____		3 p.m. _____
7 a.m. _____		4 p.m. _____
8 a.m _____		5 p.m. _____
9 a.m. _____		6 p.m. _____
10 a.m. _____		7 p.m. _____
11 a.m. _____		8 p.m. _____
12 p.m. _____		9 p.m. _____
1 p.m. _____		10 p.m. _____

my training journal

my training log

SWIMMING WORKOUT: distance

a.m.	
p.m.	
	total

BIKING WORKOUT: distance

a.m.	
p.m.	
	total

RUNNING WORKOUT: distance

a.m.	
p.m.	
	total

CROSS-TRAINING: time

a.m.	
p.m.	
	total

TOMORROW'S To Do

223

✓RUNALOG® FOR TRIATHLETES

TODAY'S DATE _____

MY LONG-TERM GOAL(S) _____

TODAY'S MEAL PLAN	BREAKFAST	SNACK	LUNCH	SNACK	DINNER
	_____	_____	_____	_____	_____
	_____	_____	_____	_____	_____

weekly planner

	SUNDAY	MONDAY	TUESDAY	WEDNESDAY	THURSDAY	FRIDAY	SATURDAY	TOTAL
a.m.								
p.m.								

🕐 daily planner

5 a.m. _____	2 p.m. _____
6 a.m. _____	3 p.m. _____
7 a.m. _____	4 p.m. _____
8 a.m _____	5 p.m. _____
9 a.m. _____	6 p.m. _____
10 a.m. _____	7 p.m. _____
11 a.m. _____	8 p.m. _____
12 p.m. _____	9 p.m. _____
1 p.m. _____	10 p.m. _____

✍ my training journal

my training log

SWIMMING WORKOUT: *distance*

a.m.	
p.m.	
	total

BIKING WORKOUT: *distance*

a.m.	
p.m.	
	total

RUNNING WORKOUT: *distance*

a.m.	
p.m.	
	total

CROSS-TRAINING: *time*

a.m.	
p.m.	
	total

TOMORROW'S To Do

RUNALOG® FOR TRIATHLETES

TODAY'S DATE _____

MY LONG-TERM GOAL(S) _____

_____

TODAY'S MEAL PLAN	BREAKFAST	SNACK	LUNCH	SNACK	DINNER
	_____	_____	_____	_____	_____
	_____	_____	_____	_____	_____

weekly planner

	SUNDAY	MONDAY	TUESDAY	WEDNESDAY	THURSDAY	FRIDAY	SATURDAY	TOTAL
a.m.								
p.m.								

daily planner

5 a.m. _____		2 p.m. _____	
6 a.m. _____		3 p.m. _____	
7 a.m. _____		4 p.m. _____	
8 a.m _____		5 p.m. _____	
9 a.m. _____		6 p.m. _____	
10 a.m. _____		7 p.m. _____	
11 a.m. _____		8 p.m. _____	
12 p.m. _____		9 p.m. _____	
1 p.m. _____		10 p.m. _____	

my training journal

_____

_____

_____

_____

_____

_____

_____

_____

_____

_____

_____

_____

_____

_____

_____

_____

_____

_____

my training log

SWIMMING WORKOUT:	distance
a.m.	
p.m.	
	total

BIKING WORKOUT:	distance
a.m.	
p.m.	
	total

RUNNING WORKOUT:	distance
a.m.	
p.m.	
	total

CROSS-TRAINING:	time
a.m.	
p.m.	
	total

TOMORROW'S To Do

225

ⱽRUNALOG® FOR TRIATHLETES

TODAY'S DATE _____

MY LONG-TERM GOAL(S) _____

TODAY'S MEAL PLAN	BREAKFAST	SNACK	LUNCH	SNACK	DINNER
	_____	_____	_____	_____	_____
	_____	_____	_____	_____	_____

weekly planner

	SUNDAY	MONDAY	TUESDAY	WEDNESDAY	THURSDAY	FRIDAY	SATURDAY	TOTAL
a.m.								
p.m.								

daily planner

5 a.m. _____	2 p.m. _____
6 a.m. _____	3 p.m. _____
7 a.m. _____	4 p.m. _____
8 a.m _____	5 p.m. _____
9 a.m. _____	6 p.m. _____
10 a.m. _____	7 p.m. _____
11 a.m. _____	8 p.m. _____
12 p.m. _____	9 p.m. _____
1 p.m. _____	10 p.m. _____

my training journal

my training log

SWIMMING WORKOUT:	*distance*
a.m.	
p.m.	
	total

BIKING WORKOUT:	*distance*
a.m.	
p.m.	
	total

RUNNING WORKOUT:	*distance*
a.m.	
p.m.	
	total

CROSS-TRAINING:	*time*
a.m.	
p.m.	
	total

TOMORROW'S TO DO

⩔RUNALOG® FOR TRIATHLETES

TODAY'S DATE _____

MY LONG-TERM GOAL(S) _____

Today's Meal Plan	BREAKFAST	SNACK	LUNCH	SNACK	DINNER
	_____	_____	_____	_____	_____
	_____	_____	_____	_____	_____

weekly planner

	SUNDAY	MONDAY	TUESDAY	WEDNESDAY	THURSDAY	FRIDAY	SATURDAY	TOTAL
a.m.								
p.m.								

daily planner

5 a.m. _____	2 p.m. _____
6 a.m. _____	3 p.m. _____
7 a.m. _____	4 p.m. _____
8 a.m _____	5 p.m. _____
9 a.m. _____	6 p.m. _____
10 a.m. _____	7 p.m. _____
11 a.m. _____	8 p.m. _____
12 p.m. _____	9 p.m. _____
1 p.m. _____	10 p.m. _____

my training journal

my training log

SWIMMING WORKOUT:	*distance*
a.m.	
p.m.	
	total

BIKING WORKOUT:	*distance*
a.m.	
p.m.	
	total

RUNNING WORKOUT:	*distance*
a.m.	
p.m.	
	total

CROSS-TRAINING:	*time*
a.m.	
p.m.	
	total

TOMORROW'S TO DO

227

ⱱRUNALOG° FOR TRIATHLETES

TODAY'S DATE _____

MY LONG-TERM GOAL(S) _____

TODAY'S MEAL PLAN	BREAKFAST	SNACK	LUNCH	SNACK	DINNER

weekly planner

	SUNDAY	MONDAY	TUESDAY	WEDNESDAY	THURSDAY	FRIDAY	SATURDAY	TOTAL
a.m.								
p.m.								

🕐 daily planner

5 a.m. _____	2 p.m. _____
6 a.m. _____	3 p.m. _____
7 a.m. _____	4 p.m. _____
8 a.m _____	5 p.m. _____
9 a.m. _____	6 p.m. _____
10 a.m. _____	7 p.m. _____
11 a.m. _____	8 p.m. _____
12 p.m. _____	9 p.m. _____
1 p.m. _____	10 p.m. _____

✍ my training journal

my training log

SWIMMING WORKOUT:	*distance*
a.m.	
p.m.	
	total

BIKING WORKOUT:	*distance*
a.m.	
p.m.	
	total

RUNNING WORKOUT:	*distance*
a.m.	
p.m.	
	total

CROSS-TRAINING:	*time*
a.m.	
p.m.	
	total

TOMORROW'S TO DO

ⱽRUNALOG® FOR TRIATHLETES

TODAY'S DATE _____

MY LONG-TERM GOAL(S) _____
_____

TODAY'S MEAL PLAN	BREAKFAST	SNACK	LUNCH	SNACK	DINNER
	_____	_____	_____	_____	_____

weekly planner

	SUNDAY	MONDAY	TUESDAY	WEDNESDAY	THURSDAY	FRIDAY	SATURDAY	TOTAL
a.m.								
p.m.								

daily planner

5 a.m. _____	2 p.m. _____
6 a.m. _____	3 p.m. _____
7 a.m. _____	4 p.m. _____
8 a.m _____	5 p.m. _____
9 a.m. _____	6 p.m. _____
10 a.m. _____	7 p.m. _____
11 a.m. _____	8 p.m. _____
12 p.m. _____	9 p.m. _____
1 p.m. _____	10 p.m. _____

my training journal

my training log

SWIMMING WORKOUT:	*distance*
a.m.	
p.m.	
	total

BIKING WORKOUT:	*distance*
a.m.	
p.m.	
	total

RUNNING WORKOUT:	*distance*
a.m.	
p.m.	
	total

CROSS-TRAINING:	*time*
a.m.	
p.m.	
	total

TOMORROW'S TO DO

√RUNALOG® *FOR TRIATHLETES*   TODAY'S DATE _____

MY LONG-TERM GOAL(S) _____
_____

TODAY'S MEAL PLAN	BREAKFAST	SNACK	LUNCH	SNACK	DINNER
	_____	_____	_____	_____	_____
	_____	_____	_____	_____	_____

weekly planner

	SUNDAY	MONDAY	TUESDAY	WEDNESDAY	THURSDAY	FRIDAY	SATURDAY	TOTAL
a.m.								
p.m.								

daily planner

5 a.m. _____	2 p.m. _____
6 a.m. _____	3 p.m. _____
7 a.m. _____	4 p.m. _____
8 a.m _____	5 p.m. _____
9 a.m. _____	6 p.m. _____
10 a.m. _____	7 p.m. _____
11 a.m. _____	8 p.m. _____
12 p.m. _____	9 p.m. _____
1 p.m. _____	10 p.m. _____

my training journal

my training log

SWIMMING WORKOUT: *distance*

a.m.	
p.m.	
	total

BIKING WORKOUT: *distance*

a.m.	
p.m.	
	total

RUNNING WORKOUT: *distance*

a.m.	
p.m.	
	total

CROSS-TRAINING: *time*

a.m.	
p.m.	
	total

TOMORROW'S To Do

√RUNALOG® FOR TRIATHLETES

TODAY'S DATE _____

MY LONG-TERM GOAL(S) _____
_____

TODAY'S MEAL PLAN	BREAKFAST	SNACK	LUNCH	SNACK	DINNER
	_____	_____	_____	_____	_____

weekly planner

	SUNDAY	MONDAY	TUESDAY	WEDNESDAY	THURSDAY	FRIDAY	SATURDAY	TOTAL
a.m.								
p.m.								

daily planner

5 a.m. _____	2 p.m. _____
6 a.m. _____	3 p.m. _____
7 a.m. _____	4 p.m. _____
8 a.m _____	5 p.m. _____
9 a.m. _____	6 p.m. _____
10 a.m. _____	7 p.m. _____
11 a.m. _____	8 p.m. _____
12 p.m. _____	9 p.m. _____
1 p.m. _____	10 p.m. _____

my training journal

my training log

SWIMMING WORKOUT:	distance
a.m.	
p.m.	
	total

BIKING WORKOUT:	distance
a.m.	
p.m.	
	total

RUNNING WORKOUT:	distance
a.m.	
p.m.	
	total

CROSS-TRAINING:	time
a.m.	
p.m.	
	total

TOMORROW'S TO DO

231

ⱽRUNALOG® *For Triathletes*

TODAY'S DATE _____

MY LONG-TERM GOAL(S) _____

TODAY'S MEAL PLAN	BREAKFAST	SNACK	LUNCH	SNACK	DINNER
	_____	_____	_____	_____	_____
	_____	_____	_____	_____	_____

weekly planner

SUNDAY	MONDAY	TUESDAY	WEDNESDAY	THURSDAY	FRIDAY	SATURDAY	TOTAL
a.m.							
p.m.							

🕐 *daily planner*

5 a.m.	_____	2 p.m.	_____
6 a.m.	_____	3 p.m.	_____
7 a.m.	_____	4 p.m.	_____
8 a.m	_____	5 p.m.	_____
9 a.m.	_____	6 p.m.	_____
10 a.m.	_____	7 p.m.	_____
11 a.m.	_____	8 p.m.	_____
12 p.m.	_____	9 p.m.	_____
1 p.m.	_____	10 p.m.	_____

✍ *my training journal*

my training log

🏊 SWIMMING WORKOUT:	*distance*
a.m.	
p.m.	
	total

🚴 BIKING WORKOUT:	*distance*
a.m.	
p.m.	
	total

🏃 RUNNING WORKOUT:	*distance*
a.m.	
p.m.	
	total

CROSS-TRAINING:	*time*
a.m.	
p.m.	
	total

TOMORROW'S TO DO

Today's Date _____

MY LONG-TERM GOAL(S) _____

_____

Today's Meal Plan	Breakfast	Snack	Lunch	Snack	Dinner
	_____	_____	_____	_____	_____
	_____	_____	_____	_____	_____

weekly planner

	SUNDAY	MONDAY	TUESDAY	WEDNESDAY	THURSDAY	FRIDAY	SATURDAY	TOTAL
a.m.								
p.m.								

🕐 *daily planner*

5 a.m. _____	2 p.m. _____
6 a.m. _____	3 p.m. _____
7 a.m. _____	4 p.m. _____
8 a.m _____	5 p.m. _____
9 a.m. _____	6 p.m. _____
10 a.m. _____	7 p.m. _____
11 a.m. _____	8 p.m. _____
12 p.m. _____	9 p.m. _____
1 p.m. _____	10 p.m. _____

✍ *my training journal*

my training log

SWIMMING WORKOUT: *distance*

a.m.	
p.m.	
	total

BIKING WORKOUT: *distance*

a.m.	
p.m.	
	total

RUNNING WORKOUT: *distance*

a.m.	
p.m.	
	total

CROSS-TRAINING: *time*

a.m.	
p.m.	
	total

Tomorrow's To Do

✓RUNALOG® FOR TRIATHLETES

TODAY'S DATE _____

MY LONG-TERM GOAL(S) _____

TODAY'S MEAL PLAN	BREAKFAST	SNACK	LUNCH	SNACK	DINNER
	_____	_____	_____	_____	_____
	_____	_____	_____	_____	_____

weekly planner

	SUNDAY	MONDAY	TUESDAY	WEDNESDAY	THURSDAY	FRIDAY	SATURDAY	TOTAL
a.m.								
p.m.								

🕐 daily planner

5 a.m.	_____	2 p.m.	_____
6 a.m.	_____	3 p.m.	_____
7 a.m.	_____	4 p.m.	_____
8 a.m	_____	5 p.m.	_____
9 a.m.	_____	6 p.m.	_____
10 a.m.	_____	7 p.m.	_____
11 a.m.	_____	8 p.m.	_____
12 p.m.	_____	9 p.m.	_____
1 p.m.	_____	10 p.m.	_____

✍ my training journal

my training log

SWIMMING WORKOUT: *distance*

a.m.		
p.m.		
		total

BIKING WORKOUT: *distance*

a.m.		
p.m.		
		total

RUNNING WORKOUT: *distance*

a.m.		
p.m.		
		total

CROSS-TRAINING: *time*

a.m.		
p.m.		
		total

TOMORROW'S TO DO

√RUNALOG® FOR TRIATHLETES

TODAY'S DATE _____

MY LONG-TERM GOAL(S) _____

TODAY'S MEAL PLAN	BREAKFAST	SNACK	LUNCH	SNACK	DINNER
	_____	_____	_____	_____	_____
	_____	_____	_____	_____	_____

weekly planner

	SUNDAY	MONDAY	TUESDAY	WEDNESDAY	THURSDAY	FRIDAY	SATURDAY	TOTAL
a.m.								
p.m.								

daily planner

5 a.m. _____	2 p.m. _____
6 a.m. _____	3 p.m. _____
7 a.m. _____	4 p.m. _____
8 a.m _____	5 p.m. _____
9 a.m. _____	6 p.m. _____
10 a.m. _____	7 p.m. _____
11 a.m. _____	8 p.m. _____
12 p.m. _____	9 p.m. _____
1 p.m. _____	10 p.m. _____

my training journal

my training log

SWIMMING WORKOUT:	*distance*
a.m.	
p.m.	
	total

BIKING WORKOUT:	*distance*
a.m.	
p.m.	
	total

RUNNING WORKOUT:	*distance*
a.m.	
p.m.	
	total

CROSS-TRAINING:	*time*
a.m.	
p.m.	
	total

TOMORROW'S TO DO

ⱽRUNALOG® *For Triathletes*   **TODAY'S DATE** _____

MY LONG-TERM GOAL(S) _____

TODAY'S MEAL PLAN	BREAKFAST	SNACK	LUNCH	SNACK	DINNER
	_____	_____	_____	_____	_____
	_____	_____	_____	_____	_____

weekly planner

	SUNDAY	MONDAY	TUESDAY	WEDNESDAY	THURSDAY	FRIDAY	SATURDAY	TOTAL
a.m.								
p.m.								

🕐 *daily planner*

5 a.m.	_____	2 p.m.	_____
6 a.m.	_____	3 p.m.	_____
7 a.m.	_____	4 p.m.	_____
8 a.m	_____	5 p.m.	_____
9 a.m.	_____	6 p.m.	_____
10 a.m.	_____	7 p.m.	_____
11 a.m.	_____	8 p.m.	_____
12 p.m.	_____	9 p.m.	_____
1 p.m.	_____	10 p.m.	_____

✍ *my training journal*

my training log

SWIMMING WORKOUT:	*distance*
a.m.	
p.m.	
	total

BIKING WORKOUT:	*distance*
a.m.	
p.m.	
	total

RUNNING WORKOUT:	*distance*
a.m.	
p.m.	
	total

CROSS-TRAINING:	*time*
a.m.	
p.m.	
	total

TOMORROW'S TO DO

√RUNALOG® FOR TRIATHLETES

TODAY'S DATE _____

MY LONG-TERM GOAL(S) _____

TODAY'S MEAL PLAN	BREAKFAST	SNACK	LUNCH	SNACK	DINNER
	_____	_____	_____	_____	_____

weekly planner

	SUNDAY	MONDAY	TUESDAY	WEDNESDAY	THURSDAY	FRIDAY	SATURDAY	TOTAL
a.m.								
p.m.								

daily planner

5 a.m. _____	2 p.m. _____
6 a.m. _____	3 p.m. _____
7 a.m. _____	4 p.m. _____
8 a.m _____	5 p.m. _____
9 a.m. _____	6 p.m. _____
10 a.m. _____	7 p.m. _____
11 a.m. _____	8 p.m. _____
12 p.m. _____	9 p.m. _____
1 p.m. _____	10 p.m. _____

my training journal

my training log

SWIMMING WORKOUT:	distance
a.m.	
p.m.	
	total

BIKING WORKOUT:	distance
a.m.	
p.m.	
	total

RUNNING WORKOUT:	distance
a.m.	
p.m.	
	total

CROSS-TRAINING:	time
a.m.	
p.m.	
	total

TOMORROW'S TO DO

√RUNALOG® *For Triathletes*   TODAY'S DATE _____

MY LONG-TERM GOAL(S) _____

TODAY'S MEAL PLAN	BREAKFAST	SNACK	LUNCH	SNACK	DINNER
	_____	_____	_____	_____	_____
	_____	_____	_____	_____	_____

weekly planner

	SUNDAY	MONDAY	TUESDAY	WEDNESDAY	THURSDAY	FRIDAY	SATURDAY	TOTAL
a.m.								
p.m.								

daily planner

5 a.m. _____	2 p.m. _____
6 a.m. _____	3 p.m. _____
7 a.m. _____	4 p.m. _____
8 a.m _____	5 p.m. _____
9 a.m. _____	6 p.m. _____
10 a.m. _____	7 p.m. _____
11 a.m. _____	8 p.m. _____
12 p.m. _____	9 p.m. _____
1 p.m. _____	10 p.m. _____

my training journal

my training log

SWIMMING WORKOUT: *distance*

a.m.	
p.m.	
	total

BIKING WORKOUT: *distance*

a.m.	
p.m.	
	total

RUNNING WORKOUT: *distance*

a.m.	
p.m.	
	total

CROSS-TRAINING: *time*

a.m.	
p.m.	
	total

TOMORROW'S TO DO

ⱽRUNALOG® *FOR TRIATHLETES*

TODAY'S DATE _____

MY LONG-TERM GOAL(S) _____

TODAY'S MEAL PLAN	BREAKFAST	SNACK	LUNCH	SNACK	DINNER
	_____	_____	_____	_____	_____
	_____	_____	_____	_____	_____

weekly planner

	SUNDAY	MONDAY	TUESDAY	WEDNESDAY	THURSDAY	FRIDAY	SATURDAY	TOTAL
a.m.								
p.m.								

🕐 *daily planner*

5 a.m. _____	2 p.m. _____
6 a.m. _____	3 p.m. _____
7 a.m. _____	4 p.m. _____
8 a.m _____	5 p.m. _____
9 a.m. _____	6 p.m. _____
10 a.m. _____	7 p.m. _____
11 a.m. _____	8 p.m. _____
12 p.m. _____	9 p.m. _____
1 p.m. _____	10 p.m. _____

✍ *my training journal*

my training log

🏊 SWIMMING WORKOUT: *distance*

a.m.	
p.m.	
	total

🚴 BIKING WORKOUT: *distance*

a.m.	
p.m.	
	total

🏃 RUNNING WORKOUT: *distance*

a.m.	
p.m.	
	total

CROSS-TRAINING: *time*

a.m.	
p.m.	
	total

TOMORROW'S TO DO

√RUNALOG® FOR TRIATHLETES   TODAY'S DATE _____

MY LONG-TERM GOAL(S) _____

TODAY'S MEAL PLAN	BREAKFAST	SNACK	LUNCH	SNACK	DINNER
	_____	_____	_____	_____	_____
	_____	_____	_____	_____	_____

weekly planner

	SUNDAY	MONDAY	TUESDAY	WEDNESDAY	THURSDAY	FRIDAY	SATURDAY	TOTAL
a.m.								
p.m.								

daily planner

5 a.m. _____	2 p.m. _____
6 a.m. _____	3 p.m. _____
7 a.m. _____	4 p.m. _____
8 a.m _____	5 p.m. _____
9 a.m. _____	6 p.m. _____
10 a.m. _____	7 p.m. _____
11 a.m. _____	8 p.m. _____
12 p.m. _____	9 p.m. _____
1 p.m. _____	10 p.m. _____

my training journal

my training log

SWIMMING WORKOUT: *distance*

a.m.	
p.m.	
	total

BIKING WORKOUT: *distance*

a.m.	
p.m.	
	total

RUNNING WORKOUT: *distance*

a.m.	
p.m.	
	total

CROSS-TRAINING: *time*

a.m.	
p.m.	
	total

TOMORROW'S TO DO

RUNALOG® FOR TRIATHLETES

TODAY'S DATE _____

MY LONG-TERM GOAL(S) _____
_____

TODAY'S MEAL PLAN	BREAKFAST	SNACK	LUNCH	SNACK	DINNER
	_____	_____	_____	_____	_____
	_____	_____	_____	_____	_____

weekly planner

	SUNDAY	MONDAY	TUESDAY	WEDNESDAY	THURSDAY	FRIDAY	SATURDAY	TOTAL
a.m.								
p.m.								

daily planner

5 a.m. _____	2 p.m. _____
6 a.m. _____	3 p.m. _____
7 a.m. _____	4 p.m. _____
8 a.m _____	5 p.m. _____
9 a.m. _____	6 p.m. _____
10 a.m. _____	7 p.m. _____
11 a.m. _____	8 p.m. _____
12 p.m. _____	9 p.m. _____
1 p.m. _____	10 p.m. _____

my training journal

my training log

SWIMMING WORKOUT:	*distance*
a.m.	
p.m.	
	total

BIKING WORKOUT:	*distance*
a.m.	
p.m.	
	total

RUNNING WORKOUT:	*distance*
a.m.	
p.m.	
	total

CROSS-TRAINING:	*time*
a.m.	
p.m.	
	total

TOMORROW'S TO DO

241

© 2009 www.RUNALOGS.com

RUNALOG® FOR TRIATHLETES

TODAY'S DATE _____

MY LONG-TERM GOAL(S) _____

TODAY'S MEAL PLAN	BREAKFAST	SNACK	LUNCH	SNACK	DINNER
	_____	_____	_____	_____	_____

weekly planner

	SUNDAY	MONDAY	TUESDAY	WEDNESDAY	THURSDAY	FRIDAY	SATURDAY	TOTAL
a.m.								
p.m.								

daily planner

5 a.m.	_____	2 p.m.	_____
6 a.m.	_____	3 p.m.	_____
7 a.m.	_____	4 p.m.	_____
8 a.m	_____	5 p.m.	_____
9 a.m.	_____	6 p.m.	_____
10 a.m.	_____	7 p.m.	_____
11 a.m.	_____	8 p.m.	_____
12 p.m.	_____	9 p.m.	_____
1 p.m.	_____	10 p.m.	_____

my training journal

my training log

SWIMMING WORKOUT: *distance*

a.m.	
p.m.	
	total

BIKING WORKOUT: *distance*

a.m.	
p.m.	
	total

RUNNING WORKOUT: *distance*

a.m.	
p.m.	
	total

CROSS-TRAINING: *time*

a.m.	
p.m.	
	total

TOMORROW'S To Do

ⓥRUNALOG® FOR TRIATHLETES

TODAY'S DATE _____

MY LONG-TERM GOAL(S) _____

TODAY'S MEAL PLAN	BREAKFAST	SNACK	LUNCH	SNACK	DINNER
	_____	_____	_____	_____	_____
	_____	_____	_____	_____	_____

weekly planner

	SUNDAY	MONDAY	TUESDAY	WEDNESDAY	THURSDAY	FRIDAY	SATURDAY	TOTAL
a.m.								
p.m.								

daily planner

5 a.m. _____	2 p.m. _____
6 a.m. _____	3 p.m. _____
7 a.m. _____	4 p.m. _____
8 a.m _____	5 p.m. _____
9 a.m. _____	6 p.m. _____
10 a.m. _____	7 p.m. _____
11 a.m. _____	8 p.m. _____
12 p.m. _____	9 p.m. _____
1 p.m. _____	10 p.m. _____

my training journal

my training log

SWIMMING WORKOUT:	distance
a.m.	
p.m.	
	total

BIKING WORKOUT:	distance
a.m.	
p.m.	
	total

RUNNING WORKOUT:	distance
a.m.	
p.m.	
	total

CROSS-TRAINING:	time
a.m.	
p.m.	
	total

TOMORROW'S To Do

√RUNALOG® FOR TRIATHLETES

TODAY'S DATE _____

MY LONG-TERM GOAL(S) _____

TODAY'S MEAL PLAN	BREAKFAST	SNACK	LUNCH	SNACK	DINNER
	_____	_____	_____	_____	_____
	_____	_____	_____	_____	_____

weekly planner

	SUNDAY	MONDAY	TUESDAY	WEDNESDAY	THURSDAY	FRIDAY	SATURDAY	TOTAL
a.m.								
p.m.								

daily planner

5 a.m. _____	2 p.m. _____
6 a.m. _____	3 p.m. _____
7 a.m. _____	4 p.m. _____
8 a.m _____	5 p.m. _____
9 a.m. _____	6 p.m. _____
10 a.m. _____	7 p.m. _____
11 a.m. _____	8 p.m. _____
12 p.m. _____	9 p.m. _____
1 p.m. _____	10 p.m. _____

my training journal

my training log

SWIMMING WORKOUT:	*distance*
a.m.	
p.m.	
	total

BIKING WORKOUT:	*distance*
a.m.	
p.m.	
	total

RUNNING WORKOUT:	*distance*
a.m.	
p.m.	
	total

CROSS-TRAINING:	*time*
a.m.	
p.m.	
	total

TOMORROW'S To Do

244

ᒾRUNALOG® FOR TRIATHLETES

TODAY'S DATE _____

MY LONG-TERM GOAL(S) _____

TODAY'S MEAL PLAN	BREAKFAST	SNACK	LUNCH	SNACK	DINNER
	_____	_____	_____	_____	_____
	_____	_____	_____	_____	_____

weekly planner

	SUNDAY	MONDAY	TUESDAY	WEDNESDAY	THURSDAY	FRIDAY	SATURDAY	TOTAL
a.m.								
p.m.								

daily planner

5 a.m. _____	2 p.m. _____
6 a.m. _____	3 p.m. _____
7 a.m. _____	4 p.m. _____
8 a.m _____	5 p.m. _____
9 a.m. _____	6 p.m. _____
10 a.m. _____	7 p.m. _____
11 a.m. _____	8 p.m. _____
12 p.m. _____	9 p.m. _____
1 p.m. _____	10 p.m. _____

my training journal

my training log

SWIMMING WORKOUT:	*distance*
a.m.	
p.m.	
	total

BIKING WORKOUT:	*distance*
a.m.	
p.m.	
	total

RUNNING WORKOUT:	*distance*
a.m.	
p.m.	
	total

CROSS-TRAINING:	*time*
a.m.	
p.m.	
	total

Tomorrow's To Do

245

ᐯRUNALOG® *For Triathletes*   *Today's Date* _____

MY LONG-TERM GOAL(S) _____

TODAY'S MEAL PLAN	BREAKFAST	SNACK	LUNCH	SNACK	DINNER
	_____	_____	_____	_____	_____
	_____	_____	_____	_____	_____

weekly planner

SUNDAY	MONDAY	TUESDAY	WEDNESDAY	THURSDAY	FRIDAY	SATURDAY	TOTAL
a.m.							
p.m.							

daily planner

5 a.m.	_____	2 p.m.	_____
6 a.m.	_____	3 p.m.	_____
7 a.m.	_____	4 p.m.	_____
8 a.m	_____	5 p.m.	_____
9 a.m.	_____	6 p.m.	_____
10 a.m.	_____	7 p.m.	_____
11 a.m.	_____	8 p.m.	_____
12 p.m.	_____	9 p.m.	_____
1 p.m.	_____	10 p.m.	_____

my training journal

my training log

SWIMMING WORKOUT: *distance*

a.m.	
p.m.	
	total

BIKING WORKOUT: *distance*

a.m.	
p.m.	
	total

RUNNING WORKOUT: *distance*

a.m.	
p.m.	
	total

CROSS-TRAINING: *time*

a.m.	
p.m.	
	total

Tomorrow's To Do

ᐁRUNALOG° FOR TRIATHLETES

TODAY'S DATE _____

MY LONG-TERM GOAL(S) _____

TODAY'S MEAL PLAN	BREAKFAST	SNACK	LUNCH	SNACK	DINNER

weekly planner

	SUNDAY	MONDAY	TUESDAY	WEDNESDAY	THURSDAY	FRIDAY	SATURDAY	TOTAL
a.m.								
p.m.								

🕐 daily planner

5 a.m. _____		2 p.m. _____
6 a.m. _____		3 p.m. _____
7 a.m. _____		4 p.m. _____
8 a.m _____		5 p.m. _____
9 a.m. _____		6 p.m. _____
10 a.m. _____		7 p.m. _____
11 a.m. _____		8 p.m. _____
12 p.m. _____		9 p.m. _____
1 p.m. _____		10 p.m. _____

✍ my training journal

my training log

SWIMMING WORKOUT:	distance
a.m.	
p.m.	
	total

BIKING WORKOUT:	distance
a.m.	
p.m.	
	total

RUNNING WORKOUT:	distance
a.m.	
p.m.	
	total

CROSS-TRAINING:	time
a.m.	
p.m.	
	total

TOMORROW'S TO DO

247

√RUNALOG® FOR TRIATHLETES

TODAY'S DATE _____

MY LONG-TERM GOAL(S) _____

TODAY'S MEAL PLAN	BREAKFAST	SNACK	LUNCH	SNACK	DINNER

weekly planner

	SUNDAY	MONDAY	TUESDAY	WEDNESDAY	THURSDAY	FRIDAY	SATURDAY	TOTAL
a.m.								
p.m.								

daily planner

5 a.m. _____	2 p.m. _____
6 a.m. _____	3 p.m. _____
7 a.m. _____	4 p.m. _____
8 a.m _____	5 p.m. _____
9 a.m. _____	6 p.m. _____
10 a.m. _____	7 p.m. _____
11 a.m. _____	8 p.m. _____
12 p.m. _____	9 p.m. _____
1 p.m. _____	10 p.m. _____

my training journal

my training log

SWIMMING WORKOUT:	distance
a.m.	
p.m.	
	total

BIKING WORKOUT:	distance
a.m.	
p.m.	
	total

RUNNING WORKOUT:	distance
a.m.	
p.m.	
	total

CROSS-TRAINING:	time
a.m.	
p.m.	
	total

TOMORROW'S TO DO

ꭓRUNALOG® FOR TRIATHLETES

TODAY'S DATE _____

MY LONG-TERM GOAL(S) _____
_____

TODAY'S MEAL PLAN	BREAKFAST	SNACK	LUNCH	SNACK	DINNER
	_____	_____	_____	_____	_____
	_____	_____	_____	_____	_____

weekly planner

	SUNDAY	MONDAY	TUESDAY	WEDNESDAY	THURSDAY	FRIDAY	SATURDAY	TOTAL
a.m.								
p.m.								

daily planner

5 a.m. _____	2 p.m. _____
6 a.m. _____	3 p.m. _____
7 a.m. _____	4 p.m. _____
8 a.m _____	5 p.m. _____
9 a.m. _____	6 p.m. _____
10 a.m. _____	7 p.m. _____
11 a.m. _____	8 p.m. _____
12 p.m. _____	9 p.m. _____
1 p.m. _____	10 p.m. _____

my training journal

my training log

SWIMMING WORKOUT:	*distance*
a.m.	
p.m.	
	total

BIKING WORKOUT:	*distance*
a.m.	
p.m.	
	total

RUNNING WORKOUT:	*distance*
a.m.	
p.m.	
	total

CROSS-TRAINING:	*time*
a.m.	
p.m.	
	total

TOMORROW'S TO DO

⚕RUNALOG® FOR TRIATHLETES

TODAY'S DATE _____

MY LONG-TERM GOAL(S) _____

TODAY'S MEAL PLAN	BREAKFAST	SNACK	LUNCH	SNACK	DINNER
	_____	_____	_____	_____	_____

weekly planner

	SUNDAY	MONDAY	TUESDAY	WEDNESDAY	THURSDAY	FRIDAY	SATURDAY	TOTAL
a.m.								
p.m.								

🕐 *daily planner*

5 a.m. _____	2 p.m. _____
6 a.m. _____	3 p.m. _____
7 a.m. _____	4 p.m. _____
8 a.m _____	5 p.m. _____
9 a.m. _____	6 p.m. _____
10 a.m. _____	7 p.m. _____
11 a.m. _____	8 p.m. _____
12 p.m. _____	9 p.m. _____
1 p.m. _____	10 p.m. _____

✍ *my training journal*

my training log

SWIMMING WORKOUT:	*distance*
a.m.	
p.m.	
	total

BIKING WORKOUT:	*distance*
a.m.	
p.m.	
	total

RUNNING WORKOUT:	*distance*
a.m.	
p.m.	
	total

CROSS-TRAINING:	*time*
a.m.	
p.m.	
	total

TOMORROW'S TO DO

RUNALOG® FOR TRIATHLETES

TODAY'S DATE _____

MY LONG-TERM GOAL(S) _____

TODAY'S MEAL PLAN	BREAKFAST	SNACK	LUNCH	SNACK	DINNER
	_____	_____	_____	_____	_____
	_____	_____	_____	_____	_____

weekly planner

	SUNDAY	MONDAY	TUESDAY	WEDNESDAY	THURSDAY	FRIDAY	SATURDAY	TOTAL
a.m.								
p.m.								

daily planner

5 a.m. _____	2 p.m. _____
6 a.m. _____	3 p.m. _____
7 a.m. _____	4 p.m. _____
8 a.m _____	5 p.m. _____
9 a.m. _____	6 p.m. _____
10 a.m. _____	7 p.m. _____
11 a.m. _____	8 p.m. _____
12 p.m. _____	9 p.m. _____
1 p.m. _____	10 p.m. _____

my training journal

my training log

SWIMMING WORKOUT: distance

a.m.	
p.m.	
	total

BIKING WORKOUT: distance

a.m.	
p.m.	
	total

RUNNING WORKOUT: distance

a.m.	
p.m.	
	total

CROSS-TRAINING: time

a.m.	
p.m.	
	total

TOMORROW'S TO DO

251

© 2009 www.RUNALOGS.com

MY LONG-TERM GOAL(S) _____

TODAY'S MEAL PLAN	BREAKFAST	SNACK	LUNCH	SNACK	DINNER
	_____	_____	_____	_____	_____
	_____	_____	_____	_____	_____

weekly planner

	SUNDAY	MONDAY	TUESDAY	WEDNESDAY	THURSDAY	FRIDAY	SATURDAY	TOTAL
a.m.								
p.m.								

daily planner

5 a.m. _____	2 p.m. _____
6 a.m. _____	3 p.m. _____
7 a.m. _____	4 p.m. _____
8 a.m _____	5 p.m. _____
9 a.m. _____	6 p.m. _____
10 a.m. _____	7 p.m. _____
11 a.m. _____	8 p.m. _____
12 p.m. _____	9 p.m. _____
1 p.m. _____	10 p.m. _____

my training journal

my training log

SWIMMING WORKOUT:	*distance*
a.m.	
p.m.	
	total

BIKING WORKOUT:	*distance*
a.m.	
p.m.	
	total

RUNNING WORKOUT:	*distance*
a.m.	
p.m.	
	total

CROSS-TRAINING:	*time*
a.m.	
p.m.	
	total

TOMORROW'S TO DO

MY LONG-TERM GOAL(S) _____

TODAY'S MEAL PLAN	BREAKFAST	SNACK	LUNCH	SNACK	DINNER
	_____	_____	_____	_____	_____
	_____	_____	_____	_____	_____

weekly planner

	SUNDAY	MONDAY	TUESDAY	WEDNESDAY	THURSDAY	FRIDAY	SATURDAY	TOTAL
a.m.								
p.m.								

daily planner

5 a.m. _____	2 p.m. _____
6 a.m. _____	3 p.m. _____
7 a.m. _____	4 p.m. _____
8 a.m _____	5 p.m. _____
9 a.m. _____	6 p.m. _____
10 a.m. _____	7 p.m. _____
11 a.m. _____	8 p.m. _____
12 p.m. _____	9 p.m. _____
1 p.m. _____	10 p.m. _____

my training journal

my training log

SWIMMING WORKOUT: *distance*

a.m.	
p.m.	
	total

BIKING WORKOUT: *distance*

a.m.	
p.m.	
	total

RUNNING WORKOUT: *distance*

a.m.	
p.m.	
	total

CROSS-TRAINING: *time*

a.m.	
p.m.	
	total

TOMORROW'S TO DO

RUNALOG® FOR TRIATHLETES

TODAY'S DATE _____

MY LONG-TERM GOAL(S) _____

TODAY'S MEAL PLAN	BREAKFAST	SNACK	LUNCH	SNACK	DINNER

weekly planner

	SUNDAY	MONDAY	TUESDAY	WEDNESDAY	THURSDAY	FRIDAY	SATURDAY	TOTAL
a.m.								
p.m.								

daily planner

5 a.m.	_____	2 p.m.	_____
6 a.m.	_____	3 p.m.	_____
7 a.m.	_____	4 p.m.	_____
8 a.m	_____	5 p.m.	_____
9 a.m.	_____	6 p.m.	_____
10 a.m.	_____	7 p.m.	_____
11 a.m.	_____	8 p.m.	_____
12 p.m.	_____	9 p.m.	_____
1 p.m.	_____	10 p.m.	_____

my training journal

my training log

SWIMMING WORKOUT:	*distance*
a.m.	
p.m.	
	total

BIKING WORKOUT:	*distance*
a.m.	
p.m.	
	total

RUNNING WORKOUT:	*distance*
a.m.	
p.m.	
	total

CROSS-TRAINING:	*time*
a.m.	
p.m.	
	total

TOMORROW'S TO DO

✔RUNALOG® FOR TRIATHLETES

TODAY'S DATE _____

MY LONG-TERM GOAL(S) _____

_____

TODAY'S MEAL PLAN	BREAKFAST	SNACK	LUNCH	SNACK	DINNER
	_____	_____	_____	_____	_____
	_____	_____	_____	_____	_____

weekly planner

	SUNDAY	MONDAY	TUESDAY	WEDNESDAY	THURSDAY	FRIDAY	SATURDAY	TOTAL
a.m.								
p.m.								

daily planner

5 a.m. _____	2 p.m. _____
6 a.m. _____	3 p.m. _____
7 a.m. _____	4 p.m. _____
8 a.m _____	5 p.m. _____
9 a.m. _____	6 p.m. _____
10 a.m. _____	7 p.m. _____
11 a.m. _____	8 p.m. _____
12 p.m. _____	9 p.m. _____
1 p.m. _____	10 p.m. _____

my training journal

my training log

SWIMMING WORKOUT:	distance
a.m.	
p.m.	
	total

BIKING WORKOUT:	distance
a.m.	
p.m.	
	total

RUNNING WORKOUT:	distance
a.m.	
p.m.	
	total

CROSS-TRAINING:	time
a.m.	
p.m.	
	total

TOMORROW'S TO DO

√RUNALOG® *FOR TRIATHLETES*   TODAY'S DATE _____

MY LONG-TERM GOAL(S) _____
_____

TODAY'S MEAL PLAN	BREAKFAST	SNACK	LUNCH	SNACK	DINNER
	_____	_____	_____	_____	_____
	_____	_____	_____	_____	_____

weekly planner

	SUNDAY	MONDAY	TUESDAY	WEDNESDAY	THURSDAY	FRIDAY	SATURDAY	TOTAL
a.m.								
p.m.								

daily planner

5 a.m.	_____	2 p.m.	_____
6 a.m.	_____	3 p.m.	_____
7 a.m.	_____	4 p.m.	_____
8 a.m	_____	5 p.m.	_____
9 a.m.	_____	6 p.m.	_____
10 a.m.	_____	7 p.m.	_____
11 a.m.	_____	8 p.m.	_____
12 p.m.	_____	9 p.m.	_____
1 p.m.	_____	10 p.m.	_____

my training journal

my training log

SWIMMING WORKOUT:	*distance*
a.m.	
p.m.	
	total

BIKING WORKOUT:	*distance*
a.m.	
p.m.	
	total

RUNNING WORKOUT:	*distance*
a.m.	
p.m.	
	total

CROSS-TRAINING:	*time*
a.m.	
p.m.	
	total

TOMORROW'S To Do

ᐤ RUNALOG® FOR TRIATHLETES

TODAY'S DATE _____

MY LONG-TERM GOAL(S) _____

_____

TODAY'S MEAL PLAN	BREAKFAST	SNACK	LUNCH	SNACK	DINNER
	_____	_____	_____	_____	_____
	_____	_____	_____	_____	_____

weekly planner

	SUNDAY	MONDAY	TUESDAY	WEDNESDAY	THURSDAY	FRIDAY	SATURDAY	TOTAL
a.m.								
p.m.								

🕐 *daily planner*

5 a.m. _____	2 p.m. _____
6 a.m. _____	3 p.m. _____
7 a.m. _____	4 p.m. _____
8 a.m _____	5 p.m. _____
9 a.m. _____	6 p.m. _____
10 a.m. _____	7 p.m. _____
11 a.m. _____	8 p.m. _____
12 p.m. _____	9 p.m. _____
1 p.m. _____	10 p.m. _____

✍ *my training journal*

my training log

SWIMMING WORKOUT:	*distance*
a.m.	
p.m.	
	total

BIKING WORKOUT:	*distance*
a.m.	
p.m.	
	total

RUNNING WORKOUT:	*distance*
a.m.	
p.m.	
	total

CROSS-TRAINING:	*time*
a.m.	
p.m.	
	total

TOMORROW'S TO DO

✔RUNALOG® *For Triathletes*

TODAY'S DATE _____

MY LONG-TERM GOAL(S) _____

TODAY'S MEAL PLAN	BREAKFAST	SNACK	LUNCH	SNACK	DINNER
	_____	_____	_____	_____	_____
	_____	_____	_____	_____	_____

weekly planner

	SUNDAY	MONDAY	TUESDAY	WEDNESDAY	THURSDAY	FRIDAY	SATURDAY	TOTAL
a.m.								
p.m.								

🕐 *daily planner*

5 a.m. _____	2 p.m. _____
6 a.m. _____	3 p.m. _____
7 a.m. _____	4 p.m. _____
8 a.m _____	5 p.m. _____
9 a.m. _____	6 p.m. _____
10 a.m. _____	7 p.m. _____
11 a.m. _____	8 p.m. _____
12 p.m. _____	9 p.m. _____
1 p.m. _____	10 p.m. _____

✍ *my training journal*

my training log

SWIMMING WORKOUT: *distance*

a.m.	
p.m.	
	total

BIKING WORKOUT: *distance*

a.m.	
p.m.	
	total

RUNNING WORKOUT: *distance*

a.m.	
p.m.	
	total

CROSS-TRAINING: *time*

a.m.	
p.m.	
	total

TOMORROW'S TO DO

✔RUNALOG® For Triathletes

Today's Date _____

MY LONG-TERM GOAL(S) _____

_____

Today's Meal Plan	Breakfast	Snack	Lunch	Snack	Dinner
	_____	_____	_____	_____	_____
	_____	_____	_____	_____	_____

weekly planner

	SUNDAY	MONDAY	TUESDAY	WEDNESDAY	THURSDAY	FRIDAY	SATURDAY	TOTAL
a.m.								
p.m.								

🕐 *daily planner*

5 a.m. _____	2 p.m. _____
6 a.m. _____	3 p.m. _____
7 a.m. _____	4 p.m. _____
8 a.m _____	5 p.m. _____
9 a.m. _____	6 p.m. _____
10 a.m. _____	7 p.m. _____
11 a.m. _____	8 p.m. _____
12 p.m. _____	9 p.m. _____
1 p.m. _____	10 p.m. _____

✍ *my training journal*

my training log

SWIMMING WORKOUT: *distance*

a.m.	
p.m.	
	total

BIKING WORKOUT: *distance*

a.m.	
p.m.	
	total

RUNNING WORKOUT: *distance*

a.m.	
p.m.	
	total

CROSS-TRAINING: *time*

a.m.	
p.m.	
	total

Tomorrow's To Do

259

RUNALOG® FOR TRIATHLETES

TODAY'S DATE _____

MY LONG-TERM GOAL(S) _____

TODAY'S MEAL PLAN	BREAKFAST	SNACK	LUNCH	SNACK	DINNER
	_____	_____	_____	_____	_____

weekly planner

	SUNDAY	MONDAY	TUESDAY	WEDNESDAY	THURSDAY	FRIDAY	SATURDAY	TOTAL
a.m.								
p.m.								

daily planner

5 a.m.	_____	2 p.m.	_____
6 a.m.	_____	3 p.m.	_____
7 a.m.	_____	4 p.m.	_____
8 a.m	_____	5 p.m.	_____
9 a.m.	_____	6 p.m.	_____
10 a.m.	_____	7 p.m.	_____
11 a.m.	_____	8 p.m.	_____
12 p.m.	_____	9 p.m.	_____
1 p.m.	_____	10 p.m.	_____

my training journal

my training log

SWIMMING WORKOUT:	*distance*
a.m.	
p.m.	
	total

BIKING WORKOUT:	*distance*
a.m.	
p.m.	
	total

RUNNING WORKOUT:	*distance*
a.m.	
p.m.	
	total

CROSS-TRAINING:	*time*
a.m.	
p.m.	
	total

TOMORROW'S TO DO

ᐯRUNALOG® FOR TRIATHLETES

TODAY'S DATE _____

MY LONG-TERM GOAL(S) _____

_____

TODAY'S MEAL PLAN	BREAKFAST	SNACK	LUNCH	SNACK	DINNER
	_____	_____	_____	_____	_____
	_____	_____	_____	_____	_____

weekly planner

	SUNDAY	MONDAY	TUESDAY	WEDNESDAY	THURSDAY	FRIDAY	SATURDAY	TOTAL
a.m.								
p.m.								

🕐 daily planner

5 a.m. _____	2 p.m. _____
6 a.m. _____	3 p.m. _____
7 a.m. _____	4 p.m. _____
8 a.m _____	5 p.m. _____
9 a.m. _____	6 p.m. _____
10 a.m. _____	7 p.m. _____
11 a.m. _____	8 p.m. _____
12 p.m. _____	9 p.m. _____
1 p.m. _____	10 p.m. _____

✍ my training journal

my training log

SWIMMING WORKOUT:	*distance*
a.m.	
p.m.	
	total

BIKING WORKOUT:	*distance*
a.m.	
p.m.	
	total

RUNNING WORKOUT:	*distance*
a.m.	
p.m.	
	total

CROSS-TRAINING:	*time*
a.m.	
p.m.	
	total

TOMORROW'S TO DO

ᐱRUNALOG® *For Triathletes*

TODAY'S DATE _____

MY LONG-TERM GOAL(S) _____

TODAY'S MEAL PLAN	BREAKFAST	SNACK	LUNCH	SNACK	DINNER
	_____	_____	_____	_____	_____
	_____	_____	_____	_____	_____

weekly planner

SUNDAY	MONDAY	TUESDAY	WEDNESDAY	THURSDAY	FRIDAY	SATURDAY	TOTAL
a.m.							
p.m.							

🕐 *daily planner*

5 a.m. _____	2 p.m. _____
6 a.m. _____	3 p.m. _____
7 a.m. _____	4 p.m. _____
8 a.m _____	5 p.m. _____
9 a.m. _____	6 p.m. _____
10 a.m. _____	7 p.m. _____
11 a.m. _____	8 p.m. _____
12 p.m. _____	9 p.m. _____
1 p.m. _____	10 p.m. _____

☞ *my training journal*

my training log

SWIMMING WORKOUT: *distance*

a.m.	
p.m.	
	total

BIKING WORKOUT: *distance*

a.m.	
p.m.	
	total

RUNNING WORKOUT: *distance*

a.m.	
p.m.	
	total

CROSS-TRAINING: *time*

a.m.	
p.m.	
	total

TOMORROW'S To Do

⩒RUNALOG® FOR TRIATHLETES

TODAY'S DATE _____

MY LONG-TERM GOAL(S) _____

	BREAKFAST	SNACK	LUNCH	SNACK	DINNER
TODAY'S MEAL PLAN	_____	_____	_____	_____	_____
	_____	_____	_____	_____	_____

weekly planner

	SUNDAY	MONDAY	TUESDAY	WEDNESDAY	THURSDAY	FRIDAY	SATURDAY	TOTAL
a.m.								
p.m.								

🕐 *daily planner*

5 a.m. _____	2 p.m. _____
6 a.m. _____	3 p.m. _____
7 a.m. _____	4 p.m. _____
8 a.m _____	5 p.m. _____
9 a.m. _____	6 p.m. _____
10 a.m. _____	7 p.m. _____
11 a.m. _____	8 p.m. _____
12 p.m. _____	9 p.m. _____
1 p.m. _____	10 p.m. _____

✍ *my training journal*

my training log

SWIMMING WORKOUT:	*distance*
a.m.	
p.m.	
	total

BIKING WORKOUT:	*distance*
a.m.	
p.m.	
	total

RUNNING WORKOUT:	*distance*
a.m.	
p.m.	
	total

CROSS-TRAINING:	*time*
a.m.	
p.m.	
	total

TOMORROW'S TO DO

RUNALOG® FOR TRIATHLETES

TODAY'S DATE _____

MY LONG-TERM GOAL(S) _____

TODAY'S MEAL PLAN	BREAKFAST	SNACK	LUNCH	SNACK	DINNER
	_____	_____	_____	_____	_____
	_____	_____	_____	_____	_____

weekly planner

SUNDAY	MONDAY	TUESDAY	WEDNESDAY	THURSDAY	FRIDAY	SATURDAY	TOTAL
a.m.							
p.m.							

daily planner

5 a.m. _____	2 p.m. _____
6 a.m. _____	3 p.m. _____
7 a.m. _____	4 p.m. _____
8 a.m _____	5 p.m. _____
9 a.m. _____	6 p.m. _____
10 a.m. _____	7 p.m. _____
11 a.m. _____	8 p.m. _____
12 p.m. _____	9 p.m. _____
1 p.m. _____	10 p.m. _____

my training journal

my training log

SWIMMING WORKOUT:	*distance*
a.m.	
p.m.	
	total

BIKING WORKOUT:	*distance*
a.m.	
p.m.	
	total

RUNNING WORKOUT:	*distance*
a.m.	
p.m.	
	total

CROSS-TRAINING:	*time*
a.m.	
p.m.	
	total

TOMORROW's To Do

264

ᴠRUNALOG® FOR TRIATHLETES

TODAY'S DATE _____

MY LONG-TERM GOAL(S) _____

_____

TODAY'S MEAL PLAN	BREAKFAST	SNACK	LUNCH	SNACK	DINNER
	_____	_____	_____	_____	_____
	_____	_____	_____	_____	_____

weekly planner

	SUNDAY	MONDAY	TUESDAY	WEDNESDAY	THURSDAY	FRIDAY	SATURDAY	TOTAL
a.m.								
p.m.								

daily planner

5 a.m. _____	2 p.m. _____
6 a.m. _____	3 p.m. _____
7 a.m. _____	4 p.m. _____
8 a.m _____	5 p.m. _____
9 a.m. _____	6 p.m. _____
10 a.m. _____	7 p.m. _____
11 a.m. _____	8 p.m. _____
12 p.m. _____	9 p.m. _____
1 p.m. _____	10 p.m. _____

my training journal

my training log

SWIMMING WORKOUT:	*distance*
a.m.	
p.m.	
	total

BIKING WORKOUT:	*distance*
a.m.	
p.m.	
	total

RUNNING WORKOUT:	*distance*
a.m.	
p.m.	
	total

CROSS-TRAINING:	*time*
a.m.	
p.m.	
	total

TOMORROW'S To Do

265

√RUNALOG® FOR TRIATHLETES   TODAY'S DATE _____

MY LONG-TERM GOAL(S) _____
_____

TODAY'S MEAL PLAN	BREAKFAST	SNACK	LUNCH	SNACK	DINNER
	_____	_____	_____	_____	_____
	_____	_____	_____	_____	_____

weekly planner

	SUNDAY	MONDAY	TUESDAY	WEDNESDAY	THURSDAY	FRIDAY	SATURDAY	TOTAL
a.m.								
p.m.								

daily planner

5 a.m. _____	2 p.m. _____
6 a.m. _____	3 p.m. _____
7 a.m. _____	4 p.m. _____
8 a.m _____	5 p.m. _____
9 a.m. _____	6 p.m. _____
10 a.m. _____	7 p.m. _____
11 a.m. _____	8 p.m. _____
12 p.m. _____	9 p.m. _____
1 p.m. _____	10 p.m. _____

my training journal

my training log

SWIMMING WORKOUT:	*distance*
a.m.	
p.m.	
	total

BIKING WORKOUT:	*distance*
a.m.	
p.m.	
	total

RUNNING WORKOUT:	*distance*
a.m.	
p.m.	
	total

CROSS-TRAINING:	*time*
a.m.	
p.m.	
	total

TOMORROW'S TO DO

ᐱRUNALOG® FOR TRIATHLETES

TODAY'S DATE _____

MY LONG-TERM GOAL(S) _____
_____

TODAY'S MEAL PLAN	BREAKFAST	SNACK	LUNCH	SNACK	DINNER
	_____	_____	_____	_____	_____
	_____	_____	_____	_____	_____

weekly planner

	SUNDAY	MONDAY	TUESDAY	WEDNESDAY	THURSDAY	FRIDAY	SATURDAY	TOTAL
a.m.								
p.m.								

🕐 *daily planner*

5 a.m. _____		2 p.m. _____	
6 a.m. _____		3 p.m. _____	
7 a.m. _____		4 p.m. _____	
8 a.m _____		5 p.m. _____	
9 a.m. _____		6 p.m. _____	
10 a.m. _____		7 p.m. _____	
11 a.m. _____		8 p.m. _____	
12 p.m. _____		9 p.m. _____	
1 p.m. _____		10 p.m. _____	

✍ *my training journal*

my training log

SWIMMING WORKOUT:	*distance*
a.m.	
p.m.	
	total

🚴 BIKING WORKOUT:	*distance*
a.m.	
p.m.	
	total

🏃 RUNNING WORKOUT:	*distance*
a.m.	
p.m.	
	total

CROSS-TRAINING:	*time*
a.m.	
p.m.	
	total

TOMORROW'S TO DO

⩛RUNALOG® FOR TRIATHLETES

TODAY'S DATE _____

MY LONG-TERM GOAL(S) _____

TODAY'S MEAL PLAN	BREAKFAST	SNACK	LUNCH	SNACK	DINNER
	_____	_____	_____	_____	_____
	_____	_____	_____	_____	_____

weekly planner

	SUNDAY	MONDAY	TUESDAY	WEDNESDAY	THURSDAY	FRIDAY	SATURDAY	TOTAL
a.m.								
p.m.								

🕐 *daily planner*

5 a.m. _____		2 p.m. _____	
6 a.m. _____		3 p.m. _____	
7 a.m. _____		4 p.m. _____	
8 a.m _____		5 p.m. _____	
9 a.m. _____		6 p.m. _____	
10 a.m. _____		7 p.m. _____	
11 a.m. _____		8 p.m. _____	
12 p.m. _____		9 p.m. _____	
1 p.m. _____		10 p.m. _____	

✍ *my training journal*

my training log

SWIMMING WORKOUT:	*distance*
a.m.	
p.m.	
	total

BIKING WORKOUT:	*distance*
a.m.	
p.m.	
	total

RUNNING WORKOUT:	*distance*
a.m.	
p.m.	
	total

CROSS-TRAINING:	*time*
a.m.	
p.m.	
	total

TOMORROW'S To Do

TODAY'S DATE _____

MY LONG-TERM GOAL(S) _____
_____

TODAY'S MEAL PLAN	BREAKFAST	SNACK	LUNCH	SNACK	DINNER
	_____	_____	_____	_____	_____
	_____	_____	_____	_____	_____

weekly planner

	SUNDAY	MONDAY	TUESDAY	WEDNESDAY	THURSDAY	FRIDAY	SATURDAY	TOTAL
a.m.								
p.m.								

🕐 *daily planner*

5 a.m. _____	2 p.m. _____
6 a.m. _____	3 p.m. _____
7 a.m. _____	4 p.m. _____
8 a.m _____	5 p.m. _____
9 a.m. _____	6 p.m. _____
10 a.m. _____	7 p.m. _____
11 a.m. _____	8 p.m. _____
12 p.m. _____	9 p.m. _____
1 p.m. _____	10 p.m. _____

✍ *my training journal*

my training log

🏊 SWIMMING WORKOUT:	*distance*
a.m.	
p.m.	
	total

🚴 BIKING WORKOUT:	*distance*
a.m.	
p.m.	
	total

🏃 RUNNING WORKOUT:	*distance*
a.m.	
p.m.	
	total

CROSS-TRAINING:	*time*
a.m.	
p.m.	
	total

TOMORROW'S TO DO

⅋RUNALOG® FOR TRIATHLETES

TODAY'S DATE _____

MY LONG-TERM GOAL(S) _____

TODAY'S MEAL PLAN	BREAKFAST	SNACK	LUNCH	SNACK	DINNER
	_____	_____	_____	_____	_____
	_____	_____	_____	_____	_____

weekly planner

	SUNDAY	MONDAY	TUESDAY	WEDNESDAY	THURSDAY	FRIDAY	SATURDAY	TOTAL
a.m.								
p.m.								

daily planner

5 a.m. _____	2 p.m. _____
6 a.m. _____	3 p.m. _____
7 a.m. _____	4 p.m. _____
8 a.m _____	5 p.m. _____
9 a.m. _____	6 p.m. _____
10 a.m. _____	7 p.m. _____
11 a.m. _____	8 p.m. _____
12 p.m. _____	9 p.m. _____
1 p.m. _____	10 p.m. _____

my training journal

my training log

SWIMMING WORKOUT:	distance
a.m.	
p.m.	
	total

BIKING WORKOUT:	distance
a.m.	
p.m.	
	total

RUNNING WORKOUT:	distance
a.m.	
p.m.	
	total

CROSS-TRAINING:	time
a.m.	
p.m.	
	total

TOMORROW'S To Do

✓RUNALOG® FOR TRIATHLETES

TODAY'S DATE _____

MY LONG-TERM GOAL(S) _____

_____

TODAY'S MEAL PLAN	BREAKFAST	SNACK	LUNCH	SNACK	DINNER
	_____	_____	_____	_____	_____
	_____	_____	_____	_____	_____

weekly planner

	SUNDAY	MONDAY	TUESDAY	WEDNESDAY	THURSDAY	FRIDAY	SATURDAY	TOTAL
a.m.								
p.m.								

🕐 daily planner

5 a.m. _____	2 p.m. _____
6 a.m. _____	3 p.m. _____
7 a.m. _____	4 p.m. _____
8 a.m _____	5 p.m. _____
9 a.m. _____	6 p.m. _____
10 a.m. _____	7 p.m. _____
11 a.m. _____	8 p.m. _____
12 p.m. _____	9 p.m. _____
1 p.m. _____	10 p.m. _____

✍ my training journal

my training log

SWIMMING WORKOUT:	*distance*
a.m.	
p.m.	
	total

BIKING WORKOUT:	*distance*
a.m.	
p.m.	
	total

RUNNING WORKOUT:	*distance*
a.m.	
p.m.	
	total

CROSS-TRAINING:	*time*
a.m.	
p.m.	
	total

TOMORROW'S TO DO

271

RUNALOG® FOR TRIATHLETES   TODAY'S DATE _____

MY LONG-TERM GOAL(S) _____

TODAY'S MEAL PLAN	BREAKFAST	SNACK	LUNCH	SNACK	DINNER
	_____	_____	_____	_____	_____
	_____	_____	_____	_____	_____

weekly planner

	SUNDAY	MONDAY	TUESDAY	WEDNESDAY	THURSDAY	FRIDAY	SATURDAY	TOTAL
a.m.								
p.m.								

daily planner

5 a.m. _____	2 p.m. _____
6 a.m. _____	3 p.m. _____
7 a.m. _____	4 p.m. _____
8 a.m _____	5 p.m. _____
9 a.m. _____	6 p.m. _____
10 a.m. _____	7 p.m. _____
11 a.m. _____	8 p.m. _____
12 p.m. _____	9 p.m. _____
1 p.m. _____	10 p.m. _____

my training journal

my training log

SWIMMING WORKOUT:	distance
a.m.	
p.m.	
	total

BIKING WORKOUT:	distance
a.m.	
p.m.	
	total

RUNNING WORKOUT:	distance
a.m.	
p.m.	
	total

CROSS-TRAINING:	time
a.m.	
p.m.	
	total

TOMORROW'S TO DO

272

⩔RUNALOG® FOR TRIATHLETES

TODAY'S DATE _____

MY LONG-TERM GOAL(S) _____

_____

TODAY'S MEAL PLAN	BREAKFAST	SNACK	LUNCH	SNACK	DINNER
	_____	_____	_____	_____	_____
	_____	_____	_____	_____	_____

weekly planner

	SUNDAY	MONDAY	TUESDAY	WEDNESDAY	THURSDAY	FRIDAY	SATURDAY	TOTAL
a.m.								
p.m.								

daily planner

5 a.m. _____	2 p.m. _____
6 a.m. _____	3 p.m. _____
7 a.m. _____	4 p.m. _____
8 a.m _____	5 p.m. _____
9 a.m. _____	6 p.m. _____
10 a.m. _____	7 p.m. _____
11 a.m. _____	8 p.m. _____
12 p.m. _____	9 p.m. _____
1 p.m. _____	10 p.m. _____

my training journal

my training log

SWIMMING WORKOUT:	*distance*
a.m.	
p.m.	
	total

BIKING WORKOUT:	*distance*
a.m.	
p.m.	
	total

RUNNING WORKOUT:	*distance*
a.m.	
p.m.	
	total

CROSS-TRAINING:	*time*
a.m.	
p.m.	
	total

TOMORROW'S To Do

ᐯRUNALOG® *For Triathletes*

TODAY'S DATE _____

MY LONG-TERM GOAL(S) _____

TODAY'S MEAL PLAN	**BREAKFAST**	**SNACK**	**LUNCH**	**SNACK**	**DINNER**
	_____	_____	_____	_____	_____
	_____	_____	_____	_____	_____

weekly planner

	SUNDAY	MONDAY	TUESDAY	WEDNESDAY	THURSDAY	FRIDAY	SATURDAY	TOTAL
a.m.								
p.m.								

daily planner

5 a.m. _____	2 p.m. _____
6 a.m. _____	3 p.m. _____
7 a.m. _____	4 p.m. _____
8 a.m _____	5 p.m. _____
9 a.m. _____	6 p.m. _____
10 a.m. _____	7 p.m. _____
11 a.m. _____	8 p.m. _____
12 p.m. _____	9 p.m. _____
1 p.m. _____	10 p.m. _____

my training journal

my training log

SWIMMING WORKOUT:	*distance*
a.m.	
p.m.	
	total

BIKING WORKOUT:	*distance*
a.m.	
p.m.	
	total

RUNNING WORKOUT:	*distance*
a.m.	
p.m.	
	total

CROSS-TRAINING:	*time*
a.m.	
p.m.	
	total

TOMORROW'S TO DO

ᐯRUNALOG® FOR TRIATHLETES

TODAY'S DATE _____

MY LONG-TERM GOAL(S) _____

_____

TODAY'S MEAL PLAN	BREAKFAST	SNACK	LUNCH	SNACK	DINNER
	_____	_____	_____	_____	_____
	_____	_____	_____	_____	_____

weekly planner

	SUNDAY	MONDAY	TUESDAY	WEDNESDAY	THURSDAY	FRIDAY	SATURDAY	TOTAL
a.m.								
p.m.								

daily planner

5 a.m. _____	2 p.m. _____
6 a.m. _____	3 p.m. _____
7 a.m. _____	4 p.m. _____
8 a.m _____	5 p.m. _____
9 a.m. _____	6 p.m. _____
10 a.m. _____	7 p.m. _____
11 a.m. _____	8 p.m. _____
12 p.m. _____	9 p.m. _____
1 p.m. _____	10 p.m. _____

my training journal

my training log

SWIMMING WORKOUT:	*distance*
a.m.	
p.m.	
	total

BIKING WORKOUT:	*distance*
a.m.	
p.m.	
	total

RUNNING WORKOUT:	*distance*
a.m.	
p.m.	
	total

CROSS-TRAINING:	*time*
a.m.	
p.m.	
	total

TOMORROW'S To Do

√RUNALOG® FOR TRIATHLETES

TODAY'S DATE _____

MY LONG-TERM GOAL(S) _____

TODAY'S MEAL PLAN	BREAKFAST	SNACK	LUNCH	SNACK	DINNER
	_____	_____	_____	_____	_____
	_____	_____	_____	_____	_____

weekly planner

SUNDAY	MONDAY	TUESDAY	WEDNESDAY	THURSDAY	FRIDAY	SATURDAY	TOTAL
a.m.							
p.m.							

daily planner

5 a.m. _____	2 p.m. _____
6 a.m. _____	3 p.m. _____
7 a.m. _____	4 p.m. _____
8 a.m _____	5 p.m. _____
9 a.m. _____	6 p.m. _____
10 a.m. _____	7 p.m. _____
11 a.m. _____	8 p.m. _____
12 p.m. _____	9 p.m. _____
1 p.m. _____	10 p.m. _____

my training journal

my training log

SWIMMING WORKOUT:	*distance*
a.m.	
p.m.	
	total

BIKING WORKOUT:	*distance*
a.m.	
p.m.	
	total

RUNNING WORKOUT:	*distance*
a.m.	
p.m.	
	total

CROSS-TRAINING:	*time*
a.m.	
p.m.	
	total

TOMORROW'S TO DO

√RUNALOG° *FOR TRIATHLETES*   TODAY'S DATE _____

MY LONG-TERM GOAL(S) _____
_____

TODAY'S MEAL PLAN	BREAKFAST	SNACK	LUNCH	SNACK	DINNER
	_____	_____	_____	_____	_____
	_____	_____	_____	_____	_____

weekly planner

	SUNDAY	MONDAY	TUESDAY	WEDNESDAY	THURSDAY	FRIDAY	SATURDAY	TOTAL
a.m.								
p.m.								

daily planner

5 a.m. _____	2 p.m. _____
6 a.m. _____	3 p.m. _____
7 a.m. _____	4 p.m. _____
8 a.m _____	5 p.m. _____
9 a.m. _____	6 p.m. _____
10 a.m. _____	7 p.m. _____
11 a.m. _____	8 p.m. _____
12 p.m. _____	9 p.m. _____
1 p.m. _____	10 p.m. _____

my training journal

my training log

SWIMMING WORKOUT: *distance*

a.m.

p.m.

total

BIKING WORKOUT: *distance*

a.m.

p.m.

total

RUNNING WORKOUT: *distance*

a.m.

p.m.

total

CROSS-TRAINING: *time*

a.m.

p.m.

total

TOMORROW'S To Do

277

√RUNALOG° FOR TRIATHLETES

TODAY'S DATE _____

MY LONG-TERM GOAL(S) _____

TODAY'S MEAL PLAN	BREAKFAST	SNACK	LUNCH	SNACK	DINNER
	_____	_____	_____	_____	_____
	_____	_____	_____	_____	_____

weekly planner

	SUNDAY	MONDAY	TUESDAY	WEDNESDAY	THURSDAY	FRIDAY	SATURDAY	TOTAL
a.m.								
p.m.								

daily planner

5 a.m. _____	2 p.m. _____
6 a.m. _____	3 p.m. _____
7 a.m. _____	4 p.m. _____
8 a.m _____	5 p.m. _____
9 a.m. _____	6 p.m. _____
10 a.m. _____	7 p.m. _____
11 a.m. _____	8 p.m. _____
12 p.m. _____	9 p.m. _____
1 p.m. _____	10 p.m. _____

my training journal

my training log

SWIMMING WORKOUT:	*distance*
a.m.	
p.m.	
	total

BIKING WORKOUT:	*distance*
a.m.	
p.m.	
	total

RUNNING WORKOUT:	*distance*
a.m.	
p.m.	
	total

CROSS-TRAINING:	*time*
a.m.	
p.m.	
	total

TOMORROW'S To Do

TODAY'S DATE _____

MY LONG-TERM GOAL(S) _____

_____

TODAY'S MEAL PLAN	BREAKFAST	SNACK	LUNCH	SNACK	DINNER
	_____	_____	_____	_____	_____
	_____	_____	_____	_____	_____

weekly planner

	SUNDAY	MONDAY	TUESDAY	WEDNESDAY	THURSDAY	FRIDAY	SATURDAY	TOTAL
a.m.								
p.m.								

daily planner

5 a.m. _____	2 p.m. _____
6 a.m. _____	3 p.m. _____
7 a.m. _____	4 p.m. _____
8 a.m _____	5 p.m. _____
9 a.m. _____	6 p.m. _____
10 a.m. _____	7 p.m. _____
11 a.m. _____	8 p.m. _____
12 p.m. _____	9 p.m. _____
1 p.m. _____	10 p.m. _____

my training journal

my training log

SWIMMING WORKOUT:	*distance*
a.m.	
p.m.	
	total

BIKING WORKOUT:	*distance*
a.m.	
p.m.	
	total

RUNNING WORKOUT:	*distance*
a.m.	
p.m.	
	total

CROSS-TRAINING:	*time*
a.m.	
p.m.	
	total

TOMORROW'S TO DO

ᛏRUNALOG° *FOR TRIATHLETES*

TODAY'S DATE _____

MY LONG-TERM GOAL(S) _____

_____

TODAY'S MEAL PLAN	BREAKFAST	SNACK	LUNCH	SNACK	DINNER
	_____	_____	_____	_____	_____
	_____	_____	_____	_____	_____

weekly planner

	SUNDAY	MONDAY	TUESDAY	WEDNESDAY	THURSDAY	FRIDAY	SATURDAY	TOTAL
a.m.								
p.m.								

🕐 *daily planner*

5 a.m. _____	2 p.m. _____
6 a.m. _____	3 p.m. _____
7 a.m. _____	4 p.m. _____
8 a.m _____	5 p.m. _____
9 a.m. _____	6 p.m. _____
10 a.m. _____	7 p.m. _____
11 a.m. _____	8 p.m. _____
12 p.m. _____	9 p.m. _____
1 p.m. _____	10 p.m. _____

🖎 *my training journal*

my training log

SWIMMING WORKOUT: *distance*

a.m.		
p.m.		
		total

BIKING WORKOUT: *distance*

a.m.		
p.m.		
		total

RUNNING WORKOUT: *distance*

a.m.		
p.m.		
		total

CROSS-TRAINING: *time*

a.m.		
p.m.		
		total

TOMORROW'S To Do

√RUNALOG® FOR TRIATHLETES   TODAY'S DATE _____

MY LONG-TERM GOAL(S) _____
_____

TODAY'S MEAL PLAN	BREAKFAST	SNACK	LUNCH	SNACK	DINNER
	_____	_____	_____	_____	_____
	_____	_____	_____	_____	_____

weekly planner

	SUNDAY	MONDAY	TUESDAY	WEDNESDAY	THURSDAY	FRIDAY	SATURDAY	TOTAL
a.m.								
p.m.								

daily planner

5 a.m. _____	2 p.m. _____
6 a.m. _____	3 p.m. _____
7 a.m. _____	4 p.m. _____
8 a.m _____	5 p.m. _____
9 a.m. _____	6 p.m. _____
10 a.m. _____	7 p.m. _____
11 a.m. _____	8 p.m. _____
12 p.m. _____	9 p.m. _____
1 p.m. _____	10 p.m. _____

my training journal

my training log

SWIMMING WORKOUT:	distance
a.m.	
p.m.	
	total

BIKING WORKOUT:	distance
a.m.	
p.m.	
	total

RUNNING WORKOUT:	distance
a.m.	
p.m.	
	total

CROSS-TRAINING:	time
a.m.	
p.m.	
	total

TOMORROW'S TO DO

√RUNALOG° *For Triathletes*   TODAY'S DATE _____

MY LONG-TERM GOAL(S) _____

TODAY'S MEAL PLAN	BREAKFAST	SNACK	LUNCH	SNACK	DINNER
	_____	_____	_____	_____	_____
	_____	_____	_____	_____	_____

weekly planner

	SUNDAY	MONDAY	TUESDAY	WEDNESDAY	THURSDAY	FRIDAY	SATURDAY	TOTAL
a.m.								
p.m.								

daily planner

5 a.m. _____	2 p.m. _____
6 a.m. _____	3 p.m. _____
7 a.m. _____	4 p.m. _____
8 a.m _____	5 p.m. _____
9 a.m. _____	6 p.m. _____
10 a.m. _____	7 p.m. _____
11 a.m. _____	8 p.m. _____
12 p.m. _____	9 p.m. _____
1 p.m. _____	10 p.m. _____

my training journal

my training log

SWIMMING WORKOUT: *distance*

a.m.	
p.m.	
	total

BIKING WORKOUT: *distance*

a.m.	
p.m.	
	total

RUNNING WORKOUT: *distance*

a.m.	
p.m.	
	total

CROSS-TRAINING: *time*

a.m.	
p.m.	
	total

TOMORROW'S To Do

MY LONG-TERM GOAL(S) _____

TODAY'S **MEAL** **PLAN**	**BREAKFAST**	**SNACK**	**LUNCH**	**SNACK**	**DINNER**
	_____	_____	_____	_____	_____

weekly planner

	SUNDAY	MONDAY	TUESDAY	WEDNESDAY	THURSDAY	FRIDAY	SATURDAY	TOTAL
a.m.								
p.m.								

🕐 *daily planner*

5 a.m. _____	2 p.m. _____
6 a.m. _____	3 p.m. _____
7 a.m. _____	4 p.m. _____
8 a.m _____	5 p.m. _____
9 a.m. _____	6 p.m. _____
10 a.m. _____	7 p.m. _____
11 a.m. _____	8 p.m. _____
12 p.m. _____	9 p.m. _____
1 p.m. _____	10 p.m. _____

✍ *my training journal*

my training log

🏊 SWIMMING WORKOUT:	*distance*
a.m.	
p.m.	
	total

🚴 BIKING WORKOUT:	*distance*
a.m.	
p.m.	
	total

🏃 RUNNING WORKOUT:	*distance*
a.m.	
p.m.	
	total

CROSS-TRAINING:	*time*
a.m.	
p.m.	
	total

TOMORROW'S TO DO

RUNALOG® FOR TRIATHLETES

TODAY'S DATE _____

MY LONG-TERM GOAL(S) _____

_____

TODAY'S MEAL PLAN	BREAKFAST	SNACK	LUNCH	SNACK	DINNER
	_____	_____	_____	_____	_____
	_____	_____	_____	_____	_____

weekly planner

SUNDAY	MONDAY	TUESDAY	WEDNESDAY	THURSDAY	FRIDAY	SATURDAY	TOTAL
a.m.							
p.m.							

daily planner

5 a.m. _____	2 p.m. _____
6 a.m. _____	3 p.m. _____
7 a.m. _____	4 p.m. _____
8 a.m _____	5 p.m. _____
9 a.m. _____	6 p.m. _____
10 a.m. _____	7 p.m. _____
11 a.m. _____	8 p.m. _____
12 p.m. _____	9 p.m. _____
1 p.m. _____	10 p.m. _____

my training journal

my training log

SWIMMING WORKOUT: *distance*

a.m.	
p.m.	
	total

BIKING WORKOUT: *distance*

a.m.	
p.m.	
	total

RUNNING WORKOUT: *distance*

a.m.	
p.m.	
	total

CROSS-TRAINING: *time*

a.m.	
p.m.	
	total

Tomorrow's To Do

√RUNALOG® FOR TRIATHLETES

TODAY'S DATE _____

MY LONG-TERM GOAL(S) _____

TODAY'S MEAL PLAN	BREAKFAST	SNACK	LUNCH	SNACK	DINNER
	_____	_____	_____	_____	_____

weekly planner

	SUNDAY	MONDAY	TUESDAY	WEDNESDAY	THURSDAY	FRIDAY	SATURDAY	TOTAL
a.m.								
p.m.								

daily planner

5 a.m. _____	2 p.m. _____
6 a.m. _____	3 p.m. _____
7 a.m. _____	4 p.m. _____
8 a.m _____	5 p.m. _____
9 a.m. _____	6 p.m. _____
10 a.m. _____	7 p.m. _____
11 a.m. _____	8 p.m. _____
12 p.m. _____	9 p.m. _____
1 p.m. _____	10 p.m. _____

my training journal

my training log

SWIMMING WORKOUT:	distance
a.m.	
p.m.	
	total

BIKING WORKOUT:	distance
a.m.	
p.m.	
	total

RUNNING WORKOUT:	distance
a.m.	
p.m.	
	total

CROSS-TRAINING:	time
a.m.	
p.m.	
	total

TOMORROW'S To Do

✓RUNALOG® *FOR TRIATHLETES*

TODAY'S DATE _____

MY LONG-TERM GOAL(S) _____

_____

TODAY'S MEAL PLAN	BREAKFAST	SNACK	LUNCH	SNACK	DINNER
	_____	_____	_____	_____	_____
	_____	_____	_____	_____	_____

weekly planner

SUNDAY	MONDAY	TUESDAY	WEDNESDAY	THURSDAY	FRIDAY	SATURDAY	TOTAL
a.m.							
p.m.							

🕐 *daily planner*

5 a.m. _____	2 p.m. _____
6 a.m. _____	3 p.m. _____
7 a.m. _____	4 p.m. _____
8 a.m _____	5 p.m. _____
9 a.m. _____	6 p.m. _____
10 a.m. _____	7 p.m. _____
11 a.m. _____	8 p.m. _____
12 p.m. _____	9 p.m. _____
1 p.m. _____	10 p.m. _____

✍ *my training journal*

my training log

SWIMMING WORKOUT: *distance*

a.m.	
p.m.	
	total

BIKING WORKOUT: *distance*

a.m.	
p.m.	
	total

RUNNING WORKOUT: *distance*

a.m.	
p.m.	
	total

CROSS-TRAINING: *time*

a.m.	
p.m.	
	total

TOMORROW'S TO DO

286

√RUNALOG® FOR TRIATHLETES

TODAY'S DATE _____

MY LONG-TERM GOAL(S) _____

_____

TODAY'S MEAL PLAN	BREAKFAST	SNACK	LUNCH	SNACK	DINNER
	_____	_____	_____	_____	_____
	_____	_____	_____	_____	_____

weekly planner

	SUNDAY	MONDAY	TUESDAY	WEDNESDAY	THURSDAY	FRIDAY	SATURDAY	TOTAL
a.m.								
p.m.								

daily planner

5 a.m. _____	2 p.m. _____
6 a.m. _____	3 p.m. _____
7 a.m. _____	4 p.m. _____
8 a.m _____	5 p.m. _____
9 a.m. _____	6 p.m. _____
10 a.m. _____	7 p.m. _____
11 a.m. _____	8 p.m. _____
12 p.m. _____	9 p.m. _____
1 p.m. _____	10 p.m. _____

my training journal

my training log

SWIMMING WORKOUT:	distance
a.m.	
p.m.	
	total

BIKING WORKOUT:	distance
a.m.	
p.m.	
	total

RUNNING WORKOUT:	distance
a.m.	
p.m.	
	total

CROSS-TRAINING:	time
a.m.	
p.m.	
	total

TOMORROW'S TO DO

© 2009 www.RUNALOGS.com

287

RUNALOG® FOR TRIATHLETES

TODAY'S DATE _____

MY LONG-TERM GOAL(S) _____

_____

TODAY'S MEAL PLAN	BREAKFAST	SNACK	LUNCH	SNACK	DINNER
	_____	_____	_____	_____	_____
	_____	_____	_____	_____	_____

weekly planner

	SUNDAY	MONDAY	TUESDAY	WEDNESDAY	THURSDAY	FRIDAY	SATURDAY	TOTAL
a.m.								
p.m.								

daily planner

5 a.m. _____	2 p.m. _____
6 a.m. _____	3 p.m. _____
7 a.m. _____	4 p.m. _____
8 a.m _____	5 p.m. _____
9 a.m. _____	6 p.m. _____
10 a.m. _____	7 p.m. _____
11 a.m. _____	8 p.m. _____
12 p.m. _____	9 p.m. _____
1 p.m. _____	10 p.m. _____

my training journal

my training log

SWIMMING WORKOUT:	distance
a.m.	
p.m.	
	total

BIKING WORKOUT:	distance
a.m.	
p.m.	
	total

RUNNING WORKOUT:	distance
a.m.	
p.m.	
	total

CROSS-TRAINING:	time
a.m.	
p.m.	
	total

TOMORROW'S To Do

RUNALOG® FOR TRIATHLETES

TODAY'S DATE _____

MY LONG-TERM GOAL(S) _____
_____

TODAY'S MEAL PLAN	BREAKFAST	SNACK	LUNCH	SNACK	DINNER
	_____	_____	_____	_____	_____
	_____	_____	_____	_____	_____

weekly planner

	SUNDAY	MONDAY	TUESDAY	WEDNESDAY	THURSDAY	FRIDAY	SATURDAY	TOTAL
a.m.								
p.m.								

daily planner

5 a.m.	_____	2 p.m.	_____
6 a.m.	_____	3 p.m.	_____
7 a.m.	_____	4 p.m.	_____
8 a.m	_____	5 p.m.	_____
9 a.m.	_____	6 p.m.	_____
10 a.m.	_____	7 p.m.	_____
11 a.m.	_____	8 p.m.	_____
12 p.m.	_____	9 p.m.	_____
1 p.m.	_____	10 p.m.	_____

my training journal

my training log

SWIMMING WORKOUT:	distance
a.m.	
p.m.	
	total

BIKING WORKOUT:	distance
a.m.	
p.m.	
	total

RUNNING WORKOUT:	distance
a.m.	
p.m.	
	total

CROSS-TRAINING:	time
a.m.	
p.m.	
	total

TOMORROW'S TO DO

⩗RUNALOG® FOR TRIATHLETES

TODAY'S DATE _____

MY LONG-TERM GOAL(S) _____

_____

TODAY'S MEAL PLAN	BREAKFAST	SNACK	LUNCH	SNACK	DINNER
	_____	_____	_____	_____	_____

weekly planner

	SUNDAY	MONDAY	TUESDAY	WEDNESDAY	THURSDAY	FRIDAY	SATURDAY	TOTAL
a.m.								
p.m.								

daily planner

5 a.m. _____	2 p.m. _____
6 a.m. _____	3 p.m. _____
7 a.m. _____	4 p.m. _____
8 a.m _____	5 p.m. _____
9 a.m. _____	6 p.m. _____
10 a.m. _____	7 p.m. _____
11 a.m. _____	8 p.m. _____
12 p.m. _____	9 p.m. _____
1 p.m. _____	10 p.m. _____

my training journal

my training log

SWIMMING WORKOUT:	distance
a.m.	
p.m.	
	total

BIKING WORKOUT:	distance
a.m.	
p.m.	
	total

RUNNING WORKOUT:	distance
a.m.	
p.m.	
	total

CROSS-TRAINING:	time
a.m.	
p.m.	
	total

TOMORROW'S TO DO

√RUNALOG® FOR TRIATHLETES

TODAY'S DATE _____

MY LONG-TERM GOAL(S) _____

TODAY'S MEAL PLAN	BREAKFAST	SNACK	LUNCH	SNACK	DINNER
	_____	_____	_____	_____	_____

weekly planner

	SUNDAY	MONDAY	TUESDAY	WEDNESDAY	THURSDAY	FRIDAY	SATURDAY	TOTAL
a.m.								
p.m.								

daily planner

5 a.m. _____	2 p.m. _____
6 a.m. _____	3 p.m. _____
7 a.m. _____	4 p.m. _____
8 a.m _____	5 p.m. _____
9 a.m. _____	6 p.m. _____
10 a.m. _____	7 p.m. _____
11 a.m. _____	8 p.m. _____
12 p.m. _____	9 p.m. _____
1 p.m. _____	10 p.m. _____

my training journal

my training log

SWIMMING WORKOUT:	*distance*
a.m.	
p.m.	
	total

BIKING WORKOUT:	*distance*
a.m.	
p.m.	
	total

RUNNING WORKOUT:	*distance*
a.m.	
p.m.	
	total

CROSS-TRAINING:	*time*
a.m.	
p.m.	
	total

TOMORROW'S TO DO

√RUNALOG® FOR TRIATHLETES

TODAY'S DATE _____

MY LONG-TERM GOAL(S) _____

_____

TODAY'S MEAL PLAN	BREAKFAST	SNACK	LUNCH	SNACK	DINNER
	_____	_____	_____	_____	_____
	_____	_____	_____	_____	_____

weekly planner

	SUNDAY	MONDAY	TUESDAY	WEDNESDAY	THURSDAY	FRIDAY	SATURDAY	TOTAL
a.m.								
p.m.								

daily planner

5 a.m. _____	2 p.m. _____
6 a.m. _____	3 p.m. _____
7 a.m. _____	4 p.m. _____
8 a.m _____	5 p.m. _____
9 a.m. _____	6 p.m. _____
10 a.m. _____	7 p.m. _____
11 a.m. _____	8 p.m. _____
12 p.m. _____	9 p.m. _____
1 p.m. _____	10 p.m. _____

my training journal

my training log

SWIMMING WORKOUT: *distance*

a.m.		
p.m.		
		total

BIKING WORKOUT: *distance*

a.m.		
p.m.		
		total

RUNNING WORKOUT: *distance*

a.m.		
p.m.		
		total

CROSS-TRAINING: *time*

a.m.		
p.m.		
		total

TOMORROW'S TO DO

√RUNALOG® FOR TRIATHLETES

TODAY'S DATE _____

MY LONG-TERM GOAL(S) _____

TODAY'S MEAL PLAN	BREAKFAST	SNACK	LUNCH	SNACK	DINNER
	_____	_____	_____	_____	_____
	_____	_____	_____	_____	_____

weekly planner

	SUNDAY	MONDAY	TUESDAY	WEDNESDAY	THURSDAY	FRIDAY	SATURDAY	TOTAL
a.m.								
p.m.								

daily planner

5 a.m. _____	2 p.m. _____
6 a.m. _____	3 p.m. _____
7 a.m. _____	4 p.m. _____
8 a.m _____	5 p.m. _____
9 a.m. _____	6 p.m. _____
10 a.m. _____	7 p.m. _____
11 a.m. _____	8 p.m. _____
12 p.m. _____	9 p.m. _____
1 p.m. _____	10 p.m. _____

my training journal

my training log

SWIMMING WORKOUT:	*distance*
a.m.	
p.m.	
	total

BIKING WORKOUT:	*distance*
a.m.	
p.m.	
	total

RUNNING WORKOUT:	*distance*
a.m.	
p.m.	
	total

CROSS-TRAINING:	*time*
a.m.	
p.m.	
	total

TOMORROW'S To Do

RUNALOG® FOR TRIATHLETES

TODAY'S DATE _____

MY LONG-TERM GOAL(S) _____

TODAY'S MEAL PLAN	BREAKFAST	SNACK	LUNCH	SNACK	DINNER
	_____	_____	_____	_____	_____
	_____	_____	_____	_____	_____

weekly planner

	SUNDAY	MONDAY	TUESDAY	WEDNESDAY	THURSDAY	FRIDAY	SATURDAY	TOTAL
a.m.								
p.m.								

daily planner

5 a.m. _____		2 p.m. _____	
6 a.m. _____		3 p.m. _____	
7 a.m. _____		4 p.m. _____	
8 a.m _____		5 p.m. _____	
9 a.m. _____		6 p.m. _____	
10 a.m. _____		7 p.m. _____	
11 a.m. _____		8 p.m. _____	
12 p.m. _____		9 p.m. _____	
1 p.m. _____		10 p.m. _____	

my training journal

my training log

SWIMMING WORKOUT:	*distance*
a.m.	
p.m.	
	total

BIKING WORKOUT:	*distance*
a.m.	
p.m.	
	total

RUNNING WORKOUT:	*distance*
a.m.	
p.m.	
	total

CROSS-TRAINING:	*time*
a.m.	
p.m.	
	total

TOMORROW'S To Do

ⱽRUNALOG® FOR TRIATHLETES

TODAY'S DATE _____

MY LONG-TERM GOAL(S) _____

TODAY'S MEAL PLAN	BREAKFAST	SNACK	LUNCH	SNACK	DINNER
	_____	_____	_____	_____	_____
	_____	_____	_____	_____	_____

weekly planner

	SUNDAY	MONDAY	TUESDAY	WEDNESDAY	THURSDAY	FRIDAY	SATURDAY	TOTAL
a.m.								
p.m.								

🕐 daily planner

5 a.m. _____	2 p.m. _____
6 a.m. _____	3 p.m. _____
7 a.m. _____	4 p.m. _____
8 a.m _____	5 p.m. _____
9 a.m. _____	6 p.m. _____
10 a.m. _____	7 p.m. _____
11 a.m. _____	8 p.m. _____
12 p.m. _____	9 p.m. _____
1 p.m. _____	10 p.m. _____

✍ my training journal

my training log

SWIMMING WORKOUT:	distance
a.m.	
p.m.	
	total

BIKING WORKOUT:	distance
a.m.	
p.m.	
	total

RUNNING WORKOUT:	distance
a.m.	
p.m.	
	total

CROSS-TRAINING:	time
a.m.	
p.m.	
	total

TOMORROW'S To Do

295

RUNALOG® FOR TRIATHLETES   TODAY'S DATE _____

MY LONG-TERM GOAL(S) _____

TODAY'S MEAL PLAN	BREAKFAST	SNACK	LUNCH	SNACK	DINNER

weekly planner

	SUNDAY	MONDAY	TUESDAY	WEDNESDAY	THURSDAY	FRIDAY	SATURDAY	TOTAL
a.m.								
p.m.								

daily planner

5 a.m. _____	2 p.m. _____
6 a.m. _____	3 p.m. _____
7 a.m. _____	4 p.m. _____
8 a.m _____	5 p.m. _____
9 a.m. _____	6 p.m. _____
10 a.m. _____	7 p.m. _____
11 a.m. _____	8 p.m. _____
12 p.m. _____	9 p.m. _____
1 p.m. _____	10 p.m. _____

my training journal

my training log

SWIMMING WORKOUT:	*distance*
a.m.	
p.m.	
	total

BIKING WORKOUT:	*distance*
a.m.	
p.m.	
	total

RUNNING WORKOUT:	*distance*
a.m.	
p.m.	
	total

CROSS-TRAINING:	*time*
a.m.	
p.m.	
	total

TOMORROW'S TO DO

√RUNALOG° FOR TRIATHLETES   TODAY'S DATE _____

MY LONG-TERM GOAL(S) _____
_____

TODAY'S MEAL PLAN	BREAKFAST	SNACK	LUNCH	SNACK	DINNER
	_____	_____	_____	_____	_____
	_____	_____	_____	_____	_____

weekly planner

	SUNDAY	MONDAY	TUESDAY	WEDNESDAY	THURSDAY	FRIDAY	SATURDAY	TOTAL
a.m.								
p.m.								

daily planner

5 a.m. _____	2 p.m. _____
6 a.m. _____	3 p.m. _____
7 a.m. _____	4 p.m. _____
8 a.m _____	5 p.m. _____
9 a.m. _____	6 p.m. _____
10 a.m. _____	7 p.m. _____
11 a.m. _____	8 p.m. _____
12 p.m. _____	9 p.m. _____
1 p.m. _____	10 p.m. _____

my training journal

my training log

SWIMMING WORKOUT:	*distance*
a.m.	
p.m.	
	total

BIKING WORKOUT:	*distance*
a.m.	
p.m.	
	total

RUNNING WORKOUT:	*distance*
a.m.	
p.m.	
	total

CROSS-TRAINING:	*time*
a.m.	
p.m.	
	total

TOMORROW'S TO DO

√RUNALOG® *For Triathletes*   TODAY'S DATE _____

MY LONG-TERM GOAL(S) _____

TODAY'S MEAL PLAN	BREAKFAST	SNACK	LUNCH	SNACK	DINNER
	_____	_____	_____	_____	_____
	_____	_____	_____	_____	_____

weekly planner

SUNDAY	MONDAY	TUESDAY	WEDNESDAY	THURSDAY	FRIDAY	SATURDAY	TOTAL
a.m.							
p.m.							

daily planner

5 a.m.	_____	2 p.m.	_____
6 a.m.	_____	3 p.m.	_____
7 a.m.	_____	4 p.m.	_____
8 a.m	_____	5 p.m.	_____
9 a.m.	_____	6 p.m.	_____
10 a.m.	_____	7 p.m.	_____
11 a.m.	_____	8 p.m.	_____
12 p.m.	_____	9 p.m.	_____
1 p.m.	_____	10 p.m.	_____

my training journal

my training log

SWIMMING WORKOUT:	*distance*
a.m.	
p.m.	
	total

BIKING WORKOUT:	*distance*
a.m.	
p.m.	
	total

RUNNING WORKOUT:	*distance*
a.m.	
p.m.	
	total

CROSS-TRAINING:	*time*
a.m.	
p.m.	
	total

TOMORROW'S To Do

MY LONG-TERM GOAL(S) _____
_____

TODAY'S MEAL PLAN	BREAKFAST	SNACK	LUNCH	SNACK	DINNER
	_____	_____	_____	_____	_____
	_____	_____	_____	_____	_____

weekly planner

	SUNDAY	MONDAY	TUESDAY	WEDNESDAY	THURSDAY	FRIDAY	SATURDAY	TOTAL
a.m.								
p.m.								

daily planner

5 a.m. _____	2 p.m. _____
6 a.m. _____	3 p.m. _____
7 a.m. _____	4 p.m. _____
8 a.m _____	5 p.m. _____
9 a.m. _____	6 p.m. _____
10 a.m. _____	7 p.m. _____
11 a.m. _____	8 p.m. _____
12 p.m. _____	9 p.m. _____
1 p.m. _____	10 p.m. _____

my training journal

my training log

SWIMMING WORKOUT:	distance
a.m.	
p.m.	
	total

BIKING WORKOUT:	distance
a.m.	
p.m.	
	total

RUNNING WORKOUT:	distance
a.m.	
p.m.	
	total

CROSS-TRAINING:	time
a.m.	
p.m.	
	total

TOMORROW'S To Do

ᵛRUNALOG® *For Triathletes*

Today's Date _____

MY LONG-TERM GOAL(S) _____
_____

Today's Meal Plan	Breakfast	Snack	Lunch	Snack	Dinner
	_____	_____	_____	_____	_____
	_____	_____	_____	_____	_____

weekly planner

SUNDAY	MONDAY	TUESDAY	WEDNESDAY	THURSDAY	FRIDAY	SATURDAY	TOTAL
a.m.							
p.m.							

daily planner

5 a.m. ____	2 p.m. ____
6 a.m. ____	3 p.m. ____
7 a.m. ____	4 p.m. ____
8 a.m ____	5 p.m. ____
9 a.m. ____	6 p.m. ____
10 a.m. ____	7 p.m. ____
11 a.m. ____	8 p.m. ____
12 p.m. ____	9 p.m. ____
1 p.m. ____	10 p.m. ____

my training journal

my training log

SWIMMING WORKOUT:	*distance*
a.m.	
p.m.	
	total

BIKING WORKOUT:	*distance*
a.m.	
p.m.	
	total

RUNNING WORKOUT:	*distance*
a.m.	
p.m.	
	total

CROSS-TRAINING:	*time*
a.m.	
p.m.	
	total

TOMORROW'S TO DO

√RUNALOG® FOR TRIATHLETES

TODAY'S DATE _____

MY LONG-TERM GOAL(S) _____

TODAY'S MEAL PLAN	BREAKFAST	SNACK	LUNCH	SNACK	DINNER
	_____	_____	_____	_____	_____
	_____	_____	_____	_____	_____

weekly planner

	SUNDAY	MONDAY	TUESDAY	WEDNESDAY	THURSDAY	FRIDAY	SATURDAY	TOTAL
a.m.								
p.m.								

daily planner

5 a.m. _____	2 p.m. _____
6 a.m. _____	3 p.m. _____
7 a.m. _____	4 p.m. _____
8 a.m _____	5 p.m. _____
9 a.m. _____	6 p.m. _____
10 a.m. _____	7 p.m. _____
11 a.m. _____	8 p.m. _____
12 p.m. _____	9 p.m. _____
1 p.m. _____	10 p.m. _____

my training journal

my training log

SWIMMING WORKOUT: distance

a.m.		
p.m.		
		total

BIKING WORKOUT: distance

a.m.		
p.m.		
		total

RUNNING WORKOUT: distance

a.m.		
p.m.		
		total

CROSS-TRAINING: time

a.m.		
p.m.		
		total

TOMORROW'S To Do

MY LONG-TERM GOAL(S) _____

TODAY'S DATE _____

TODAY'S MEAL PLAN	BREAKFAST	SNACK	LUNCH	SNACK	DINNER

weekly planner

	SUNDAY	MONDAY	TUESDAY	WEDNESDAY	THURSDAY	FRIDAY	SATURDAY	TOTAL
a.m.								
p.m.								

daily planner

5 a.m.	_____	2 p.m.	_____
6 a.m.	_____	3 p.m.	_____
7 a.m.	_____	4 p.m.	_____
8 a.m	_____	5 p.m.	_____
9 a.m.	_____	6 p.m.	_____
10 a.m.	_____	7 p.m.	_____
11 a.m.	_____	8 p.m.	_____
12 p.m.	_____	9 p.m.	_____
1 p.m.	_____	10 p.m.	_____

my training journal

my training log

SWIMMING WORKOUT:	*distance*
a.m.	
p.m.	
	total

BIKING WORKOUT:	*distance*
a.m.	
p.m.	
	total

RUNNING WORKOUT:	*distance*
a.m.	
p.m.	
	total

CROSS-TRAINING:	*time*
a.m.	
p.m.	
	total

TOMORROW'S TO DO

√RUNALOG® FOR TRIATHLETES

TODAY'S DATE _____

MY LONG-TERM GOAL(S) _____
_____

TODAY'S MEAL PLAN	BREAKFAST	SNACK	LUNCH	SNACK	DINNER
	_____	_____	_____	_____	_____
	_____	_____	_____	_____	_____

weekly planner

	SUNDAY	MONDAY	TUESDAY	WEDNESDAY	THURSDAY	FRIDAY	SATURDAY	TOTAL
a.m.								
p.m.								

daily planner

5 a.m. _____	2 p.m. _____
6 a.m. _____	3 p.m. _____
7 a.m. _____	4 p.m. _____
8 a.m _____	5 p.m. _____
9 a.m. _____	6 p.m. _____
10 a.m. _____	7 p.m. _____
11 a.m. _____	8 p.m. _____
12 p.m. _____	9 p.m. _____
1 p.m. _____	10 p.m. _____

my training journal

my training log

SWIMMING WORKOUT:	distance
a.m.	
p.m.	
	total

BIKING WORKOUT:	distance
a.m.	
p.m.	
	total

RUNNING WORKOUT:	distance
a.m.	
p.m.	
	total

CROSS-TRAINING:	time
a.m.	
p.m.	
	total

TOMORROW'S To Do

√RUNALOG® FOR TRIATHLETES   TODAY'S DATE _____

MY LONG-TERM GOAL(S) _____
_____

TODAY'S MEAL PLAN	BREAKFAST	SNACK	LUNCH	SNACK	DINNER
	_____	_____	_____	_____	_____
	_____	_____	_____	_____	_____

weekly planner

SUNDAY	MONDAY	TUESDAY	WEDNESDAY	THURSDAY	FRIDAY	SATURDAY	TOTAL
a.m.							
p.m.							

daily planner

5 a.m.	_____	2 p.m.	_____
6 a.m.	_____	3 p.m.	_____
7 a.m.	_____	4 p.m.	_____
8 a.m	_____	5 p.m.	_____
9 a.m.	_____	6 p.m.	_____
10 a.m.	_____	7 p.m.	_____
11 a.m.	_____	8 p.m.	_____
12 p.m.	_____	9 p.m.	_____
1 p.m.	_____	10 p.m.	_____

my training journal

my training log

SWIMMING WORKOUT:	*distance*
a.m.	
p.m.	
	total

BIKING WORKOUT:	*distance*
a.m.	
p.m.	
	total

RUNNING WORKOUT:	*distance*
a.m.	
p.m.	
	total

CROSS-TRAINING:	*time*
a.m.	
p.m.	
	total

TOMORROW'S TO DO

⚡RUNALOG® FOR TRIATHLETES

TODAY'S DATE _____

MY LONG-TERM GOAL(S) _____
_____

TODAY'S MEAL PLAN	BREAKFAST	SNACK	LUNCH	SNACK	DINNER
	_____	_____	_____	_____	_____
	_____	_____	_____	_____	_____

weekly planner

	SUNDAY	MONDAY	TUESDAY	WEDNESDAY	THURSDAY	FRIDAY	SATURDAY	TOTAL
a.m.								
p.m.								

🕐 daily planner

5 a.m. _____		2 p.m. _____	
6 a.m. _____		3 p.m. _____	
7 a.m. _____		4 p.m. _____	
8 a.m _____		5 p.m. _____	
9 a.m. _____		6 p.m. _____	
10 a.m. _____		7 p.m. _____	
11 a.m. _____		8 p.m. _____	
12 p.m. _____		9 p.m. _____	
1 p.m. _____		10 p.m. _____	

✍ my training journal

my training log

SWIMMING WORKOUT:	*distance*
a.m.	
p.m.	
	total

🚴 BIKING WORKOUT:	*distance*
a.m.	
p.m.	
	total

🏃 RUNNING WORKOUT:	*distance*
a.m.	
p.m.	
	total

CROSS-TRAINING:	*time*
a.m.	
p.m.	
	total

TOMORROW'S To Do

305

TODAY'S DATE _____

MY LONG-TERM GOAL(S) _____

TODAY'S MEAL PLAN	BREAKFAST	SNACK	LUNCH	SNACK	DINNER

weekly planner

SUNDAY	MONDAY	TUESDAY	WEDNESDAY	THURSDAY	FRIDAY	SATURDAY	TOTAL
a.m.							
p.m.							

daily planner

5 a.m. _____	2 p.m. _____
6 a.m. _____	3 p.m. _____
7 a.m. _____	4 p.m. _____
8 a.m _____	5 p.m. _____
9 a.m. _____	6 p.m. _____
10 a.m. _____	7 p.m. _____
11 a.m. _____	8 p.m. _____
12 p.m. _____	9 p.m. _____
1 p.m. _____	10 p.m. _____

my training journal

my training log

SWIMMING WORKOUT:	*distance*
a.m.	
p.m.	
	total

BIKING WORKOUT:	*distance*
a.m.	
p.m.	
	total

RUNNING WORKOUT:	*distance*
a.m.	
p.m.	
	total

CROSS-TRAINING:	*time*
a.m.	
p.m.	
	total

Tomorrow's To Do

306

√RUNALOG° FOR TRIATHLETES

TODAY'S DATE _____

MY LONG-TERM GOAL(S) _____

TODAY'S MEAL PLAN	BREAKFAST	SNACK	LUNCH	SNACK	DINNER
	_____	_____	_____	_____	_____
	_____	_____	_____	_____	_____

weekly planner

	SUNDAY	MONDAY	TUESDAY	WEDNESDAY	THURSDAY	FRIDAY	SATURDAY	TOTAL
a.m.								
p.m.								

daily planner

5 a.m. _____	2 p.m. _____
6 a.m. _____	3 p.m. _____
7 a.m. _____	4 p.m. _____
8 a.m _____	5 p.m. _____
9 a.m. _____	6 p.m. _____
10 a.m. _____	7 p.m. _____
11 a.m. _____	8 p.m. _____
12 p.m. _____	9 p.m. _____
1 p.m. _____	10 p.m. _____

my training journal

my training log

SWIMMING WORKOUT:	*distance*
a.m.	
p.m.	
	total

BIKING WORKOUT:	*distance*
a.m.	
p.m.	
	total

RUNNING WORKOUT:	*distance*
a.m.	
p.m.	
	total

CROSS-TRAINING:	*time*
a.m.	
p.m.	
	total

TOMORROW'S To Do

RUNALOG® FOR TRIATHLETES

TODAY'S DATE _____

MY LONG-TERM GOAL(S) _____

TODAY'S MEAL PLAN	BREAKFAST	SNACK	LUNCH	SNACK	DINNER
	_____	_____	_____	_____	_____
	_____	_____	_____	_____	_____

weekly planner

	SUNDAY	MONDAY	TUESDAY	WEDNESDAY	THURSDAY	FRIDAY	SATURDAY	TOTAL
a.m.								
p.m.								

daily planner

5 a.m. _____	2 p.m. _____
6 a.m. _____	3 p.m. _____
7 a.m. _____	4 p.m. _____
8 a.m _____	5 p.m. _____
9 a.m. _____	6 p.m. _____
10 a.m. _____	7 p.m. _____
11 a.m. _____	8 p.m. _____
12 p.m. _____	9 p.m. _____
1 p.m. _____	10 p.m. _____

my training journal

my training log

SWIMMING WORKOUT:	*distance*
a.m.	
p.m.	
	total

BIKING WORKOUT:	*distance*
a.m.	
p.m.	
	total

RUNNING WORKOUT:	*distance*
a.m.	
p.m.	
	total

CROSS-TRAINING:	*time*
a.m.	
p.m.	
	total

TOMORROW'S To Do

√RUNALOG® *FOR TRIATHLETES*   TODAY'S DATE _____

MY LONG-TERM GOAL(S) _____
_____

TODAY'S MEAL PLAN	BREAKFAST	SNACK	LUNCH	SNACK	DINNER
	_____	_____	_____	_____	_____
	_____	_____	_____	_____	_____

weekly planner

	SUNDAY	MONDAY	TUESDAY	WEDNESDAY	THURSDAY	FRIDAY	SATURDAY	TOTAL
a.m.								
p.m.								

daily planner

5 a.m. _____	2 p.m. _____
6 a.m. _____	3 p.m. _____
7 a.m. _____	4 p.m. _____
8 a.m _____	5 p.m. _____
9 a.m. _____	6 p.m. _____
10 a.m. _____	7 p.m. _____
11 a.m. _____	8 p.m. _____
12 p.m. _____	9 p.m. _____
1 p.m. _____	10 p.m. _____

my training journal

my training log

SWIMMING WORKOUT: *distance*

a.m.	
p.m.	
	total

BIKING WORKOUT: *distance*

a.m.	
p.m.	
	total

RUNNING WORKOUT: *distance*

a.m.	
p.m.	
	total

CROSS-TRAINING: *time*

a.m.	
p.m.	
	total

TOMORROW'S TO DO

ⱽRUNALOG® FOR TRIATHLETES

TODAY'S DATE _____

MY LONG-TERM GOAL(S) _____

TODAY'S MEAL PLAN	BREAKFAST	SNACK	LUNCH	SNACK	DINNER
	_____	_____	_____	_____	_____
	_____	_____	_____	_____	_____

weekly planner

	SUNDAY	MONDAY	TUESDAY	WEDNESDAY	THURSDAY	FRIDAY	SATURDAY	TOTAL
a.m.								
p.m.								

daily planner

5 a.m.	_____	2 p.m.	_____
6 a.m.	_____	3 p.m.	_____
7 a.m.	_____	4 p.m.	_____
8 a.m	_____	5 p.m.	_____
9 a.m.	_____	6 p.m.	_____
10 a.m.	_____	7 p.m.	_____
11 a.m.	_____	8 p.m.	_____
12 p.m.	_____	9 p.m.	_____
1 p.m.	_____	10 p.m.	_____

my training log

SWIMMING WORKOUT: distance

a.m.		
p.m.		
		total

BIKING WORKOUT: distance

a.m.		
p.m.		
		total

RUNNING WORKOUT: distance

a.m.		
p.m.		
		total

CROSS-TRAINING: time

a.m.		
p.m.		
		total

my training journal

TOMORROW'S To Do

⩔RUNALOG® FOR TRIATHLETES

TODAY'S DATE _____

MY LONG-TERM GOAL(S) _____

_____

TODAY'S MEAL PLAN	BREAKFAST	SNACK	LUNCH	SNACK	DINNER
	_____	_____	_____	_____	_____
	_____	_____	_____	_____	_____

weekly planner

	SUNDAY	MONDAY	TUESDAY	WEDNESDAY	THURSDAY	FRIDAY	SATURDAY	TOTAL
a.m.								
p.m.								

daily planner

5 a.m. _____		2 p.m. _____
6 a.m. _____		3 p.m. _____
7 a.m. _____		4 p.m. _____
8 a.m _____		5 p.m. _____
9 a.m. _____		6 p.m. _____
10 a.m. _____		7 p.m. _____
11 a.m. _____		8 p.m. _____
12 p.m. _____		9 p.m. _____
1 p.m. _____		10 p.m. _____

my training journal

my training log

SWIMMING WORKOUT:	*distance*
a.m.	
p.m.	
	total

BIKING WORKOUT:	*distance*
a.m.	
p.m.	
	total

RUNNING WORKOUT:	*distance*
a.m.	
p.m.	
	total

CROSS-TRAINING:	*time*
a.m.	
p.m.	
	total

TOMORROW'S TO DO

311

√RUNALOG® *For Triathletes*

TODAY'S DATE _____

MY LONG-TERM GOAL(S) _____
_____

TODAY'S MEAL PLAN	BREAKFAST	SNACK	LUNCH	SNACK	DINNER
	_____	_____	_____	_____	_____
	_____	_____	_____	_____	_____

weekly planner

	SUNDAY	MONDAY	TUESDAY	WEDNESDAY	THURSDAY	FRIDAY	SATURDAY	TOTAL
a.m.								
p.m.								

daily planner

5 a.m.	_____	2 p.m.	_____
6 a.m.	_____	3 p.m.	_____
7 a.m.	_____	4 p.m.	_____
8 a.m	_____	5 p.m.	_____
9 a.m.	_____	6 p.m.	_____
10 a.m.	_____	7 p.m.	_____
11 a.m.	_____	8 p.m.	_____
12 p.m.	_____	9 p.m.	_____
1 p.m.	_____	10 p.m.	_____

my training journal

my training log

SWIMMING WORKOUT:	*distance*
a.m.	
p.m.	
	total

BIKING WORKOUT:	*distance*
a.m.	
p.m.	
	total

RUNNING WORKOUT:	*distance*
a.m.	
p.m.	
	total

CROSS-TRAINING:	*time*
a.m.	
p.m.	
	total

TOMORROW'S TO DO

MY LONG-TERM GOAL(S) _____
_____

TODAY'S MEAL PLAN	BREAKFAST	SNACK	LUNCH	SNACK	DINNER
	_____	_____	_____	_____	_____
	_____	_____	_____	_____	_____

weekly planner

	SUNDAY	MONDAY	TUESDAY	WEDNESDAY	THURSDAY	FRIDAY	SATURDAY	TOTAL
a.m.								
p.m.								

daily planner

5 a.m. _____	2 p.m. _____
6 a.m. _____	3 p.m. _____
7 a.m. _____	4 p.m. _____
8 a.m _____	5 p.m. _____
9 a.m. _____	6 p.m. _____
10 a.m. _____	7 p.m. _____
11 a.m. _____	8 p.m. _____
12 p.m. _____	9 p.m. _____
1 p.m. _____	10 p.m. _____

my training journal

my training log

SWIMMING WORKOUT:	distance
a.m.	
p.m.	
	total

BIKING WORKOUT:	distance
a.m.	
p.m.	
	total

RUNNING WORKOUT:	distance
a.m.	
p.m.	
	total

CROSS-TRAINING:	time
a.m.	
p.m.	
	total

TOMORROW'S To Do

RUNALOG® FOR TRIATHLETES

TODAY'S DATE _____

MY LONG-TERM GOAL(S) _____

_____

TODAY'S MEAL PLAN	BREAKFAST	SNACK	LUNCH	SNACK	DINNER

weekly planner

	SUNDAY	MONDAY	TUESDAY	WEDNESDAY	THURSDAY	FRIDAY	SATURDAY	TOTAL
a.m.								
p.m.								

daily planner

5 a.m. _____	2 p.m. _____
6 a.m. _____	3 p.m. _____
7 a.m. _____	4 p.m. _____
8 a.m _____	5 p.m. _____
9 a.m. _____	6 p.m. _____
10 a.m. _____	7 p.m. _____
11 a.m. _____	8 p.m. _____
12 p.m. _____	9 p.m. _____
1 p.m. _____	10 p.m. _____

my training journal

my training log

SWIMMING WORKOUT:	distance
a.m.	
p.m.	
	total

BIKING WORKOUT:	distance
a.m.	
p.m.	
	total

RUNNING WORKOUT:	distance
a.m.	
p.m.	
	total

CROSS-TRAINING:	time
a.m.	
p.m.	
	total

TOMORROW'S To Do

ᐯRUNALOG® FOR TRIATHLETES

Today's Date _____

MY LONG-TERM GOAL(S) _____

_____

Today's Meal Plan	Breakfast	Snack	Lunch	Snack	Dinner
	_____	_____	_____	_____	_____
	_____	_____	_____	_____	_____

weekly planner

	SUNDAY	MONDAY	TUESDAY	WEDNESDAY	THURSDAY	FRIDAY	SATURDAY	TOTAL
a.m.								
p.m.								

daily planner

5 a.m. _____	2 p.m. _____
6 a.m. _____	3 p.m. _____
7 a.m. _____	4 p.m. _____
8 a.m _____	5 p.m. _____
9 a.m. _____	6 p.m. _____
10 a.m. _____	7 p.m. _____
11 a.m. _____	8 p.m. _____
12 p.m. _____	9 p.m. _____
1 p.m. _____	10 p.m. _____

my training journal

my training log

SWIMMING WORKOUT:	distance
a.m.	
p.m.	
	total

BIKING WORKOUT:	distance
a.m.	
p.m.	
	total

RUNNING WORKOUT:	distance
a.m.	
p.m.	
	total

CROSS-TRAINING:	time
a.m.	
p.m.	
	total

Tomorrow's To Do

© 2009 www.RUNALOGS.com

315

RUNALOG® FOR TRIATHLETES

TODAY'S DATE _____

MY LONG-TERM GOAL(S) _____
_____

TODAY'S MEAL PLAN	BREAKFAST	SNACK	LUNCH	SNACK	DINNER
	_____	_____	_____	_____	_____
	_____	_____	_____	_____	_____
	_____	_____	_____	_____	_____

weekly planner

	SUNDAY	MONDAY	TUESDAY	WEDNESDAY	THURSDAY	FRIDAY	SATURDAY	TOTAL
a.m.								
p.m.								

daily planner

5 a.m. _____	2 p.m. _____
6 a.m. _____	3 p.m. _____
7 a.m. _____	4 p.m. _____
8 a.m _____	5 p.m. _____
9 a.m. _____	6 p.m. _____
10 a.m. _____	7 p.m. _____
11 a.m. _____	8 p.m. _____
12 p.m. _____	9 p.m. _____
1 p.m. _____	10 p.m. _____

my training journal

my training log

SWIMMING WORKOUT:	*distance*
a.m.	
p.m.	
	total

BIKING WORKOUT:	*distance*
a.m.	
p.m.	
	total

RUNNING WORKOUT:	*distance*
a.m.	
p.m.	
	total

CROSS-TRAINING:	*time*
a.m.	
p.m.	
	total

TOMORROW'S To Do

MY LONG-TERM GOAL(S) _____
_____

	BREAKFAST	SNACK	LUNCH	SNACK	DINNER
TODAY'S MEAL PLAN	_____	_____	_____	_____	_____
	_____	_____	_____	_____	_____

weekly planner

	SUNDAY	MONDAY	TUESDAY	WEDNESDAY	THURSDAY	FRIDAY	SATURDAY	TOTAL
a.m.								
p.m.								

🕐 daily planner

5 a.m. _____	2 p.m. _____
6 a.m. _____	3 p.m. _____
7 a.m. _____	4 p.m. _____
8 a.m _____	5 p.m. _____
9 a.m. _____	6 p.m. _____
10 a.m. _____	7 p.m. _____
11 a.m. _____	8 p.m. _____
12 p.m. _____	9 p.m. _____
1 p.m. _____	10 p.m. _____

✍ my training journal

my training log

SWIMMING WORKOUT: *distance*

a.m.	
p.m.	
	total

BIKING WORKOUT: *distance*

a.m.	
p.m.	
	total

RUNNING WORKOUT: *distance*

a.m.	
p.m.	
	total

CROSS-TRAINING: *time*

a.m.	
p.m.	
	total

Tomorrow's To Do

⚡RUNALOG® FOR TRIATHLETES

TODAY'S DATE _____

MY LONG-TERM GOAL(S) _____

TODAY'S MEAL PLAN	BREAKFAST	SNACK	LUNCH	SNACK	DINNER
	_____	_____	_____	_____	_____
	_____	_____	_____	_____	_____

weekly planner

	SUNDAY	MONDAY	TUESDAY	WEDNESDAY	THURSDAY	FRIDAY	SATURDAY	TOTAL
a.m.								
p.m.								

🕐 *daily planner*

5 a.m.	_____	2 p.m.	_____
6 a.m.	_____	3 p.m.	_____
7 a.m.	_____	4 p.m.	_____
8 a.m	_____	5 p.m.	_____
9 a.m.	_____	6 p.m.	_____
10 a.m.	_____	7 p.m.	_____
11 a.m.	_____	8 p.m.	_____
12 p.m.	_____	9 p.m.	_____
1 p.m.	_____	10 p.m.	_____

☞ *my training journal*

my training log

SWIMMING WORKOUT:	*distance*
a.m.	
p.m.	
	total

BIKING WORKOUT:	*distance*
a.m.	
p.m.	
	total

RUNNING WORKOUT:	*distance*
a.m.	
p.m.	
	total

CROSS-TRAINING:	*time*
a.m.	
p.m.	
	total

TOMORROW'S To Do

⩔RUNALOG® FOR TRIATHLETES

TODAY'S DATE _____

MY LONG-TERM GOAL(S) _____
_____

TODAY'S MEAL PLAN	BREAKFAST	SNACK	LUNCH	SNACK	DINNER
	_____	_____	_____	_____	_____
	_____	_____	_____	_____	_____

weekly planner

	SUNDAY	MONDAY	TUESDAY	WEDNESDAY	THURSDAY	FRIDAY	SATURDAY	TOTAL
a.m.								
p.m.								

daily planner

5 a.m. _____	2 p.m. _____
6 a.m. _____	3 p.m. _____
7 a.m. _____	4 p.m. _____
8 a.m _____	5 p.m. _____
9 a.m. _____	6 p.m. _____
10 a.m. _____	7 p.m. _____
11 a.m. _____	8 p.m. _____
12 p.m. _____	9 p.m. _____
1 p.m. _____	10 p.m. _____

my training journal

my training log

SWIMMING WORKOUT:	*distance*
a.m.	
p.m.	
	total

BIKING WORKOUT:	*distance*
a.m.	
p.m.	
	total

RUNNING WORKOUT:	*distance*
a.m.	
p.m.	
	total

CROSS-TRAINING:	*time*
a.m.	
p.m.	
	total

TOMORROW'S TO DO

√RUNALOG® FOR TRIATHLETES

TODAY'S DATE _____

MY LONG-TERM GOAL(S) _____

TODAY'S MEAL PLAN	BREAKFAST	SNACK	LUNCH	SNACK	DINNER
	_____	_____	_____	_____	_____
	_____	_____	_____	_____	_____

weekly planner

	SUNDAY	MONDAY	TUESDAY	WEDNESDAY	THURSDAY	FRIDAY	SATURDAY	TOTAL
a.m.								
p.m.								

daily planner

5 a.m. _____	2 p.m. _____
6 a.m. _____	3 p.m. _____
7 a.m. _____	4 p.m. _____
8 a.m _____	5 p.m. _____
9 a.m. _____	6 p.m. _____
10 a.m. _____	7 p.m. _____
11 a.m. _____	8 p.m. _____
12 p.m. _____	9 p.m. _____
1 p.m. _____	10 p.m. _____

my training journal

my training log

SWIMMING WORKOUT:	distance
a.m.	
p.m.	
	total

BIKING WORKOUT:	distance
a.m.	
p.m.	
	total

RUNNING WORKOUT:	distance
a.m.	
p.m.	
	total

CROSS-TRAINING:	time
a.m.	
p.m.	
	total

TOMORROW'S To Do

√RUNALOG° FOR TRIATHLETES

TODAY'S DATE _____

MY LONG-TERM GOAL(S) _____

_____

TODAY'S MEAL PLAN	BREAKFAST	SNACK	LUNCH	SNACK	DINNER
	_____	_____	_____	_____	_____
	_____	_____	_____	_____	_____

weekly planner

	SUNDAY	MONDAY	TUESDAY	WEDNESDAY	THURSDAY	FRIDAY	SATURDAY	TOTAL
a.m.								
p.m.								

daily planner

5 a.m. _____	2 p.m. _____
6 a.m. _____	3 p.m. _____
7 a.m. _____	4 p.m. _____
8 a.m _____	5 p.m. _____
9 a.m. _____	6 p.m. _____
10 a.m. _____	7 p.m. _____
11 a.m. _____	8 p.m. _____
12 p.m. _____	9 p.m. _____
1 p.m. _____	10 p.m. _____

my training journal

my training log

SWIMMING WORKOUT:	*distance*
a.m.	
p.m.	
	total

BIKING WORKOUT:	*distance*
a.m.	
p.m.	
	total

RUNNING WORKOUT:	*distance*
a.m.	
p.m.	
	total

CROSS-TRAINING:	*time*
a.m.	
p.m.	
	total

Tomorrow's To Do

321

ᵛ̌RUNALOG® *FOR TRIATHLETES*

TODAY'S DATE _____

MY LONG-TERM GOAL(S) _____

_____

TODAY'S MEAL PLAN	BREAKFAST	SNACK	LUNCH	SNACK	DINNER
	_____	_____	_____	_____	_____
	_____	_____	_____	_____	_____
	_____	_____	_____	_____	_____

weekly planner

	SUNDAY	MONDAY	TUESDAY	WEDNESDAY	THURSDAY	FRIDAY	SATURDAY	TOTAL
a.m.								
p.m.								

🕐 *daily planner*

5 a.m. _____	2 p.m. _____
6 a.m. _____	3 p.m. _____
7 a.m. _____	4 p.m. _____
8 a.m _____	5 p.m. _____
9 a.m. _____	6 p.m. _____
10 a.m. _____	7 p.m. _____
11 a.m. _____	8 p.m. _____
12 p.m. _____	9 p.m. _____
1 p.m. _____	10 p.m. _____

☛ *my training journal*

my training log

SWIMMING WORKOUT:	*distance*
a.m.	
p.m.	
	total

BIKING WORKOUT:	*distance*
a.m.	
p.m.	
	total

RUNNING WORKOUT:	*distance*
a.m.	
p.m.	
	total

CROSS-TRAINING:	*time*
a.m.	
p.m.	
	total

TOMORROW'S To Do

ⱽRUNALOG® For Triathletes

Today's Date _____

MY LONG-TERM GOAL(S) _____
_____

Today's Meal Plan	Breakfast	Snack	Lunch	Snack	Dinner
	_____	_____	_____	_____	_____
	_____	_____	_____	_____	_____

weekly planner

	SUNDAY	MONDAY	TUESDAY	WEDNESDAY	THURSDAY	FRIDAY	SATURDAY	TOTAL
a.m.								
p.m.								

daily planner

5 a.m. _____	2 p.m. _____
6 a.m. _____	3 p.m. _____
7 a.m. _____	4 p.m. _____
8 a.m _____	5 p.m. _____
9 a.m. _____	6 p.m. _____
10 a.m. _____	7 p.m. _____
11 a.m. _____	8 p.m. _____
12 p.m. _____	9 p.m. _____
1 p.m. _____	10 p.m. _____

my training journal

my training log

SWIMMING WORKOUT: distance

a.m.	
p.m.	
	total

BIKING WORKOUT: distance

a.m.	
p.m.	
	total

RUNNING WORKOUT: distance

a.m.	
p.m.	
	total

CROSS-TRAINING: time

a.m.	
p.m.	
	total

Tomorrow's To Do

√RUNALOG® *For Triathletes*   **Today's Date** _____

MY LONG-TERM GOAL(S) _____
_____

Today's Meal Plan	Breakfast	Snack	Lunch	Snack	Dinner
	_____	_____	_____	_____	_____
	_____	_____	_____	_____	_____

weekly planner

	SUNDAY	MONDAY	TUESDAY	WEDNESDAY	THURSDAY	FRIDAY	SATURDAY	TOTAL
a.m.								
p.m.								

daily planner

5 a.m.	_____	2 p.m.	_____
6 a.m.	_____	3 p.m.	_____
7 a.m.	_____	4 p.m.	_____
8 a.m	_____	5 p.m.	_____
9 a.m.	_____	6 p.m.	_____
10 a.m.	_____	7 p.m.	_____
11 a.m.	_____	8 p.m.	_____
12 p.m.	_____	9 p.m.	_____
1 p.m.	_____	10 p.m.	_____

my training journal

my training log

SWIMMING WORKOUT:	*distance*
a.m.	
p.m.	
	total

BIKING WORKOUT:	*distance*
a.m.	
p.m.	
	total

RUNNING WORKOUT:	*distance*
a.m.	
p.m.	
	total

CROSS-TRAINING:	*time*
a.m.	
p.m.	
	total

Tomorrow's To Do

ⱱRUNALOG® FOR TRIATHLETES

TODAY'S DATE _____

MY LONG-TERM GOAL(S) _____

_____

TODAY'S MEAL PLAN	BREAKFAST	SNACK	LUNCH	SNACK	DINNER
	_____	_____	_____	_____	_____
	_____	_____	_____	_____	_____

weekly planner

	SUNDAY	MONDAY	TUESDAY	WEDNESDAY	THURSDAY	FRIDAY	SATURDAY	TOTAL
a.m.								
p.m.								

🕐 daily planner

5 a.m. _____		2 p.m. _____	
6 a.m. _____		3 p.m. _____	
7 a.m. _____		4 p.m. _____	
8 a.m _____		5 p.m. _____	
9 a.m. _____		6 p.m. _____	
10 a.m. _____		7 p.m. _____	
11 a.m. _____		8 p.m. _____	
12 p.m. _____		9 p.m. _____	
1 p.m. _____		10 p.m. _____	

✍ my training journal

_____

_____

_____

_____

_____

_____

_____

_____

_____

_____

_____

_____

_____

_____

_____

_____

_____

my training log

SWIMMING WORKOUT:	distance
a.m.	
p.m.	
	total

🚴 BIKING WORKOUT:	distance
a.m.	
p.m.	
	total

🏃 RUNNING WORKOUT:	distance
a.m.	
p.m.	
	total

CROSS-TRAINING:	time
a.m.	
p.m.	
	total

TOMORROW'S TO DO

⚡RUNALOG° *FOR TRIATHLETES*   **TODAY'S DATE** _____

MY LONG-TERM GOAL(S) _____

TODAY'S MEAL PLAN	BREAKFAST	SNACK	LUNCH	SNACK	DINNER
	_____	_____	_____	_____	_____
	_____	_____	_____	_____	_____

weekly planner

	SUNDAY	MONDAY	TUESDAY	WEDNESDAY	THURSDAY	FRIDAY	SATURDAY	TOTAL
a.m.								
p.m.								

🕐 *daily planner*

5 a.m. _____	2 p.m. _____
6 a.m. _____	3 p.m. _____
7 a.m. _____	4 p.m. _____
8 a.m _____	5 p.m. _____
9 a.m. _____	6 p.m. _____
10 a.m. _____	7 p.m. _____
11 a.m. _____	8 p.m. _____
12 p.m. _____	9 p.m. _____
1 p.m. _____	10 p.m. _____

✍ *my training journal*

my training log

SWIMMING WORKOUT:	*distance*
a.m.	
p.m.	
	total

BIKING WORKOUT:	*distance*
a.m.	
p.m.	
	total

RUNNING WORKOUT:	*distance*
a.m.	
p.m.	
	total

CROSS-TRAINING:	*time*
a.m.	
p.m.	
	total

TOMORROW'S TO DO

RUNALOG® FOR TRIATHLETES

TODAY'S DATE _____

MY LONG-TERM GOAL(S) _____
_____

TODAY'S MEAL PLAN	BREAKFAST	SNACK	LUNCH	SNACK	DINNER
	_____	_____	_____	_____	_____
	_____	_____	_____	_____	_____

weekly planner

	SUNDAY	MONDAY	TUESDAY	WEDNESDAY	THURSDAY	FRIDAY	SATURDAY	TOTAL
a.m.								
p.m.								

daily planner

5 a.m. _____	2 p.m. _____
6 a.m. _____	3 p.m. _____
7 a.m. _____	4 p.m. _____
8 a.m _____	5 p.m. _____
9 a.m. _____	6 p.m. _____
10 a.m. _____	7 p.m. _____
11 a.m. _____	8 p.m. _____
12 p.m. _____	9 p.m. _____
1 p.m. _____	10 p.m. _____

my training journal

my training log

SWIMMING WORKOUT:	distance
a.m.	
p.m.	
	total

BIKING WORKOUT:	distance
a.m.	
p.m.	
	total

RUNNING WORKOUT:	distance
a.m.	
p.m.	
	total

CROSS-TRAINING:	time
a.m.	
p.m.	
	total

TOMORROW'S TO DO

© 2009 www.RUNALOGS.com

327

ⱽRUNALOG° FOR TRIATHLETES

MY LONG-TERM GOAL(S) _____

TODAY'S MEAL PLAN	BREAKFAST	SNACK	LUNCH	SNACK	DINNER
	_____	_____	_____	_____	_____
	_____	_____	_____	_____	_____

weekly planner

	SUNDAY	MONDAY	TUESDAY	WEDNESDAY	THURSDAY	FRIDAY	SATURDAY	TOTAL
a.m.								
p.m.								

🕐 daily planner

5 a.m. _____	2 p.m. _____
6 a.m. _____	3 p.m. _____
7 a.m. _____	4 p.m. _____
8 a.m _____	5 p.m. _____
9 a.m. _____	6 p.m. _____
10 a.m. _____	7 p.m. _____
11 a.m. _____	8 p.m. _____
12 p.m. _____	9 p.m. _____
1 p.m. _____	10 p.m. _____

✍ my training journal

my training log

SWIMMING WORKOUT:	distance
a.m.	
p.m.	
	total

BIKING WORKOUT:	distance
a.m.	
p.m.	
	total

RUNNING WORKOUT:	distance
a.m.	
p.m.	
	total

CROSS-TRAINING:	time
a.m.	
p.m.	
	total

TOMORROW'S To Do

MY LONG-TERM GOAL(S) _____
_____

TODAY'S MEAL PLAN	**BREAKFAST**	**SNACK**	**LUNCH**	**SNACK**	**DINNER**
	_____	_____	_____	_____	_____
	_____	_____	_____	_____	_____

weekly planner

	SUNDAY	MONDAY	TUESDAY	WEDNESDAY	THURSDAY	FRIDAY	SATURDAY	TOTAL
a.m.								
p.m.								

🕐 *daily planner*

5 a.m. _____	2 p.m. _____
6 a.m. _____	3 p.m. _____
7 a.m. _____	4 p.m. _____
8 a.m _____	5 p.m. _____
9 a.m. _____	6 p.m. _____
10 a.m. _____	7 p.m. _____
11 a.m. _____	8 p.m. _____
12 p.m. _____	9 p.m. _____
1 p.m. _____	10 p.m. _____

✍ *my training journal*

my training log

SWIMMING WORKOUT:	*distance*
a.m.	
p.m.	
	total

🚲 BIKING WORKOUT:	*distance*
a.m.	
p.m.	
	total

🏃 RUNNING WORKOUT:	*distance*
a.m.	
p.m.	
	total

CROSS-TRAINING:	*time*
a.m.	
p.m.	
	total

TOMORROW'S To Do

√RUNALOG® FOR TRIATHLETES

TODAY'S DATE _____

MY LONG-TERM GOAL(S) _____

_____

TODAY'S MEAL PLAN	BREAKFAST	SNACK	LUNCH	SNACK	DINNER
	_____	_____	_____	_____	_____
	_____	_____	_____	_____	_____

weekly planner

SUNDAY	MONDAY	TUESDAY	WEDNESDAY	THURSDAY	FRIDAY	SATURDAY	TOTAL
a.m.							
p.m.							

🕐 daily planner

5 a.m. _____	2 p.m. _____
6 a.m. _____	3 p.m. _____
7 a.m. _____	4 p.m. _____
8 a.m _____	5 p.m. _____
9 a.m. _____	6 p.m. _____
10 a.m. _____	7 p.m. _____
11 a.m. _____	8 p.m. _____
12 p.m. _____	9 p.m. _____
1 p.m. _____	10 p.m. _____

✍ my training journal

my training log

SWIMMING WORKOUT:	*distance*
a.m.	
p.m.	
	total

BIKING WORKOUT:	*distance*
a.m.	
p.m.	
	total

RUNNING WORKOUT:	*distance*
a.m.	
p.m.	
	total

CROSS-TRAINING:	*time*
a.m.	
p.m.	
	total

TOMORROW'S TO DO

ᐯRUNALOG° *For Triathletes*

Today's Date _____

MY LONG-TERM GOAL(S) _____

_____

Today's Meal Plan	Breakfast	Snack	Lunch	Snack	Dinner
	_____	_____	_____	_____	_____
	_____	_____	_____	_____	_____

weekly planner

	SUNDAY	MONDAY	TUESDAY	WEDNESDAY	THURSDAY	FRIDAY	SATURDAY	TOTAL
a.m.								
p.m.								

daily planner

5 a.m. _____	2 p.m. _____
6 a.m. _____	3 p.m. _____
7 a.m. _____	4 p.m. _____
8 a.m _____	5 p.m. _____
9 a.m. _____	6 p.m. _____
10 a.m. _____	7 p.m. _____
11 a.m. _____	8 p.m. _____
12 p.m. _____	9 p.m. _____
1 p.m. _____	10 p.m. _____

my training journal

my training log

SWIMMING WORKOUT: *distance*

a.m.	
p.m.	
	total

BIKING WORKOUT: *distance*

a.m.	
p.m.	
	total

RUNNING WORKOUT: *distance*

a.m.	
p.m.	
	total

CROSS-TRAINING: *time*

a.m.	
p.m.	
	total

Tomorrow's To Do

RUNALOG® FOR TRIATHLETES

TODAY'S DATE _____

MY LONG-TERM GOAL(S) _____

TODAY'S MEAL PLAN	BREAKFAST	SNACK	LUNCH	SNACK	DINNER
	_____	_____	_____	_____	_____
	_____	_____	_____	_____	_____

weekly planner

	SUNDAY	MONDAY	TUESDAY	WEDNESDAY	THURSDAY	FRIDAY	SATURDAY	TOTAL
a.m.								
p.m.								

daily planner

5 a.m.	_____	2 p.m.	_____
6 a.m.	_____	3 p.m.	_____
7 a.m.	_____	4 p.m.	_____
8 a.m	_____	5 p.m.	_____
9 a.m.	_____	6 p.m.	_____
10 a.m.	_____	7 p.m.	_____
11 a.m.	_____	8 p.m.	_____
12 p.m.	_____	9 p.m.	_____
1 p.m.	_____	10 p.m.	_____

my training journal

my training log

SWIMMING WORKOUT:	distance
a.m.	
p.m.	
	total

BIKING WORKOUT:	distance
a.m.	
p.m.	
	total

RUNNING WORKOUT:	distance
a.m.	
p.m.	
	total

CROSS-TRAINING:	time
a.m.	
p.m.	
	total

TOMORROW'S TO DO

ᐯRUNALOG® FOR TRIATHLETES

TODAY'S DATE _____

MY LONG-TERM GOAL(S) _____

_____

TODAY'S MEAL PLAN	BREAKFAST	SNACK	LUNCH	SNACK	DINNER
	_____	_____	_____	_____	_____
	_____	_____	_____	_____	_____

weekly planner

	SUNDAY	MONDAY	TUESDAY	WEDNESDAY	THURSDAY	FRIDAY	SATURDAY	TOTAL
a.m.								
p.m.								

daily planner

5 a.m. _____	2 p.m. _____
6 a.m. _____	3 p.m. _____
7 a.m. _____	4 p.m. _____
8 a.m _____	5 p.m. _____
9 a.m. _____	6 p.m. _____
10 a.m. _____	7 p.m. _____
11 a.m. _____	8 p.m. _____
12 p.m. _____	9 p.m. _____
1 p.m. _____	10 p.m. _____

my training journal

my training log

SWIMMING WORKOUT:	distance
a.m.	
p.m.	
	total

BIKING WORKOUT:	distance
a.m.	
p.m.	
	total

RUNNING WORKOUT:	distance
a.m.	
p.m.	
	total

CROSS-TRAINING:	time
a.m.	
p.m.	
	total

TOMORROW'S TO DO

RUNALOG® FOR TRIATHLETES

TODAY'S DATE _____

MY LONG-TERM GOAL(S) _____

TODAY'S MEAL PLAN	BREAKFAST	SNACK	LUNCH	SNACK	DINNER
	_____	_____	_____	_____	_____

weekly planner

	SUNDAY	MONDAY	TUESDAY	WEDNESDAY	THURSDAY	FRIDAY	SATURDAY	TOTAL
a.m.								
p.m.								

daily planner

5 a.m. _____	2 p.m. _____
6 a.m. _____	3 p.m. _____
7 a.m. _____	4 p.m. _____
8 a.m _____	5 p.m. _____
9 a.m. _____	6 p.m. _____
10 a.m. _____	7 p.m. _____
11 a.m. _____	8 p.m. _____
12 p.m. _____	9 p.m. _____
1 p.m. _____	10 p.m. _____

my training journal

my training log

SWIMMING WORKOUT:		*distance*
a.m.		
p.m.		
		total

BIKING WORKOUT:		*distance*
a.m.		
p.m.		
		total

RUNNING WORKOUT:		*distance*
a.m.		
p.m.		
		total

CROSS-TRAINING:		*time*
a.m.		
p.m.		
		total

TOMORROW'S TO DO

✔RUNALOG® FOR TRIATHLETES

TODAY'S DATE _____

MY LONG-TERM GOAL(S) _____
_____

TODAY'S MEAL PLAN	BREAKFAST	SNACK	LUNCH	SNACK	DINNER
	_____	_____	_____	_____	_____
	_____	_____	_____	_____	_____

weekly planner

	SUNDAY	MONDAY	TUESDAY	WEDNESDAY	THURSDAY	FRIDAY	SATURDAY	TOTAL
a.m.								
p.m.								

🕐 daily planner

5 a.m. _____	2 p.m. _____
6 a.m. _____	3 p.m. _____
7 a.m. _____	4 p.m. _____
8 a.m _____	5 p.m. _____
9 a.m. _____	6 p.m. _____
10 a.m. _____	7 p.m. _____
11 a.m. _____	8 p.m. _____
12 p.m. _____	9 p.m. _____
1 p.m. _____	10 p.m. _____

✍ my training journal

my training log

SWIMMING WORKOUT:	distance
a.m.	
p.m.	
	total

🚴 BIKING WORKOUT:	distance
a.m.	
p.m.	
	total

🏃 RUNNING WORKOUT:	distance
a.m.	
p.m.	
	total

CROSS-TRAINING:	time
a.m.	
p.m.	
	total

TOMORROW'S TO DO

RUNALOG® FOR TRIATHLETES

TODAY'S DATE _____

MY LONG-TERM GOAL(S) _____

TODAY'S MEAL PLAN	BREAKFAST	SNACK	LUNCH	SNACK	DINNER
	_____	_____	_____	_____	_____
	_____	_____	_____	_____	_____

weekly planner

	SUNDAY	MONDAY	TUESDAY	WEDNESDAY	THURSDAY	FRIDAY	SATURDAY	TOTAL
a.m.								
p.m.								

daily planner

5 a.m. _____	2 p.m. _____
6 a.m. _____	3 p.m. _____
7 a.m. _____	4 p.m. _____
8 a.m _____	5 p.m. _____
9 a.m. _____	6 p.m. _____
10 a.m. _____	7 p.m. _____
11 a.m. _____	8 p.m. _____
12 p.m. _____	9 p.m. _____
1 p.m. _____	10 p.m. _____

my training journal

my training log

SWIMMING WORKOUT:	*distance*
a.m.	
p.m.	
	total

BIKING WORKOUT:	*distance*
a.m.	
p.m.	
	total

RUNNING WORKOUT:	*distance*
a.m.	
p.m.	
	total

CROSS-TRAINING:	*time*
a.m.	
p.m.	
	total

TOMORROW'S TO DO

⩔RUNALOG® FOR TRIATHLETES

TODAY'S DATE _____

MY LONG-TERM GOAL(S) _____
_____

TODAY'S MEAL PLAN	BREAKFAST	SNACK	LUNCH	SNACK	DINNER
	_____	_____	_____	_____	_____
	_____	_____	_____	_____	_____

weekly planner

	SUNDAY	MONDAY	TUESDAY	WEDNESDAY	THURSDAY	FRIDAY	SATURDAY	TOTAL
a.m.								
p.m.								

🕐 daily planner

5 a.m. _____	2 p.m. _____
6 a.m. _____	3 p.m. _____
7 a.m. _____	4 p.m. _____
8 a.m _____	5 p.m. _____
9 a.m. _____	6 p.m. _____
10 a.m. _____	7 p.m. _____
11 a.m. _____	8 p.m. _____
12 p.m. _____	9 p.m. _____
1 p.m. _____	10 p.m. _____

✍ my training journal

my training log

SWIMMING WORKOUT:	distance
a.m.	
p.m.	
	total

🚲 BIKING WORKOUT:	distance
a.m.	
p.m.	
	total

🏃 RUNNING WORKOUT:	distance
a.m.	
p.m.	
	total

CROSS-TRAINING:	time
a.m.	
p.m.	
	total

TOMORROW'S TO DO

√RUNALOG® FOR TRIATHLETES

TODAY'S DATE _____

MY LONG-TERM GOAL(S) _____
_____

TODAY'S MEAL PLAN	BREAKFAST	SNACK	LUNCH	SNACK	DINNER
	_____	_____	_____	_____	_____
	_____	_____	_____	_____	_____

weekly planner

	SUNDAY	MONDAY	TUESDAY	WEDNESDAY	THURSDAY	FRIDAY	SATURDAY	TOTAL
a.m.								
p.m.								

daily planner

5 a.m. _____	2 p.m. _____
6 a.m. _____	3 p.m. _____
7 a.m. _____	4 p.m. _____
8 a.m _____	5 p.m. _____
9 a.m. _____	6 p.m. _____
10 a.m. _____	7 p.m. _____
11 a.m. _____	8 p.m. _____
12 p.m. _____	9 p.m. _____
1 p.m. _____	10 p.m. _____

my training journal

my training log

SWIMMING WORKOUT:	*distance*
a.m.	
p.m.	
	total

BIKING WORKOUT:	*distance*
a.m.	
p.m.	
	total

RUNNING WORKOUT:	*distance*
a.m.	
p.m.	
	total

CROSS-TRAINING:	*time*
a.m.	
p.m.	
	total

TOMORROW'S TO DO

MY LONG-TERM GOAL(S) _____
_____

TODAY'S MEAL PLAN	BREAKFAST	SNACK	LUNCH	SNACK	DINNER
	_____	_____	_____	_____	_____
	_____	_____	_____	_____	_____

weekly planner

	SUNDAY	MONDAY	TUESDAY	WEDNESDAY	THURSDAY	FRIDAY	SATURDAY	TOTAL
a.m.								
p.m.								

🕐 daily planner

5 a.m.	_____	2 p.m.	_____
6 a.m.	_____	3 p.m.	_____
7 a.m.	_____	4 p.m.	_____
8 a.m	_____	5 p.m.	_____
9 a.m.	_____	6 p.m.	_____
10 a.m.	_____	7 p.m.	_____
11 a.m.	_____	8 p.m.	_____
12 p.m.	_____	9 p.m.	_____
1 p.m.	_____	10 p.m.	_____

🖊 my training journal

my training log

SWIMMING WORKOUT:	*distance*
a.m.	
p.m.	
	total

🚴 BIKING WORKOUT:	*distance*
a.m.	
p.m.	
	total

🏃 RUNNING WORKOUT:	*distance*
a.m.	
p.m.	
	total

CROSS-TRAINING:	*time*
a.m.	
p.m.	
	total

TOMORROW'S TO DO

♈RUNALOG® FOR TRIATHLETES

TODAY'S DATE _____

MY LONG-TERM GOAL(S) _____

TODAY'S MEAL PLAN	BREAKFAST	SNACK	LUNCH	SNACK	DINNER
	_____	_____	_____	_____	_____
	_____	_____	_____	_____	_____

weekly planner

	SUNDAY	MONDAY	TUESDAY	WEDNESDAY	THURSDAY	FRIDAY	SATURDAY	TOTAL
a.m.								
p.m.								

🕐 daily planner

5 a.m. _____	2 p.m. _____
6 a.m. _____	3 p.m. _____
7 a.m. _____	4 p.m. _____
8 a.m _____	5 p.m. _____
9 a.m. _____	6 p.m. _____
10 a.m. _____	7 p.m. _____
11 a.m. _____	8 p.m. _____
12 p.m. _____	9 p.m. _____
1 p.m. _____	10 p.m. _____

✍ my training journal

my training log

SWIMMING WORKOUT: *distance*

a.m.	
p.m.	
	total

BIKING WORKOUT: *distance*

a.m.	
p.m.	
	total

RUNNING WORKOUT: *distance*

a.m.	
p.m.	
	total

CROSS-TRAINING: *time*

a.m.	
p.m.	
	total

TOMORROW'S To Do

✓RUNALOG® FOR TRIATHLETES

TODAY'S DATE _____

MY LONG-TERM GOAL(S) _____
_____

TODAY'S MEAL PLAN	BREAKFAST	SNACK	LUNCH	SNACK	DINNER
	_____	_____	_____	_____	_____
	_____	_____	_____	_____	_____

weekly planner

	SUNDAY	MONDAY	TUESDAY	WEDNESDAY	THURSDAY	FRIDAY	SATURDAY	TOTAL
a.m.								
p.m.								

🕐 daily planner

5 a.m. _____	2 p.m. _____
6 a.m. _____	3 p.m. _____
7 a.m. _____	4 p.m. _____
8 a.m _____	5 p.m. _____
9 a.m. _____	6 p.m. _____
10 a.m. _____	7 p.m. _____
11 a.m. _____	8 p.m. _____
12 p.m. _____	9 p.m. _____
1 p.m. _____	10 p.m. _____

✍ my training journal

my training log

SWIMMING WORKOUT:	distance
a.m.	
p.m.	
	total

BIKING WORKOUT:	distance
a.m.	
p.m.	
	total

RUNNING WORKOUT:	distance
a.m.	
p.m.	
	total

CROSS-TRAINING:	time
a.m.	
p.m.	
	total

TOMORROW'S TO DO

√RUNALOG® FOR TRIATHLETES

TODAY'S DATE _____

MY LONG-TERM GOAL(S) _____

TODAY'S MEAL PLAN	BREAKFAST	SNACK	LUNCH	SNACK	DINNER

weekly planner

	SUNDAY	MONDAY	TUESDAY	WEDNESDAY	THURSDAY	FRIDAY	SATURDAY	TOTAL
a.m.								
p.m.								

daily planner

5 a.m. _____	2 p.m. _____
6 a.m. _____	3 p.m. _____
7 a.m. _____	4 p.m. _____
8 a.m _____	5 p.m. _____
9 a.m. _____	6 p.m. _____
10 a.m. _____	7 p.m. _____
11 a.m. _____	8 p.m. _____
12 p.m. _____	9 p.m. _____
1 p.m. _____	10 p.m. _____

my training log

SWIMMING WORKOUT:	distance
a.m.	
p.m.	
	total

BIKING WORKOUT:	distance
a.m.	
p.m.	
	total

RUNNING WORKOUT:	distance
a.m.	
p.m.	
	total

CROSS-TRAINING:	time
a.m.	
p.m.	
	total

my training journal

TOMORROW'S TO DO

ⱽRUNALOG® FOR TRIATHLETES

TODAY'S DATE _____

MY LONG-TERM GOAL(S) _____

_____

TODAY'S MEAL PLAN	BREAKFAST	SNACK	LUNCH	SNACK	DINNER
	_____	_____	_____	_____	_____
	_____	_____	_____	_____	_____

weekly planner

	SUNDAY	MONDAY	TUESDAY	WEDNESDAY	THURSDAY	FRIDAY	SATURDAY	TOTAL
a.m.								
p.m.								

🕐 *daily planner*

5 a.m. _____	2 p.m. _____
6 a.m. _____	3 p.m. _____
7 a.m. _____	4 p.m. _____
8 a.m _____	5 p.m. _____
9 a.m. _____	6 p.m. _____
10 a.m. _____	7 p.m. _____
11 a.m. _____	8 p.m. _____
12 p.m. _____	9 p.m. _____
1 p.m. _____	10 p.m. _____

✍ *my training journal*

my training log

🏊 SWIMMING WORKOUT:	*distance*
a.m.	
p.m.	
	total

🚴 BIKING WORKOUT:	*distance*
a.m.	
p.m.	
	total

🏃 RUNNING WORKOUT:	*distance*
a.m.	
p.m.	
	total

CROSS-TRAINING:	*time*
a.m.	
p.m.	
	total

TOMORROW'S TO DO

RUNALOG® FOR TRIATHLETES

TODAY'S DATE _____

MY LONG-TERM GOAL(S) _____
_____

TODAY'S MEAL PLAN	BREAKFAST	SNACK	LUNCH	SNACK	DINNER

weekly planner

	SUNDAY	MONDAY	TUESDAY	WEDNESDAY	THURSDAY	FRIDAY	SATURDAY	TOTAL
a.m.								
p.m.								

daily planner

5 a.m.	_____	2 p.m.	_____
6 a.m.	_____	3 p.m.	_____
7 a.m.	_____	4 p.m.	_____
8 a.m	_____	5 p.m.	_____
9 a.m.	_____	6 p.m.	_____
10 a.m.	_____	7 p.m.	_____
11 a.m.	_____	8 p.m.	_____
12 p.m.	_____	9 p.m.	_____
1 p.m.	_____	10 p.m.	_____

my training journal

my training log

SWIMMING WORKOUT:	distance
a.m.	
p.m.	
	total

BIKING WORKOUT:	distance
a.m.	
p.m.	
	total

RUNNING WORKOUT:	distance
a.m.	
p.m.	
	total

CROSS-TRAINING:	time
a.m.	
p.m.	
	total

TOMORROW'S TO DO

RUNALOG® FOR TRIATHLETES

TODAY'S DATE _____

MY LONG-TERM GOAL(S) _____

TODAY'S MEAL PLAN	BREAKFAST	SNACK	LUNCH	SNACK	DINNER
	_____	_____	_____	_____	_____
	_____	_____	_____	_____	_____

weekly planner

	SUNDAY	MONDAY	TUESDAY	WEDNESDAY	THURSDAY	FRIDAY	SATURDAY	TOTAL
a.m.								
p.m.								

daily planner

5 a.m. _____	2 p.m. _____
6 a.m. _____	3 p.m. _____
7 a.m. _____	4 p.m. _____
8 a.m _____	5 p.m. _____
9 a.m. _____	6 p.m. _____
10 a.m. _____	7 p.m. _____
11 a.m. _____	8 p.m. _____
12 p.m. _____	9 p.m. _____
1 p.m. _____	10 p.m. _____

my training journal

my training log

SWIMMING WORKOUT:	distance
a.m.	
p.m.	
	total

BIKING WORKOUT:	distance
a.m.	
p.m.	
	total

RUNNING WORKOUT:	distance
a.m.	
p.m.	
	total

CROSS-TRAINING:	time
a.m.	
p.m.	
	total

TOMORROW'S To Do

⚡RUNALOG® FOR TRIATHLETES

TODAY'S DATE _____

MY LONG-TERM GOAL(S) _____
_____

TODAY'S MEAL PLAN	**BREAKFAST**	**SNACK**	**LUNCH**	**SNACK**	**DINNER**
	_____	_____	_____	_____	_____
	_____	_____	_____	_____	_____

weekly planner

	SUNDAY	MONDAY	TUESDAY	WEDNESDAY	THURSDAY	FRIDAY	SATURDAY	TOTAL
a.m.								
p.m.								

🕐 *daily planner*

5 a.m. _____	2 p.m. _____
6 a.m. _____	3 p.m. _____
7 a.m. _____	4 p.m. _____
8 a.m _____	5 p.m. _____
9 a.m. _____	6 p.m. _____
10 a.m. _____	7 p.m. _____
11 a.m. _____	8 p.m. _____
12 p.m. _____	9 p.m. _____
1 p.m. _____	10 p.m. _____

✍ *my training journal*

my training log

SWIMMING WORKOUT:	*distance*
a.m.	
p.m.	
	total

BIKING WORKOUT:	*distance*
a.m.	
p.m.	
	total

RUNNING WORKOUT:	*distance*
a.m.	
p.m.	
	total

CROSS-TRAINING:	*time*
a.m.	
p.m.	
	total

TOMORROW'S TO DO

∜RUNALOG® FOR TRIATHLETES

MY LONG-TERM GOAL(S) _____

TODAY'S MEAL PLAN	BREAKFAST	SNACK	LUNCH	SNACK	DINNER
	_____	_____	_____	_____	_____

weekly planner

	SUNDAY	MONDAY	TUESDAY	WEDNESDAY	THURSDAY	FRIDAY	SATURDAY	TOTAL
a.m.								
p.m.								

daily planner

5 a.m. _____	2 p.m. _____
6 a.m. _____	3 p.m. _____
7 a.m. _____	4 p.m. _____
8 a.m _____	5 p.m. _____
9 a.m. _____	6 p.m. _____
10 a.m. _____	7 p.m. _____
11 a.m. _____	8 p.m. _____
12 p.m. _____	9 p.m. _____
1 p.m. _____	10 p.m. _____

my training journal

my training log

SWIMMING WORKOUT:	distance
a.m.	
p.m.	
	total

BIKING WORKOUT:	distance
a.m.	
p.m.	
	total

RUNNING WORKOUT:	distance
a.m.	
p.m.	
	total

CROSS-TRAINING:	time
a.m.	
p.m.	
	total

TOMORROW'S To Do

347

√RUNALOG® *FOR TRIATHLETES*   TODAY'S DATE _____

MY LONG-TERM GOAL(S)_____
_____

TODAY'S MEAL PLAN	BREAKFAST	SNACK	LUNCH	SNACK	DINNER
	_____	_____	_____	_____	_____
	_____	_____	_____	_____	_____

weekly planner

	SUNDAY	MONDAY	TUESDAY	WEDNESDAY	THURSDAY	FRIDAY	SATURDAY	TOTAL
a.m.								
p.m.								

🕐 *daily planner*

5 a.m. _____	2 p.m. _____
6 a.m. _____	3 p.m. _____
7 a.m. _____	4 p.m. _____
8 a.m _____	5 p.m. _____
9 a.m. _____	6 p.m. _____
10 a.m. _____	7 p.m. _____
11 a.m. _____	8 p.m. _____
12 p.m. _____	9 p.m. _____
1 p.m. _____	10 p.m. _____

✍ *my training journal*

my training log

SWIMMING WORKOUT:	*distance*
a.m.	
p.m.	
	total

BIKING WORKOUT:	*distance*
a.m.	
p.m.	
	total

RUNNING WORKOUT:	*distance*
a.m.	
p.m.	
	total

CROSS-TRAINING:	*time*
a.m.	
p.m.	
	total

TOMORROW'S TO DO

RUNALOG® FOR TRIATHLETES

TODAY'S DATE _____

MY LONG-TERM GOAL(S) _____

TODAY'S MEAL PLAN	BREAKFAST	SNACK	LUNCH	SNACK	DINNER
	_____	_____	_____	_____	_____
	_____	_____	_____	_____	_____

weekly planner

	SUNDAY	MONDAY	TUESDAY	WEDNESDAY	THURSDAY	FRIDAY	SATURDAY	TOTAL
a.m.								
p.m.								

daily planner

5 a.m. _____	2 p.m. _____
6 a.m. _____	3 p.m. _____
7 a.m. _____	4 p.m. _____
8 a.m _____	5 p.m. _____
9 a.m. _____	6 p.m. _____
10 a.m. _____	7 p.m. _____
11 a.m. _____	8 p.m. _____
12 p.m. _____	9 p.m. _____
1 p.m. _____	10 p.m. _____

my training journal

my training log

SWIMMING WORKOUT: *distance*

a.m.	
p.m.	
	total

BIKING WORKOUT: *distance*

a.m.	
p.m.	
	total

RUNNING WORKOUT: *distance*

a.m.	
p.m.	
	total

CROSS-TRAINING: *time*

a.m.	
p.m.	
	total

TOMORROW'S To Do

⩜RUNALOG® FOR TRIATHLETES

TODAY'S DATE _____

MY LONG-TERM GOAL(S) _____

TODAY'S MEAL PLAN	BREAKFAST	SNACK	LUNCH	SNACK	DINNER
	_____	_____	_____	_____	_____
	_____	_____	_____	_____	_____

weekly planner

	SUNDAY	MONDAY	TUESDAY	WEDNESDAY	THURSDAY	FRIDAY	SATURDAY	TOTAL
a.m.								
p.m.								

🕐 *daily planner*

5 a.m.	_____	2 p.m.	_____
6 a.m.	_____	3 p.m.	_____
7 a.m.	_____	4 p.m.	_____
8 a.m	_____	5 p.m.	_____
9 a.m.	_____	6 p.m.	_____
10 a.m.	_____	7 p.m.	_____
11 a.m.	_____	8 p.m.	_____
12 p.m.	_____	9 p.m.	_____
1 p.m.	_____	10 p.m.	_____

✍ *my training journal*

my training log

🏊 SWIMMING WORKOUT:	*distance*
a.m.	
p.m.	
	total

🚴 BIKING WORKOUT:	*distance*
a.m.	
p.m.	
	total

🏃 RUNNING WORKOUT:	*distance*
a.m.	
p.m.	
	total

CROSS-TRAINING:	*time*
a.m.	
p.m.	
	total

TOMORROW'S To Do

ᚢRUNALOG® *FOR TRIATHLETES*

TODAY'S DATE _____

MY LONG-TERM GOAL(S) _____

TODAY'S MEAL PLAN	**BREAKFAST**	**SNACK**	**LUNCH**	**SNACK**	**DINNER**
	_____	_____	_____	_____	_____
	_____	_____	_____	_____	_____

weekly planner

	SUNDAY	MONDAY	TUESDAY	WEDNESDAY	THURSDAY	FRIDAY	SATURDAY	TOTAL
a.m.								
p.m.								

🕐 *daily planner*

5 a.m. _____	2 p.m. _____
6 a.m. _____	3 p.m. _____
7 a.m. _____	4 p.m. _____
8 a.m _____	5 p.m. _____
9 a.m. _____	6 p.m. _____
10 a.m. _____	7 p.m. _____
11 a.m. _____	8 p.m. _____
12 p.m. _____	9 p.m. _____
1 p.m. _____	10 p.m. _____

✍ *my training journal*

my training log

SWIMMING WORKOUT:	*distance*
a.m.	
p.m.	
	total

BIKING WORKOUT:	*distance*
a.m.	
p.m.	
	total

RUNNING WORKOUT:	*distance*
a.m.	
p.m.	
	total

CROSS-TRAINING:	*time*
a.m.	
p.m.	
	total

TOMORROW'S TO DO

351

RUNALOG® FOR TRIATHLETES

TODAY'S DATE _____

MY LONG-TERM GOAL(S) _____
_____

TODAY'S MEAL PLAN	BREAKFAST	SNACK	LUNCH	SNACK	DINNER
	_____	_____	_____	_____	_____
	_____	_____	_____	_____	_____

weekly planner

	SUNDAY	MONDAY	TUESDAY	WEDNESDAY	THURSDAY	FRIDAY	SATURDAY	TOTAL
a.m.								
p.m.								

daily planner

5 a.m. _____	2 p.m. _____
6 a.m. _____	3 p.m. _____
7 a.m. _____	4 p.m. _____
8 a.m _____	5 p.m. _____
9 a.m. _____	6 p.m. _____
10 a.m. _____	7 p.m. _____
11 a.m. _____	8 p.m. _____
12 p.m. _____	9 p.m. _____
1 p.m. _____	10 p.m. _____

my training journal

my training log

SWIMMING WORKOUT:	distance
a.m.	
p.m.	
	total

BIKING WORKOUT:	distance
a.m.	
p.m.	
	total

RUNNING WORKOUT:	distance
a.m.	
p.m.	
	total

CROSS-TRAINING:	time
a.m.	
p.m.	
	total

TOMORROW'S TO DO

✓RUNALOG® FOR TRIATHLETES

TODAY'S DATE _____

MY LONG-TERM GOAL(S) _____
_____

TODAY'S MEAL PLAN	BREAKFAST	SNACK	LUNCH	SNACK	DINNER
	_____	_____	_____	_____	_____
	_____	_____	_____	_____	_____

weekly planner

	SUNDAY	MONDAY	TUESDAY	WEDNESDAY	THURSDAY	FRIDAY	SATURDAY	TOTAL
a.m.								
p.m.								

🕐 daily planner

5 a.m. _____	2 p.m. _____
6 a.m. _____	3 p.m. _____
7 a.m. _____	4 p.m. _____
8 a.m _____	5 p.m. _____
9 a.m. _____	6 p.m. _____
10 a.m. _____	7 p.m. _____
11 a.m. _____	8 p.m. _____
12 p.m. _____	9 p.m. _____
1 p.m. _____	10 p.m. _____

✍ my training journal

my training log

🏊 SWIMMING WORKOUT: *distance*

a.m.	
p.m.	
	total

🚴 BIKING WORKOUT: *distance*

a.m.	
p.m.	
	total

🏃 RUNNING WORKOUT: *distance*

a.m.	
p.m.	
	total

CROSS-TRAINING: *time*

a.m.	
p.m.	
	total

TOMORROW'S To Do

MY LONG-TERM GOAL(S) _____

TODAY'S MEAL PLAN	BREAKFAST	SNACK	LUNCH	SNACK	DINNER
	_____	_____	_____	_____	_____
	_____	_____	_____	_____	_____

weekly planner

	SUNDAY	MONDAY	TUESDAY	WEDNESDAY	THURSDAY	FRIDAY	SATURDAY	TOTAL
a.m.								
p.m.								

daily planner

5 a.m. _____	2 p.m. _____
6 a.m. _____	3 p.m. _____
7 a.m. _____	4 p.m. _____
8 a.m _____	5 p.m. _____
9 a.m. _____	6 p.m. _____
10 a.m. _____	7 p.m. _____
11 a.m. _____	8 p.m. _____
12 p.m. _____	9 p.m. _____
1 p.m. _____	10 p.m. _____

my training journal

my training log

SWIMMING WORKOUT:	*distance*
a.m.	
p.m.	
	total

BIKING WORKOUT:	*distance*
a.m.	
p.m.	
	total

RUNNING WORKOUT:	*distance*
a.m.	
p.m.	
	total

CROSS-TRAINING:	*time*
a.m.	
p.m.	
	total

TOMORROW'S TO DO

$\sqrt[V]{}$RUNALOG® FOR TRIATHLETES

TODAY'S DATE _____

MY LONG-TERM GOAL(S) _____

TODAY'S MEAL PLAN	BREAKFAST	SNACK	LUNCH	SNACK	DINNER
	_____	_____	_____	_____	_____
	_____	_____	_____	_____	_____

weekly planner

	SUNDAY	MONDAY	TUESDAY	WEDNESDAY	THURSDAY	FRIDAY	SATURDAY	TOTAL
a.m.								
p.m.								

daily planner

5 a.m. _____	2 p.m. _____
6 a.m. _____	3 p.m. _____
7 a.m. _____	4 p.m. _____
8 a.m _____	5 p.m. _____
9 a.m. _____	6 p.m. _____
10 a.m. _____	7 p.m. _____
11 a.m. _____	8 p.m. _____
12 p.m. _____	9 p.m. _____
1 p.m. _____	10 p.m. _____

my training journal

my training log

SWIMMING WORKOUT:	*distance*
a.m.	
p.m.	
	total

BIKING WORKOUT:	*distance*
a.m.	
p.m.	
	total

RUNNING WORKOUT:	*distance*
a.m.	
p.m.	
	total

CROSS-TRAINING:	*time*
a.m.	
p.m.	
	total

TOMORROW'S TO DO

⚘RUNALOG® FOR TRIATHLETES   TODAY'S DATE _____

MY LONG-TERM GOAL(S) _____

TODAY'S MEAL PLAN	BREAKFAST	SNACK	LUNCH	SNACK	DINNER
	_____	_____	_____	_____	_____

weekly planner

	SUNDAY	MONDAY	TUESDAY	WEDNESDAY	THURSDAY	FRIDAY	SATURDAY	TOTAL
a.m.								
p.m.								

daily planner

5 a.m. _____	2 p.m. _____
6 a.m. _____	3 p.m. _____
7 a.m. _____	4 p.m. _____
8 a.m _____	5 p.m. _____
9 a.m. _____	6 p.m. _____
10 a.m. _____	7 p.m. _____
11 a.m. _____	8 p.m. _____
12 p.m. _____	9 p.m. _____
1 p.m. _____	10 p.m. _____

my training journal

my training log

SWIMMING WORKOUT:	distance
a.m.	
p.m.	
	total

BIKING WORKOUT:	distance
a.m.	
p.m.	
	total

RUNNING WORKOUT:	distance
a.m.	
p.m.	
	total

CROSS-TRAINING:	time
a.m.	
p.m.	
	total

TOMORROW'S TO DO

⚡RUNALOG° FOR TRIATHLETES   ***TODAY'S DATE*** _____

MY LONG-TERM GOAL(S) _____
_____

TODAY'S MEAL PLAN	BREAKFAST	SNACK	LUNCH	SNACK	DINNER
	_____	_____	_____	_____	_____
	_____	_____	_____	_____	_____

weekly planner

	SUNDAY	MONDAY	TUESDAY	WEDNESDAY	THURSDAY	FRIDAY	SATURDAY	TOTAL
a.m.								
p.m.								

🕐 *daily planner*

5 a.m. _____		2 p.m. _____	
6 a.m. _____		3 p.m. _____	
7 a.m. _____		4 p.m. _____	
8 a.m _____		5 p.m. _____	
9 a.m. _____		6 p.m. _____	
10 a.m. _____		7 p.m. _____	
11 a.m. _____		8 p.m. _____	
12 p.m. _____		9 p.m. _____	
1 p.m. _____		10 p.m. _____	

✍ *my training journal*

my training log

SWIMMING WORKOUT: *distance*

a.m.	
p.m.	
	total

BIKING WORKOUT: *distance*

a.m.	
p.m.	
	total

RUNNING WORKOUT: *distance*

a.m.	
p.m.	
	total

CROSS-TRAINING: *time*

a.m.	
p.m.	
	total

TOMORROW'S To Do

357

© 2009 www.RUNALOGS.com

√RUNALOG® FOR TRIATHLETES

TODAY'S DATE _____

MY LONG-TERM GOAL(S) _____

TODAY'S MEAL PLAN	BREAKFAST	SNACK	LUNCH	SNACK	DINNER
	_____	_____	_____	_____	_____
	_____	_____	_____	_____	_____

weekly planner

	SUNDAY	MONDAY	TUESDAY	WEDNESDAY	THURSDAY	FRIDAY	SATURDAY	TOTAL
a.m.								
p.m.								

daily planner

5 a.m.	_____	2 p.m.	_____
6 a.m.	_____	3 p.m.	_____
7 a.m.	_____	4 p.m.	_____
8 a.m	_____	5 p.m.	_____
9 a.m.	_____	6 p.m.	_____
10 a.m.	_____	7 p.m.	_____
11 a.m.	_____	8 p.m.	_____
12 p.m.	_____	9 p.m.	_____
1 p.m.	_____	10 p.m.	_____

my training log

SWIMMING WORKOUT:	*distance*
a.m.	
p.m.	
	total

BIKING WORKOUT:	*distance*
a.m.	
p.m.	
	total

RUNNING WORKOUT:	*distance*
a.m.	
p.m.	
	total

CROSS-TRAINING:	*time*
a.m.	
p.m.	
	total

my training journal

TOMORROW'S TO DO

⩔RUNALOG® FOR TRIATHLETES

TODAY'S DATE _____

MY LONG-TERM GOAL(S) _____
_____

TODAY'S MEAL PLAN	BREAKFAST	SNACK	LUNCH	SNACK	DINNER
	_____	_____	_____	_____	_____
	_____	_____	_____	_____	_____

weekly planner

	SUNDAY	MONDAY	TUESDAY	WEDNESDAY	THURSDAY	FRIDAY	SATURDAY	TOTAL
a.m.								
p.m.								

🕐 daily planner

5 a.m. _____	2 p.m. _____
6 a.m. _____	3 p.m. _____
7 a.m. _____	4 p.m. _____
8 a.m _____	5 p.m. _____
9 a.m. _____	6 p.m. _____
10 a.m. _____	7 p.m. _____
11 a.m. _____	8 p.m. _____
12 p.m. _____	9 p.m. _____
1 p.m. _____	10 p.m. _____

✍ my training journal

my training log

SWIMMING WORKOUT:	*distance*
a.m.	
p.m.	
	total

BIKING WORKOUT:	*distance*
a.m.	
p.m.	
	total

RUNNING WORKOUT:	*distance*
a.m.	
p.m.	
	total

CROSS-TRAINING:	*time*
a.m.	
p.m.	
	total

TOMORROW'S To Do

RUNALOG® FOR TRIATHLETES

TODAY'S DATE _____

MY LONG-TERM GOAL(S) _____

TODAY'S MEAL PLAN	BREAKFAST	SNACK	LUNCH	SNACK	DINNER
	_____	_____	_____	_____	_____
	_____	_____	_____	_____	_____

weekly planner

	SUNDAY	MONDAY	TUESDAY	WEDNESDAY	THURSDAY	FRIDAY	SATURDAY	TOTAL
a.m.								
p.m.								

daily planner

5 a.m. _____	2 p.m. _____
6 a.m. _____	3 p.m. _____
7 a.m. _____	4 p.m. _____
8 a.m _____	5 p.m. _____
9 a.m. _____	6 p.m. _____
10 a.m. _____	7 p.m. _____
11 a.m. _____	8 p.m. _____
12 p.m. _____	9 p.m. _____
1 p.m. _____	10 p.m. _____

my training log

SWIMMING WORKOUT:	distance
a.m.	
p.m.	
	total

BIKING WORKOUT:	distance
a.m.	
p.m.	
	total

RUNNING WORKOUT:	distance
a.m.	
p.m.	
	total

CROSS-TRAINING:	time
a.m.	
p.m.	
	total

my training journal

TOMORROW'S TO DO

RUNALOG® FOR TRIATHLETES

TODAY'S DATE _____

MY LONG-TERM GOAL(S) _____

TODAY'S MEAL PLAN	BREAKFAST	SNACK	LUNCH	SNACK	DINNER
	_____	_____	_____	_____	_____
	_____	_____	_____	_____	_____

weekly planner

	SUNDAY	MONDAY	TUESDAY	WEDNESDAY	THURSDAY	FRIDAY	SATURDAY	TOTAL
a.m.								
p.m.								

daily planner

5 a.m. _____	2 p.m. _____
6 a.m. _____	3 p.m. _____
7 a.m. _____	4 p.m. _____
8 a.m _____	5 p.m. _____
9 a.m. _____	6 p.m. _____
10 a.m. _____	7 p.m. _____
11 a.m. _____	8 p.m. _____
12 p.m. _____	9 p.m. _____
1 p.m. _____	10 p.m. _____

my training journal

my training log

SWIMMING WORKOUT:	*distance*
a.m.	
p.m.	
	total

BIKING WORKOUT:	*distance*
a.m.	
p.m.	
	total

RUNNING WORKOUT:	*distance*
a.m.	
p.m.	
	total

CROSS-TRAINING:	*time*
a.m.	
p.m.	
	total

TOMORROW'S To Do

RUNALOG® FOR TRIATHLETES

TODAY'S DATE _____

MY LONG-TERM GOAL(S) _____

TODAY'S MEAL PLAN	BREAKFAST	SNACK	LUNCH	SNACK	DINNER
	_____	_____	_____	_____	_____
	_____	_____	_____	_____	_____

weekly planner

	SUNDAY	MONDAY	TUESDAY	WEDNESDAY	THURSDAY	FRIDAY	SATURDAY	TOTAL
a.m.								
p.m.								

daily planner

5 a.m.	_____	2 p.m.	_____
6 a.m.	_____	3 p.m.	_____
7 a.m.	_____	4 p.m.	_____
8 a.m	_____	5 p.m.	_____
9 a.m.	_____	6 p.m.	_____
10 a.m.	_____	7 p.m.	_____
11 a.m.	_____	8 p.m.	_____
12 p.m.	_____	9 p.m.	_____
1 p.m.	_____	10 p.m.	_____

my training journal

my training log

SWIMMING WORKOUT:	*distance*
a.m.	
p.m.	
	total

BIKING WORKOUT:	*distance*
a.m.	
p.m.	
	total

RUNNING WORKOUT:	*distance*
a.m.	
p.m.	
	total

CROSS-TRAINING:	*time*
a.m.	
p.m.	
	total

TOMORROW'S To Do

⩗RUNALOG® For Triathletes

Today's Date _____

MY LONG-TERM GOAL(S) _____

Today's Meal Plan	Breakfast	Snack	Lunch	Snack	Dinner

weekly planner

SUNDAY	MONDAY	TUESDAY	WEDNESDAY	THURSDAY	FRIDAY	SATURDAY	TOTAL
a.m.							
p.m.							

daily planner

5 a.m. _____	2 p.m. _____
6 a.m. _____	3 p.m. _____
7 a.m. _____	4 p.m. _____
8 a.m _____	5 p.m. _____
9 a.m. _____	6 p.m. _____
10 a.m. _____	7 p.m. _____
11 a.m. _____	8 p.m. _____
12 p.m. _____	9 p.m. _____
1 p.m. _____	10 p.m. _____

my training journal

my training log

SWIMMING WORKOUT:	distance
a.m.	
p.m.	
	total

BIKING WORKOUT:	distance
a.m.	
p.m.	
	total

RUNNING WORKOUT:	distance
a.m.	
p.m.	
	total

CROSS-TRAINING:	time
a.m.	
p.m.	
	total

Tomorrow's To Do

RUNALOG® FOR TRIATHLETES

TODAY'S DATE _____

MY LONG-TERM GOAL(S) _____

TODAY'S MEAL PLAN	BREAKFAST	SNACK	LUNCH	SNACK	DINNER
	_____	_____	_____	_____	_____
	_____	_____	_____	_____	_____

weekly planner

	SUNDAY	MONDAY	TUESDAY	WEDNESDAY	THURSDAY	FRIDAY	SATURDAY	TOTAL
a.m.								
p.m.								

daily planner

5 a.m.	_____	2 p.m.	_____
6 a.m.	_____	3 p.m.	_____
7 a.m.	_____	4 p.m.	_____
8 a.m	_____	5 p.m.	_____
9 a.m.	_____	6 p.m.	_____
10 a.m.	_____	7 p.m.	_____
11 a.m.	_____	8 p.m.	_____
12 p.m.	_____	9 p.m.	_____
1 p.m.	_____	10 p.m.	_____

my training journal

my training log

SWIMMING WORKOUT: distance

a.m.	
p.m.	
	total

BIKING WORKOUT: distance

a.m.	
p.m.	
	total

RUNNING WORKOUT: distance

a.m.	
p.m.	
	total

CROSS-TRAINING: time

a.m.	
p.m.	
	total

TOMORROW'S TO DO

⩔RUNALOG° FOR TRIATHLETES

TODAY'S DATE _____

MY LONG-TERM GOAL(S) _____

TODAY'S MEAL PLAN	BREAKFAST	SNACK	LUNCH	SNACK	DINNER
	_____	_____	_____	_____	_____
	_____	_____	_____	_____	_____

weekly planner

	SUNDAY	MONDAY	TUESDAY	WEDNESDAY	THURSDAY	FRIDAY	SATURDAY	TOTAL
a.m.								
p.m.								

🕐 daily planner

5 a.m. _____	2 p.m. _____
6 a.m. _____	3 p.m. _____
7 a.m. _____	4 p.m. _____
8 a.m _____	5 p.m. _____
9 a.m. _____	6 p.m. _____
10 a.m. _____	7 p.m. _____
11 a.m. _____	8 p.m. _____
12 p.m. _____	9 p.m. _____
1 p.m. _____	10 p.m. _____

✍ my training journal

my training log

SWIMMING WORKOUT:	*distance*
a.m.	
p.m.	
	total

BIKING WORKOUT:	*distance*
a.m.	
p.m.	
	total

RUNNING WORKOUT:	*distance*
a.m.	
p.m.	
	total

CROSS-TRAINING:	*time*
a.m.	
p.m.	
	total

TOMORROW'S To Do

RUNALOG® FOR TRIATHLETES

TODAY'S DATE _____

MY LONG-TERM GOAL(S) _____

TODAY'S MEAL PLAN	BREAKFAST	SNACK	LUNCH	SNACK	DINNER
	_____	_____	_____	_____	_____
	_____	_____	_____	_____	_____

weekly planner

	SUNDAY	MONDAY	TUESDAY	WEDNESDAY	THURSDAY	FRIDAY	SATURDAY	TOTAL
a.m.								
p.m.								

daily planner

5 a.m. _____	2 p.m. _____
6 a.m. _____	3 p.m. _____
7 a.m. _____	4 p.m. _____
8 a.m _____	5 p.m. _____
9 a.m. _____	6 p.m. _____
10 a.m. _____	7 p.m. _____
11 a.m. _____	8 p.m. _____
12 p.m. _____	9 p.m. _____
1 p.m. _____	10 p.m. _____

my training journal

my training log

SWIMMING WORKOUT:	*distance*
a.m.	
p.m.	
	total

BIKING WORKOUT:	*distance*
a.m.	
p.m.	
	total

RUNNING WORKOUT:	*distance*
a.m.	
p.m.	
	total

CROSS-TRAINING:	*time*
a.m.	
p.m.	
	total

TOMORROW'S TO DO

MY LONG-TERM GOAL(S) _____

_____

TODAY'S MEAL PLAN	BREAKFAST	SNACK	LUNCH	SNACK	DINNER
	_____	_____	_____	_____	_____
	_____	_____	_____	_____	_____

weekly planner

	SUNDAY	MONDAY	TUESDAY	WEDNESDAY	THURSDAY	FRIDAY	SATURDAY	TOTAL
a.m.								
p.m.								

daily planner

5 a.m. _____	2 p.m. _____
6 a.m. _____	3 p.m. _____
7 a.m. _____	4 p.m. _____
8 a.m _____	5 p.m. _____
9 a.m. _____	6 p.m. _____
10 a.m. _____	7 p.m. _____
11 a.m. _____	8 p.m. _____
12 p.m. _____	9 p.m. _____
1 p.m. _____	10 p.m. _____

my training journal

my training log

SWIMMING WORKOUT:	*distance*
a.m.	
p.m.	
	total

BIKING WORKOUT:	*distance*
a.m.	
p.m.	
	total

RUNNING WORKOUT:	*distance*
a.m.	
p.m.	
	total

CROSS-TRAINING:	*time*
a.m.	
p.m.	
	total

TOMORROW'S To Do

RUNALOG° FOR TRIATHLETES   **TODAY'S DATE** _____

MY LONG-TERM GOAL(S) _____

TODAY'S MEAL PLAN	BREAKFAST	SNACK	LUNCH	SNACK	DINNER

weekly planner

	SUNDAY	MONDAY	TUESDAY	WEDNESDAY	THURSDAY	FRIDAY	SATURDAY	TOTAL
a.m.								
p.m.								

daily planner

5 a.m. _____	2 p.m. _____
6 a.m. _____	3 p.m. _____
7 a.m. _____	4 p.m. _____
8 a.m _____	5 p.m. _____
9 a.m. _____	6 p.m. _____
10 a.m. _____	7 p.m. _____
11 a.m. _____	8 p.m. _____
12 p.m. _____	9 p.m. _____
1 p.m. _____	10 p.m. _____

my training journal

my training log

SWIMMING WORKOUT: *distance*

a.m.	
p.m.	
	total

BIKING WORKOUT: *distance*

a.m.	
p.m.	
	total

RUNNING WORKOUT: *distance*

a.m.	
p.m.	
	total

CROSS-TRAINING: *time*

a.m.	
p.m.	
	total

TOMORROW'S To Do

✓RUNALOG® FOR TRIATHLETES

TODAY'S DATE _____

MY LONG-TERM GOAL(S) _____

TODAY'S MEAL PLAN	BREAKFAST	SNACK	LUNCH	SNACK	DINNER
	_____	_____	_____	_____	_____
	_____	_____	_____	_____	_____

weekly planner

	SUNDAY	MONDAY	TUESDAY	WEDNESDAY	THURSDAY	FRIDAY	SATURDAY	TOTAL
a.m.								
p.m.								

🕐 daily planner

5 a.m. _____	2 p.m. _____
6 a.m. _____	3 p.m. _____
7 a.m. _____	4 p.m. _____
8 a.m _____	5 p.m. _____
9 a.m. _____	6 p.m. _____
10 a.m. _____	7 p.m. _____
11 a.m. _____	8 p.m. _____
12 p.m. _____	9 p.m. _____
1 p.m. _____	10 p.m. _____

✎ my training journal

my training log

SWIMMING WORKOUT:	*distance*
a.m.	
p.m.	
	total

BIKING WORKOUT:	*distance*
a.m.	
p.m.	
	total

RUNNING WORKOUT:	*distance*
a.m.	
p.m.	
	total

CROSS-TRAINING:	*time*
a.m.	
p.m.	
	total

TOMORROW'S To Do

MY LONG-TERM GOAL(S) _____

TODAY'S MEAL PLAN	BREAKFAST	SNACK	LUNCH	SNACK	DINNER
	_____	_____	_____	_____	_____
	_____	_____	_____	_____	_____

weekly planner

	SUNDAY	MONDAY	TUESDAY	WEDNESDAY	THURSDAY	FRIDAY	SATURDAY	TOTAL
a.m.								
p.m.								

daily planner

5 a.m. _____	2 p.m. _____
6 a.m. _____	3 p.m. _____
7 a.m. _____	4 p.m. _____
8 a.m _____	5 p.m. _____
9 a.m. _____	6 p.m. _____
10 a.m. _____	7 p.m. _____
11 a.m. _____	8 p.m. _____
12 p.m. _____	9 p.m. _____
1 p.m. _____	10 p.m. _____

my training journal

my training log

SWIMMING WORKOUT:	*distance*
a.m.	
p.m.	
	total

BIKING WORKOUT:	*distance*
a.m.	
p.m.	
	total

RUNNING WORKOUT:	*distance*
a.m.	
p.m.	
	total

CROSS-TRAINING:	*time*
a.m.	
p.m.	
	total

TOMORROW'S TO DO

⩔RUNALOG® FOR TRIATHLETES

TODAY'S DATE _____

MY LONG-TERM GOAL(S) _____

_____

TODAY'S MEAL PLAN	BREAKFAST	SNACK	LUNCH	SNACK	DINNER
	_____	_____	_____	_____	_____
	_____	_____	_____	_____	_____

weekly planner

SUNDAY	MONDAY	TUESDAY	WEDNESDAY	THURSDAY	FRIDAY	SATURDAY	TOTAL
a.m.							
p.m.							

daily planner

5 a.m. _____	2 p.m. _____
6 a.m. _____	3 p.m. _____
7 a.m. _____	4 p.m. _____
8 a.m _____	5 p.m. _____
9 a.m. _____	6 p.m. _____
10 a.m. _____	7 p.m. _____
11 a.m. _____	8 p.m. _____
12 p.m. _____	9 p.m. _____
1 p.m. _____	10 p.m. _____

my training journal

my training log

SWIMMING WORKOUT: *distance*

a.m.	
p.m.	
	total

BIKING WORKOUT: *distance*

a.m.	
p.m.	
	total

RUNNING WORKOUT: *distance*

a.m.	
p.m.	
	total

CROSS-TRAINING: *time*

a.m.	
p.m.	
	total

TOMORROW'S TO DO

371

© 2009 www.RUNALOGS.com

RUNALOG® FOR TRIATHLETES

TODAY'S DATE _____

MY LONG-TERM GOAL(S) _____

TODAY'S MEAL PLAN	BREAKFAST	SNACK	LUNCH	SNACK	DINNER
	_____	_____	_____	_____	_____
	_____	_____	_____	_____	_____

weekly planner

	SUNDAY	MONDAY	TUESDAY	WEDNESDAY	THURSDAY	FRIDAY	SATURDAY	TOTAL
a.m.								
p.m.								

daily planner

5 a.m. _____	2 p.m. _____
6 a.m. _____	3 p.m. _____
7 a.m. _____	4 p.m. _____
8 a.m. _____	5 p.m. _____
9 a.m. _____	6 p.m. _____
10 a.m. _____	7 p.m. _____
11 a.m. _____	8 p.m. _____
12 p.m. _____	9 p.m. _____
1 p.m. _____	10 p.m. _____

my training journal

my training log

SWIMMING WORKOUT: *distance*

a.m.	
p.m.	
	total

BIKING WORKOUT: *distance*

a.m.	
p.m.	
	total

RUNNING WORKOUT: *distance*

a.m.	
p.m.	
	total

CROSS-TRAINING: *time*

a.m.	
p.m.	
	total

TOMORROW'S TO DO

ᵛ̆RUNALOG® FOR TRIATHLETES

TODAY'S DATE _____

MY LONG-TERM GOAL(S) _____

TODAY'S MEAL PLAN	BREAKFAST	SNACK	LUNCH	SNACK	DINNER
	_____	_____	_____	_____	_____
	_____	_____	_____	_____	_____

weekly planner

	SUNDAY	MONDAY	TUESDAY	WEDNESDAY	THURSDAY	FRIDAY	SATURDAY	TOTAL
a.m.								
p.m.								

daily planner

5 a.m. _____	2 p.m. _____
6 a.m. _____	3 p.m. _____
7 a.m. _____	4 p.m. _____
8 a.m _____	5 p.m. _____
9 a.m. _____	6 p.m. _____
10 a.m. _____	7 p.m. _____
11 a.m. _____	8 p.m. _____
12 p.m. _____	9 p.m. _____
1 p.m. _____	10 p.m. _____

my training journal

my training log

SWIMMING WORKOUT:	distance
a.m.	
p.m.	
	total

BIKING WORKOUT:	distance
a.m.	
p.m.	
	total

RUNNING WORKOUT:	distance
a.m.	
p.m.	
	total

CROSS-TRAINING:	time
a.m.	
p.m.	
	total

TOMORROW'S TO DO

RUNALOG® FOR TRIATHLETES

TODAY'S DATE _____

MY LONG-TERM GOAL(S) _____

TODAY'S MEAL PLAN	BREAKFAST	SNACK	LUNCH	SNACK	DINNER

weekly planner

	SUNDAY	MONDAY	TUESDAY	WEDNESDAY	THURSDAY	FRIDAY	SATURDAY	TOTAL
a.m.								
p.m.								

daily planner

5 a.m.	_____	2 p.m.	_____
6 a.m.	_____	3 p.m.	_____
7 a.m.	_____	4 p.m.	_____
8 a.m	_____	5 p.m.	_____
9 a.m.	_____	6 p.m.	_____
10 a.m.	_____	7 p.m.	_____
11 a.m.	_____	8 p.m.	_____
12 p.m.	_____	9 p.m.	_____
1 p.m.	_____	10 p.m.	_____

my training log

SWIMMING WORKOUT:	distance
a.m.	
p.m.	
	total

BIKING WORKOUT:	distance
a.m.	
p.m.	
	total

RUNNING WORKOUT:	distance
a.m.	
p.m.	
	total

CROSS-TRAINING:	time
a.m.	
p.m.	
	total

my training journal

TOMORROW'S TO DO

⩗RUNALOG® *FOR TRIATHLETES*

TODAY'S DATE _____

MY LONG-TERM GOAL(S) _____

_____

TODAY'S MEAL PLAN	BREAKFAST	SNACK	LUNCH	SNACK	DINNER
	_____	_____	_____	_____	_____
	_____	_____	_____	_____	_____

weekly planner

	SUNDAY	MONDAY	TUESDAY	WEDNESDAY	THURSDAY	FRIDAY	SATURDAY	TOTAL
a.m.								
p.m.								

daily planner

5 a.m. _____		2 p.m. _____	
6 a.m. _____		3 p.m. _____	
7 a.m. _____		4 p.m. _____	
8 a.m _____		5 p.m. _____	
9 a.m. _____		6 p.m. _____	
10 a.m. _____		7 p.m. _____	
11 a.m. _____		8 p.m. _____	
12 p.m. _____		9 p.m. _____	
1 p.m. _____		10 p.m. _____	

my training journal

my training log

SWIMMING WORKOUT:	*distance*
a.m.	
p.m.	
	total

BIKING WORKOUT:	*distance*
a.m.	
p.m.	
	total

RUNNING WORKOUT:	*distance*
a.m.	
p.m.	
	total

CROSS-TRAINING:	*time*
a.m.	
p.m.	
	total

TOMORROW'S To Do

RUNALOG® FOR TRIATHLETES

TODAY'S DATE _____

MY LONG-TERM GOAL(S) _____

TODAY'S MEAL PLAN	BREAKFAST	SNACK	LUNCH	SNACK	DINNER

weekly planner

SUNDAY	MONDAY	TUESDAY	WEDNESDAY	THURSDAY	FRIDAY	SATURDAY	TOTAL
a.m.							
p.m.							

daily planner

5 a.m. _____	2 p.m. _____
6 a.m. _____	3 p.m. _____
7 a.m. _____	4 p.m. _____
8 a.m. _____	5 p.m. _____
9 a.m. _____	6 p.m. _____
10 a.m. _____	7 p.m. _____
11 a.m. _____	8 p.m. _____
12 p.m. _____	9 p.m. _____
1 p.m. _____	10 p.m. _____

my training journal

my training log

SWIMMING WORKOUT:	*distance*
a.m.	
p.m.	
	total

BIKING WORKOUT:	*distance*
a.m.	
p.m.	
	total

RUNNING WORKOUT:	*distance*
a.m.	
p.m.	
	total

CROSS-TRAINING:	*time*
a.m.	
p.m.	
	total

TOMORROW'S To Do

376

⩗RUNALOG® FOR TRIATHLETES

TODAY'S DATE _____

MY LONG-TERM GOAL(S) _____
_____

TODAY'S MEAL PLAN	BREAKFAST	SNACK	LUNCH	SNACK	DINNER
	_____	_____	_____	_____	_____

weekly planner

	SUNDAY	MONDAY	TUESDAY	WEDNESDAY	THURSDAY	FRIDAY	SATURDAY	TOTAL
a.m.								
p.m.								

daily planner

5 a.m.	_____	2 p.m.	_____
6 a.m.	_____	3 p.m.	_____
7 a.m.	_____	4 p.m.	_____
8 a.m	_____	5 p.m.	_____
9 a.m.	_____	6 p.m.	_____
10 a.m.	_____	7 p.m.	_____
11 a.m.	_____	8 p.m.	_____
12 p.m.	_____	9 p.m.	_____
1 p.m.	_____	10 p.m.	_____

my training log

SWIMMING WORKOUT:	*distance*
a.m.	
p.m.	
	total

BIKING WORKOUT:	*distance*
a.m.	
p.m.	
	total

RUNNING WORKOUT:	*distance*
a.m.	
p.m.	
	total

CROSS-TRAINING:	*time*
a.m.	
p.m.	
	total

TOMORROW'S To Do

my training journal

RUNALOG® FOR TRIATHLETES

TODAY'S DATE _____

MY LONG-TERM GOAL(S) _____
_____

TODAY'S MEAL PLAN	BREAKFAST	SNACK	LUNCH	SNACK	DINNER
	_____	_____	_____	_____	_____
	_____	_____	_____	_____	_____

weekly planner

	SUNDAY	MONDAY	TUESDAY	WEDNESDAY	THURSDAY	FRIDAY	SATURDAY	TOTAL
a.m.								
p.m.								

daily planner

5 a.m. _____	2 p.m. _____
6 a.m. _____	3 p.m. _____
7 a.m. _____	4 p.m. _____
8 a.m _____	5 p.m. _____
9 a.m. _____	6 p.m. _____
10 a.m. _____	7 p.m. _____
11 a.m. _____	8 p.m. _____
12 p.m. _____	9 p.m. _____
1 p.m. _____	10 p.m. _____

my training journal

my training log

SWIMMING WORKOUT: *distance*

a.m.		
p.m.		
		total

BIKING WORKOUT: *distance*

a.m.		
p.m.		
		total

RUNNING WORKOUT: *distance*

a.m.		
p.m.		
		total

CROSS-TRAINING: *time*

a.m.		
p.m.		
		total

TOMORROW'S To Do

√RUNALOG® FOR TRIATHLETES

TODAY'S DATE _____

MY LONG-TERM GOAL(S) _____

_____

TODAY'S MEAL PLAN	BREAKFAST	SNACK	LUNCH	SNACK	DINNER
	_____	_____	_____	_____	_____
	_____	_____	_____	_____	_____

weekly planner

	SUNDAY	MONDAY	TUESDAY	WEDNESDAY	THURSDAY	FRIDAY	SATURDAY	TOTAL
a.m.								
p.m.								

daily planner

5 a.m. _____	2 p.m. _____
6 a.m. _____	3 p.m. _____
7 a.m. _____	4 p.m. _____
8 a.m _____	5 p.m. _____
9 a.m. _____	6 p.m. _____
10 a.m. _____	7 p.m. _____
11 a.m. _____	8 p.m. _____
12 p.m. _____	9 p.m. _____
1 p.m. _____	10 p.m. _____

my training journal

my training log

SWIMMING WORKOUT:	distance
a.m.	
p.m.	
	total

BIKING WORKOUT:	distance
a.m.	
p.m.	
	total

RUNNING WORKOUT:	distance
a.m.	
p.m.	
	total

CROSS-TRAINING:	time
a.m.	
p.m.	
	total

TOMORROW'S TO DO

APPENDIX PAGES

RUNALOG© FOR TRIATHLETES   date_____   *shopping list*

item	group	est. cost	final cost	totals	√

√RUNALOG® FOR TRIATHLETES   date_____   *shopping list*

item	group	est. cost	final cost	totals	√

Month	Week#	Mile/Km	Totals

	swim	bike	run	TOTALS
I				
II				
III				
IV				
V				
VI				
VII				
VIII				
IX				
X				
XI				
XII				

CROSS TRAINING

I				
II				
III				
IV				
V				
VI				
VII				
VIII				
IX				
X				
XI				
XII				
TOTALS				

Month	Week#	Mile/Km	Totals

	swim	bike	run	TOTALS
I				
II				
III				
IV				
V				
VI				
VII				
VIII				
IX				
X				
XI				
XII				

CROSS TRAINING

I				
II				
III				
IV				
V				
VI				
VII				
VIII				
IX				
X				
XI				
XII				
TOTALS				

RUNALOG® **FOR TRIATHLETES**

my today's training route

Today's date: _____

Training location: I am leaving at: should be back at:

_____ (TIME) _____ (TIME) _____

drawing of the map of my training's location, or the route's description:

if not back by:_____ (time), call: _____

Today's date: _____

| training location: | I am leaving at: (TIME) _____ | should be back at: (TIME)_____ |

drawing of the map of my training's location, or the route's description:

if not back by:_____(time), call: _____

#	Route's Name	Distance	Elevation	Notes

my favorite training routes

#	Route's Name	Distance	Elevation	Notes

RUNALOG® FOR TRIATHLETES   *contacts*

NAME	ADDRESS	PHONE/CELL	EMAIL

NAME	ADDRESS	PHONE/CELL	EMAIL

Made in the USA
San Bernardino, CA
19 December 2013